"Powderburns"
Cocaine, Contras & The Drug War
Celerino "Cele" Castillo, 3rd
Author

2709 N. 28 1/2 St.
McAllen, Texas 78501
Cell-Phone: 956 - 345 - 5770
E-Mail: powderburns@prodigy.net

POWDERBURNS

Cocaine, Contras & the Drug War

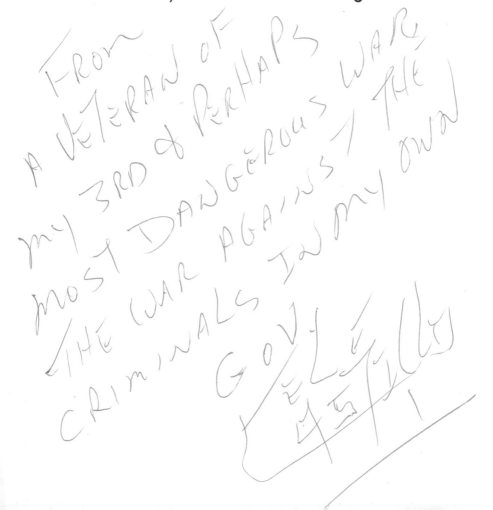

FROM A VETERAN OF my 3RD & PERHAPS MOST DANGEROUS WAR, THE WAR AGAINST CRIMINALS IN MY OWN GOV'T

CELE CASTILLO

POWDERBURNS

Cocaine, Contras & the Drug War

by
Celerino Castillo III and Dave Harmon

Sundial

an imprint of

Mosaic Press

Oakville - Buffalo - London

Canadian Cataloguing in Publication Data

Castillo, Celerino, 1949
    Powderburns

Includes bibliographical references.
ISBN 0-88962-578-6

1. Castillo, Celerino, 1949- . 2. Drug traffic- Central America.   3. Drug traffic -
United States.   4. Cocaine industry - Central America.   5. Political corruption - United
States.   6. Iran-Contra Affair, 1985-1990.   7. United States. Drug enforcement
Administration.   8. narcotic enforcement agents - United States.   I. Harmon, Dave,
1961- .II..Title.

HV5840.C45C37 1994   363.4'5'09728   C94-931968-6

Published by MOSAIC PRESS, P.O. Box 1032, Oakville, Ontario, L6J 5E9, Canada. Offices
and warehouse at 1252 Speers Road, Units #1&2, Oakville, Ontario, L6L 5N9, Canada and
Mosaic Press, 85 River Rock Drive, Suite 202, Buffalo, N.Y., 14207, USA.

Mosaic Press acknowledges the assistance of the Canada Council, the Ontario Arts Council, the
Ontario Ministry of Culture, Tourism and Recreation and the Dept. of Communications,
Government of Canada, for their support of our publishing programme.

Sundial an Imprint of Mosaic Press

In Canada:
        MOSAIC PRESS, 1252 Speers Road, Units #1&2, Oakville, Ontario, L6L 5N9,
Canada. P.O. Box 1032, Oakville, Ontario, L6J 5E9
In the United States:
        Mosaic Press, 85 River Rock Drive, Suite 202, Buffalo, N.Y., 14207

Dedication

*To Crystal Bianca, C4,
and Danny*
Celerino Castillo III

*To my parents, Philip and Barbara Harmon,
for making this book possible,
and to my brother, Chris,
for his unknowing inspiration.*
Dave Harmon

Acknowledgments

The authors would like to thank the following people:

Celerino Castillo III:
My parents, Celerino and Angie Castillo, for teaching me
what life is all about; my sisters, Diana, Melinda, and San Juanita
for being there when I needed them; Brian Casey for pointing me
to the right person; Chris Doyle for first discovering my story;
Chief Raul Garza for teaching me wat it takes to be the best; Juan
Perez for guiding me against the Gestapo; Mike Levine for his
endless encouragement; Rosa Granados for holding my hand for
the past two years (some wounds are not visible); and all the
undercover agents now being abused - "Nothing is forever"

Dave Harmon:
The proofreading squad, for their sharp eyes and vigorous
encouragement: Laura E. Keeton, Dan and Diana Dworin, Jamie
McIlvain, and Lisa DeCuir; the stalwart supporters: Steve Grey,
Sonia Sellers, Jerry and Kale Clark, Darryl Pruett, Dave "Big
Daddy" McLeod, Oscar and Tami Hinojosa, Avrel Seale, Beth
Bryant, Rob Dennett, and Robert and Viola Garza; Dr. Henry
Dietz of the University of Texas for pointers on recent Peruvian
history; the Rio Grande Book Co. for letting me run amok on their
office machines. And, most of all, Richard Derus for bringing it
all together.

FOREWORD

by
Michael Levine

Now that you've read this far I advise you to cancel any appointments you may have scheduled during the next several hours. You are not going to be able to put this book down. It will mesmerize you, enrage you and change your attitude toward the peo;le in government whom we have entrusted with our safety and security. Most importantly it will give you information that has been kept from you; information you have a riight to, because you have paid for it with your taxes, and, as many like me have done, with the blood and misery of your loved ones and friends.

There are several important facts that you must keep in mind as you read. First, that the crimes and atrocities described se vively in these in these pages, were committed by U.S. government officials using taxpayer dollars, or people undr their protection, and that, for the most part, the victims of these crimes are the very people who paid those taxes: the American people. Second, that this first hand account was written by Celerino "Cele" Castillo, a highly decorated veteran of two wars -- Vietnam and the War on Drugs; a man who has often risked his life to fulfillhis oath to protect the American people and uphold their laws, and tha Celerino Castillo is consummate professional investigator who documents every one of hs claims -- often using electronic recording devices -- so that they serve as evidence in any court in the world. Third, that every thing you are about to read was firest turned over to the upper management of DEA (The Drug Enforcement Administration), the FBI and the State Department for these pagencies to take appropriate action to sop the Oliver North/Contra operations drug smuggling activities and hat no action or investigation was ever undertaken. Fourth, that Cele Castillo persisted in pushing for an invetigationi spite of a warning from a U.S. Ambassador to back off the investigation because it was a White House Operation, and inspite of being place undr a malicious Internal Affairs investigation--DEAs classic method of silencing its outspoken agents -- that would help destroy his marriage and career and almost cost him his life. Finally, that Cele turned over all his evidence to Special Prosecutor Lawrence E. Walshs office -- then investigation Oliver North and the Contras -- and lonwhen it was clear that no investigative action would ever be taken pursuant to that evidence, and, in fact m that the Special Prosecutors final report failed to even mention the drug allegation, did Cele write this book.

When I wrote *Deep Cover* and *The Big White Lie* detailing my own deep cover experiences in South America, people were astounded by the revelations. They found it impossible to believe that their own government could tax them hundreds of billions of dollars to fight drigs andat the same time support andprotect the biggest drug dealers inthe world as they poisoned our children. It was the most despicable kind of treason. I, like many millions of Americans, was affected personally; my son Keith Richard Levine, a 27 year old NewYork City ploice officer, was murdered by crach addicts when, while off-duty, he tried to sopt and armed robbery they were committing to support their addiction; my brother David, a life long drug addict, ended his misery at 34 years of age by sucide. Our nation, thanks in large part to these criminalsn now has a homicide rate exceeding 25,000 per year, much of it drug related, and, according to some econimists, our economy is impacted by this drug plague by as much as one trillion dollars a year. Is it conceivable that so many members of our legislative, judicial and law enforcement branches of government betrayed us? No its not conceivable, but all those who read this book will find it undeniable.

In my books articles and media appearances I told of deep cover cases from Bankok to Buenos Aires, that were destroyed by the covert agencies of my own government; cases that would have exposed peo;le wohad been given a license to sell massive amounts of drugs to Americans in return for their support of Oliver Norths contras. I could easily prove that these investigations were intenetionally destroyed and that our cover was blown by our own government, but I only had circumstantial evidence linking the events to the Contras. Celerino Castillo, as you will see in these pages, had the smoking gun. At that time, had Cele come forward with his story, I believe the publics reaction to our joint testimony would have forced our elected officials into taking the action against North and others, that they were so despeatedly afraid of taking.

But at that time, Cele was bust fighting for his family, his career and his life. wherever I want people asked, If this is true, why arent any other government agents saying waht your are? I was a lone voice.

From the moment my first book was published i began receiveng - - and still receive - - lettrs from both fedral and local law enforcement officers, government informants and contract pilots for both DEA and CIA, with their own horror stories to tell indicationg that our covert agencies andState Department were sabotaging the drug war, and that when honest officers tried to do something about it, their lives and jobs were threatened, yet none would go public with their stories. They were afraid. I pinted out to all who would listen that even our highest govenment officials are afraid to confront the cirminals in government. During the years J Edgar Hoover ran the FBI, eight Presidents were aware that he was running a political police force, in violation of evry law of the land, yet they kept their silence and did nothing to stop him. They were terrified of his secret files and the revelations they might contain. It took almost twenty years after his death before the truth finally surfaced. If one man could intimidate eight Presidents, can you imagine the kind of club the CIA has over the heads of our current crop of plitical leader? How else can you explain the difference between their rhetoric and their actions, or lack therof?

Senator John Kerry, a Democrat, spent tens of millions of taxpayer dollars investigationg the drig running activities of Oliver Norths Nicaraguan Contra effort and came to the same conclusions that Cele and I did as DEA agents in the field. He said, Our covert agencis have converted themselves to channels for drugs...they have perverted our sustem of justice. An outraged Senator Alphomse Damato, a Republican, found it mind bogling, that while we taxed Americans more than $100 billion to fight drugs, we were in bed with the biggest drug dealers in the world.

All the outrage and oratory not withstanding, noe of th evidence that the led to those statements was ever presented to a grand jury of American citizens, and not one single indictment of a U.S. laws relatint ot narcotics trafficking was ever forthcoming. Nor was there ever any house-cleaning of the agencies involved. Many of these criminals in government are still, in fact, criminals in government, and as this book goes to press there is evidence that their crives continue.

It is also important for the reader to keep in mind, that to prove a government official guilty of violations of the Federal Drug Conspiracy laws, is a relatively easy task for a professional narcotics investigator. One would only have to prove that he or she know of drug trafficking activity and failed to tade appropriate actionl. In one case I was involved in, for example, A new York City police detective was convicted of violation of the Federal Conspiracy statutes and sentenced to 8 years in prison, for not taking appropriate action against a dope-dealing friend of his. We could not even prove that he had profited form his crime. DEAs files are full of similar cases. The law is exactly as Prsident Bush once said: All those who look the other way are as guilty as the drug dealer.

The Kerry commission amassed impressive evidence that Oliver North and others had violated our drug trafficking laws; they reviewed Norths 543 pages of [ersonal notes relating to drug trafficking activity, which - - even after North blacked out many incrinimating statements - - included notatins like, $14 million to finance came from drugs; they learned that North had attempted to get leniency for General Bueso-Rosa (convicted of an assassination paid for with 700 pounds of cocaine distributed in the U.S.); they found evidence, such as Norths cahs purchase of a car from a $15.000 cash slush fund he kept in a closet, and his interest in a multi-million dollar Swiss bank account, indicationg that North, with no other source of income than his military pay check, may have profited financially from drug grafficking activities, yet none of this evidence was ever fully investigated by professional narcotics investigators, nor presented to a grand jury of American citizens as it should have been, or as it would have been had North not been given the phony Redlon shield of National Security and the protection of a President.

The evidence - - and the above is only a small sampling of what is available - -is enough to enrage career nbarcotic enforcement officers who have sent so many to jail for so much less. And when you add the evidence so powerfully presented in this book t what is already known about North and his Contra operation, you will understand why Cele Castillo put his career and life at risk to try and break through that sheild, and why he continues to risk himself to his day.

In Senator Kerrys final reprot he stated, Those U.S. officials who turned a blind eye t General Noriega, who intervened on behalf of General Bueso-Rosa and who adamantly opposed the investigations of /foreign narcotics figures by honest, hard-working law enforcement officials, *must also hear the responsibility for what is happening in the streets of the U.S. today.* By the tie you finish this book you sill know tha his accusation is aimed squarely at Oliver North, Presidents Reagan and Bush, and other high government officials, yet, and it bears repeating, none of the evidence provoking that statement was ever presented to a grand jury of American citizens.

What else but fear can account for this failure ont he part of our leaders to take appropriate action a failure, that wre thay local cops or DEA agents would have gotten them arrestee and prosecuted, along withthe people they were protection.

Jack Blum, special council for the Kerry commission, resigned his post, stateng, I am sick to death of the truths I cannot tell. But Cele Castillo, as you will soon know, is not afraid and never has been. In these pages he will reveal to you some of th msot devastating of those truths.

I now welcome Cele Castillo, *a true American hero*, to the front lines of his third and perhaps most important war - a war against the criminals within his own government.

INTRODUCTION

Dear Gerneral Noriega:
...Your long-standing support of the Drug Enforcement Administration is greatly appreciated... Thank you very much for the autographed photograp. I have ad it framed and it is proudly displayed in my office....

That letter was written in march, 1984 by DEA Administrator Francis M. Mullen, Jr. to Panamanian strongman General Manuel Noriega, who, four years later, was indicated on drug traficking charges in the United States. In december, 1989, 15 American soldiers, part of an invading force of 10,000, were killed trying to hunt down Noriega and haul him back to the U.S. The man whose aytographed prtreait once hung on the DEA Administrators wall was now, in the words of the U.S. military, a cocaine-snorting, voodoo-worshiping alcoholic despot who entertained prostitues and wore red underwear.

Such are the ironies of te drug war.

These pages contain one DEA agents account of Americas longest, most frustrating war. Celerino Cele Castillo III spent a dozen years battling the drug cartels, a manece that General Paul C. Gorman, former head of the U.S. Southern Command in Panama, called more successful at subversion in the United States than any that are centered in Moscow.

This book reveals why, after more than 20 years and billions of dollars, the drug war has filed miserably. Why DEA cannot rid the streets of pushers, why it cannot dents the burgeoning coca economy in South America, why its much-ballyhooed interdiction efforts are swatted aside like gnats by the cartels.

Put simply, when U.S. fireign policy and U.S. drug policy collide, durg plicy tields every time. People like Manuel Noriega are treasured for their strategic importance, thier long-standing support, and their demcratic ideals, however superficaial, while their back-door deals with drug traffickers are conveniently ignored. And while Communist regimes around the world have withered and collapsed under their own weight, the cartels grow stronger.

No one knows this better than Cele castillo. For every small victory during his Dea Career, a ccrushing defeat followed. As a Vietnam veterna, he knew all too well the disillusionment that accompanies messy wars led by vacillating ploticians. He shrugged off the frustrations and stubbornly fought on. Then, in Central America, he stumbled upon the Contra resupply operation, a covert network guided by Lt. Col. Oliver North. Castillos investigation of the Contra operation revealed the deepest secret of the Iran-Contra Affair: the Contras; drugs-for-guns connection.

Castillos investigation unearthed enough evidence to merit a full-scale invertigatin, yet none ovccurred. His superiors told Castillo pint-blank to leave the Contra-drug connection, headed by Sen. John Kerry of Massachusetts, concluded: ...it is clear that individuals who provided support for the Contras were involved in drug trafficking, the supply network of the Contras was used by drug trafficking organizations, and elements of the Contras themselves knowingly received financial and material assistance form drug traffickers. Yet the Kerry committees findings wee ignored by the White House, and neither the Congressional Iran-Contra committees nor the Iran-Contra special prosicutor was fit to delve into the third secret of the Iran-Contra Affair.

Throughout his DEA career, Castillo kept dteiled journals which provide the basis for the dates, names, places, and DEA file numbers cited in this book. Conversations quote inthese pages were reconstructed to the best of Castillos recollection.

DEA rejected repeated efforts ot obtain Castillos reports and cables from Central America. The material, according to the U.S. Department of Justice Ofice of Informaiton and Privacy, is not appropriate for discretionary release. Likewise, large portions of Norths diaries were censored before they were turned over to eht government, including many sections adjacent to drug references. For example, Norths June 26, 1984 entry begins DEA-- followed by two blocks of deleted text.

Important questions remain: Who in the government knew about the Contras drug ties? Why were Castillos reports ignored? And what did North, now a candidate for the United States Senate, know about the drug activities within the network he steered from Washington? The truth lies somewhere beneath a quashed investigation, a belligerent bureaucracy, and a censors pen.

--DKH
McAllen, June 15, 1994

TABLE OF CONTENTS

One
Plausible Deniability
Washington D.C. - July 7, 1987

Twenty-six Congressmen sat silently as the witness was sworn in. Shutters clicked. Papers rustled. The lawyers, government officials, spectators, reporters, and staffers packed into the Senate Caucus Room, filling the chamber with a rumble of murmured anticipation. Satellite feeds carried the scene to television screens across the country. The climax of the Iran-Contra Affair was approaching. America was watching by the millions.

The din subsided; the uniformed witness stood, staring defiantly at the members of the joint Congressional Iran-Contra committee. He was the scapegoat, there to take the fall for the Reagan Administration, which allowed its most sensitive duties to fall to a small cabal wich created a government within the Government. The rows of multi-colored ribbons on his olive-drab Marine uniform; the furrowed brow; the ramrod posture; all blended into an image that would burn its way onto TV screens, front pages, and magazine covers. Clean-cut and slim, he looked the part of the loyal soldier, someone who *would* salute, about-face, and carry out his orders in the name of patriotism. When Lt. Col. Oliver L. North raised his right hand and promised to tell the truth, people wanted to believe him.

I watched North's testimony on CNN from my living room in Guatemala City. Like millions of Americans, I sat glued to the television during the week-long political soap opera. Americans wanted to learn the truth about North's role in the nations's arms sales to Iran, and the diversion of millions of dollars from those sales to the Contras -- the Nicaraguan rebels fighting to oust the leftist Sandinista regime.

I wanted the nation to learn the truth about a third secret.

* * *

North and I had a lot in common. We were both native Texans and decorated Vietnam veterans. We both spent our post-war careers serving our country: North continued in the Marines as an instructor, and later was an NSC staffer; I, however, left the Army to follow in my father's footsteps as a cop, before joining the Drug Enforcement Administration as a special agent in 1979. We were both workaholics whose jobs took us away from our families. We both believed deeply in duty and country. But when our paths collided in Central America, North and I were on very different missions.

From early 1984 to the fall of 1986, North directed a clandestine resupply operation he dubbed "Project Democracy," which used a military airbase in El Salvador to fly weapons and supplies to the Contras.

For the better part of a year, I investigated it.

By the summer of 1987, the nation already knew most of the details of North's twin covert operations: U.S.-made missles were sold to Iran, the world's most rabidly anti-American regime, through a gaggle of shady middlemen who promised the arms would ransom American hostages held by terrorists in Lebanon; the Iranians were overcharged, with the excess funneled to the Nicaraguan Contras; and, despite a 1985 law prohibiting U.S. intelligence agencies from "supporting, directly or indirectly, military or paramilitary operations in Nicaragua," North helped raise money, plan strategy, and run guns for the rebels.

When the details spilled onto the front pages in the fall of 1986, the scandal shook Ronald Reagan's Presidency to its core. Reagan, who once boasted "America will never make concessions to terrorists," stammered before the cameras that he just was not aware of the bold foreign policy maneuvers of his underlings. His subordinates dutifully supported his claim of ignorance.

Now, before America's waiting eyes and ears, North was ready to tell his version of the story.

John W. Nields, Jr., chief counsel for the House committee, wasted no time cutting to the heart of the matter: "Colonel North, were you involved in the use of the proceeds of sales of weapons to Iran for the purpose of assisting the Contras in Nicaragua?''

North, who faced indictment for lying to Congress and shredding documents during the Administration's frantic coverup, quickly pleaded the Fifth, agreeing to answer questions only after the respective Congressional chairmen assured North his testimony could not be used against him in any criminal proceedings. The show continued.

I watched, transfixed, as North parried Nields' questions with a combination of chest-pounding eloquence and impudence. ''I came here to tell you the truth - - the good, the bad, and the ugly. I am here to tell it all, pleasant and unpleasant, and I am here to accept responsibility for that which I did. I will not accept responsibility for that which I did not do.''

Nields shrugged off North's eloquent soliloquies and stuck to his game plan, prodding North to explain his role in the missile shipments, the shredding of documents, the Contra money trail.

North hedged, dodged, and lectured: ''I think it is very important for the American people to understand that this is a dangerous world ... There is great deceit, deception practiced in the conduct of covert operations.'' North and his superior, Vice Admiral John Poindexter, compartmentalized the operations. As Reagan's National Security Advisor, Poindexter wanted to give the President ''plausible deniability.'' If Reagan could honestly say he was in the dark, his famous teflon would stand a better chance of deflecting the political consequences. North, Poindexter, and their cohorts broke laws to shield their boss. When the fallout inevitably began, North sorted through his files and dropped anything relating to the funds diverted to the Contras into the shredder. As the hearings continued, I wondered what other documents North had dropped into oblivion.

Nields: And, can you think of any document, the disclosure of which would have caused [President Reagan] more domestic political damage than a document reflecting his approval of the diversion?

North: The answer to your question is yes. I can think of a lot of documents that cause domestic political damage.

I could think of a few politically damaging documents as well. I had written them. I wondered if any of the reports I so painstakingly prepared lay sandwiched in the reams of paper accumulated by the Iran-Contra committees. As the session dragged into the afternoon, I reluctantly abandoned my cool room and fought my way through traffic to DEA's Guatemala City office, where I tried halfheartedly to attend to on my paperwork. I could not concentrate. After an hour or two, I stopped pretending and rushed home for a three-hour lunch in front of the flickering screen. I could work late. This drama was more important.

I clicked on the television. Nields' face filled the screen. He was on the right track, asking North about foreign contributions for the Contras and North's own overtures to rich widows and other wealthy American citizens. The Contras were hurting for cash after Congress cut off their funding. North badly needed more money to hold the rebels together "body and soul."

I leaned forward in my chair. *Now. Ask the damn question now, Nields,* I thought anxiously. Nields rambled on, leaving the question unasked. The Tuesday session ended with the third secret intact. I watched again Wednesday, grimacing every time the lawyers edged near the topic. On Thursday, North was quietly explaining his role in the *Achille Lauro* sea-jacking when a cry from the audience broke the decorous atmosphere: "What about the cocaine dealing the U.S. is paying for? Ask about the cocaine project ... Why don't you ask about drug deliveries?" The protestors raised a banner reading: ASK ABOUT COCAINE, ASK ABOUT THE KILLING OF NON-COMBATANTS.

I shot out of my chair. Sen. Daniel Inouye of Hawaii, the chairman of the Senate committee, was equally shocked. "We will stand in recess for ten minutes," he rumbled.

The commercial break seemed to last a year. I paced the floor, my mind racing. It was as if the protestors had read my mind and shouted my questions at the Congressmen. *Will that break the silence? Will anyone listen?*

Inouye's deep, resonant voice snapped me back in front of the screen. "The hearing will please come to order," Inouye said. "I wish to advise the audience that this panel will not tolerate demonstrations." With that, North resumed his *Achille Lauro* narrative. I slumped in my chair.

The third secret surfaced again on Monday, North's fifth day of testimony. Three lawyers had already asked North hundreds of questions, some a dozen times. But not until the members began their questioning did Sen. Orrin Hatch, the Utah Republican, finally ask the question.

Hatch: Okay. What about drug smuggling? There've been a lot of allegations thrown around that the [Contra] resupply operation was involved in cocaine trafficking. A news program over the weekend suggested that Rob Owen, who testified earlier, was involved in drug smuggling. Now is there any truth to that? Can you shed any light for us on that?

I jumped toward the TV and turned the sound up. This was it.

North: Absolutely false. Mr. Owen is the last person -- perhaps right beside me -- that would ever be engaged in those kinds of activities. And when Mr. Owen found any information pertaining to the possibility of involvement in drugs, he told me and I would tell the appropriate federal authorities. And there were several of such instances. Absolutely false, Senator.
Hatch: I believe that.

''Wait!'' I shouted at the screen, instantly feeling stupid for the outburst. North's brief statement sparked a cascade of questions: Who was involved in drugs? Which federal authorities did you report to? How many times did that happen?

Hatch immediately moved on to another topic. I stood slowly, walked to the set, and clicked it off.

* * *

For seven years, I fought on the front lines of Reagan's "Drug War", trying to stamp out what I considered America's greatest foreign threat. North fought Communism. I fought cocaine.

I could not shake the feeling I was trapped in a protracted Vietnam. The enemy was everywhere I turned, on the streetcorners of Manhattan, in the Amazon jungle of Peru, in the airy cafes of

San Salvador. They were street pushers, mobsters, coca farmers, cocaine traffickers. They blended in with the civilians, who all too often supported and protected them. No matter how many of them I threw behind bars, others appeared to take their place. And the drugs kept coming, seeping over our borders in a deadly flood.

When I was posted to Guatemala in October, 1985, I knew we were playing the Drug War Follies. While our government shouted "Just Say No," entire nations fell to traffickers' dollars. The momentum was against us. The Colombian cartels ground their home government into submission with a rain of bribes and bullets, then sucked their American customers dry to purchase other governments: A cartel-backed coup toppled the Bolivian government in 1980; the scattered islands of the Bahamas became landing pads for drug flights between Colombia and Florida shortly after; and when Manuel Noriega turned Panama into a haven for trafficking and money laundering, it took a December 1989 invasion -- the largest U.S. military operation since Vietnam -- to drag the dictator into a U.S. court to face drug charges.

The cartels had too many men, too many guns, and too many dollars. DEA had too few. President Richard Nixon declared a war on drugs in 1971; when he died, 23 years and $100 billion in drug war expenditures later, addicts in Little Rock would be plunking down five bucks for rocks of crack cocaine. From the front lines, I could see the tide turning against us as the narcotics ate their way through the country. By the end of the 1980s, a third of all robberies and burglaries in the United States would be committed for money to buy drugs. The drug crime wave would have a devastating ripple effect. By 1994, drug offenders would make up 30 percent of new inmates pouring into the nation's bursting jails, up from 7 percent in 1980.

None of this came as any surprise to me. In seven years in the trenches, I had arrested dozens of traffickers; trained anti-narcotics squads in two countries; flown aerial eradication missions; spearheaded huge cocaine busts. The drug barons barely flinched: In Peru, I watched cartel pilots playing soccer with soldiers; in El Salvador, military officers took weapons seized from the guerrillas and sold them to traffickers; in Guatemala, I discovered members of our host government running a smuggling ring for the cartels. Then I discovered the Contras' secret.

* * *

By the end of his Congressional testimony, North was crowned an American Hero. Telegrams streamed in from admirers across the country, who reached out to their new icon. I knew better.

Many of the diplomats I worked with on a daily basis in the U.S. Embassy in El Salvador regarded the hard-nosed NSC staffer running the Contra operation as "pushy and arrogant."

I thought of him as the leader, whether he knew it or not, of Latin America's most protected drug smuggling operation.

The connections piled up quickly. Contra planes flew north to the U.S., loaded with cocaine, then returned laden with cash. All under the protective umbrella of the United States Government. My informants were perfectly placed: one worked with the Contra pilots at their base, while another moved easily among the Salvadoran military officials who protected the resupply operation. They fed me the names of Contra pilots. Again and again, those names showed up in the DEA database as documented drug traffickers. When I pursued the case, my superiors quietly and firmly advised me to move on to other investigations.

In Central America, the Contras' drug connection was no secret. The Salvadoran military knew. The U.S. Embassy knew. DEA knew. The CIA knew: "With respect to (drug trafficking by) the Resistance Forces ... it is not a couple of people. It is a lot of people," the CIA's Central American Task Force chief would tell the Congressmen a month after North's testimony.

And there were indications North knew.

A Congressional subcommittee chaired by Sen. John Kerry searched North's personal notebooks and found 543 pages containing "references to drugs and drug trafficking." On many of the pages, the material adjacent to the drug references was blacked out before the pages reached the subcommittee. A few cryptic references remained, scrawled in North's shorthand:

July 9, 1984. Call from Clarridge - - *Call Michel re Narco Issue* - - RIG at 1000 tomorrow (Q0384) - - DEA Miami - - Pilot went talked to Vaughn - - *wanted A/C to go to Bolivia to p/u paste* - - *want A/C to p/u 1500 kilos* - - Bud to meet w/Group (Q0385) [italics added]

It was potentially explosive. It was provocative. It was enough to make a DEA agent drool.

It was also enough to scare the hell out of some of our elected leaders, who knew a political minefield when they saw one. Six months before North's Congressional appearance, the Senate Iran-Contra committee pondered investigating the Contras' drugs-for-guns network. A *New York Times* article on January 13, 1987 summed up their trepidation: "Some senators say that any official inquiry on this topic, and how much if anything American officials knew about it, at this time would create such an uproar that it could derail the main thrusts of the Senate inquiry: to sort out the Reagan Administration's secret arms sales to Iran and diversion of profits to the contras."

They chose to ignore the issue, and when it threatened to burst into the limelight, they buried it.

A few news reports tied the Contras to narcotics smuggling, but the accusations came from the lips of convicted traffickers whose credibility was instantly attacked, or from members of Congress whose investigations into the issue were dismissed by the Administration as partisan politics. Kerry's ill-fated investigation saw its star witnesses discredited, its biggest revelations overshadowed by the Iran-Contra circus, and its final report greeted with a collective yawn by the media.

The subcommittee report sparked no public outcry, no high-profile indictments. The senators, split by internal bickering, essentially peeked under the rug, wrinkled their noses, then moved on.

The American public would quickly lose interest in the Iran-Contra scandal, with its complicated plot twists and vague policy questions. Had they discovered our government hired and protected a squad of drug traffickers, then gave them free passes into the U.S., the story might have ended very differently.

Two
Into the Jungle
Pharr, Texas - 1970

We lived on West State Street in Pharr, next to a packing shed and an icehouse. It was like a lot of struggling small towns along the Texas-Mexico border -- nobody was really rich, but nobody was homeless either. Our neighborhood, a collection of small houses crammed together with small shops, was what passed for lower middle-class, home to a good number of migrant farmworkers, a few businessmen, and a variety of blue-collar types who worked the big farms and small factories dominating the area. The railroad tracks ran past our front door, cutting between economic classes as they did in about every small Texas town. The rumble of the 6 a.m. and 10 p.m. Southern Pacific freight cars framed each day.

Our life was idyllic, a series of scenes that Rockwell would have painted had he lived on the border. My sisters Diana, Melinda, and San Juanita (who was born with Down's Syndrom), busy mopping the wooden floors as I helped my father manicure the yard. Sunday services at St. Margaret's, where I was an altarboy. Sneaking into the packing shed with my friends on weekends to ride the wooden pallets, which seemed to glide over the wooden floors on metal rollers. Dad cooking burgers on the grill every Friday night, bringing back a grinning cow's head from the slaughterhouse for Sunday *barbacoa.*

On the border, *barbacoa* was a ritual. My father would wander into the yard and start dropping hunks of hard mesquite wood into the round pit he dug in the clay soil. When the mesquite burned down to glowing embers, he arranged bricks on top of the coals. Then came the cow's head, encased in foil and burlap. He covered it with a scrap piece of aluminum siding and layers of coals and dirt. The preparations began every Saturday night at 10. By 7 o'clock Sunday morning the head was cooked. My mother would make coffee while Dad sliced the tender meat off the head and piled it up on a plate. We circled him with hot homemade tortillas in our hands.

My mother, Angelita -- everyone called her Angie -- presided over a group of children as different as could be imagined. Diana, a year older than me, was high strung and energetic, a bubbly counterpoint to my moodiness. Melinda, who came along a year after me, was the sophisticated one, the little girl we called Miss Goody Two Shoes. She was always the best dressed, the most likely to succeed and fulfill her dream of attending college -- a difficult ring to reach in our neighborhood. San Juanita was the happiest. Down's Syndrome would tie her to my parents for the rest of her life, but she was blessed with an intense sense of caring flowing from a big heart. When she was happy, her whole being glowed.

Our prime entertainment was the movies: English titles for a quarter at the Texas Theater, and Spanish at *El Capitán*. The language was irrelevant. My family, like a lot of our neighbors on the border, switched back and forth between Spanish and English at home.

We also frequented the irrigation canals that criss-crossed the area, toting our fishing poles, hoping to snag a catfish for dinner. When it rained, we hunted big Texas frogs with flashlights and homemade spears fashioned from stolen broomsticks. We laid big nails on the railroad tracks in the evening, then picked them up the next morning, filing the flattened metal into daggers and mounting them on the sticks. My mother scolded us, but always agreed to deep-fry the legs for dinner when we marched into the kitchen with our green trophies.

* * *

Somehow, I knew I would get drafted. I was so sure of it, I was ready to enlist in the Marines in the spring of 1970 to wash away the constant foreboding. Uncle Sam beat me to it. The draft notice came in an somberly official envelope, announcing I was to report to Fort Lewis in Washington state for basic training. I stared at the card, reading the short message over and over. For a teenager living in a little border town, Vietnam was just a strange, jagged crescent on the school library's mounted globe. A senior in high school, I was just starting to think about my possibilities. Others had gone before me and died fighting the Communists, who, many learned adults assured us, were all around, waiting for an opportune moment to storm city hall and use South Texas as their beachhead to conquer America.

The fear came slowly, rocking me with waves of apprehension. Yet a part of me thrilled at the chance to prove myself, to make my family proud. My father taught me about duty and patriotism, words just beginning to erode into cynicism as the 1960s gave way to the '70s, and icons like John F. Kennedy and Martin Luther King were cut down. There was no doubt I would go.

From what we saw on the news, we all thought the war was supposed to be winding down. Nixon was pulling out troops in waves as he "Vietnamized" the war. Casualties were down by half. The number of U.S. troops in the war zone would soon drop to 413,900, the fewest since 1967. Nobody told this to the man who pulled my name out of the lottery drum.

My mother cried when the envelope arrived. The next day, she called Kika de la Garza, our local congressman, and begged him to spare me. I could hear her sobbing into the phone. "This is my only son. Who will carry the family name if something happens to him?"

My father was irate when he found out what she had done. He immediately called de la Garza and told him not to intervene.

Dad was a decorated World War II veteran, a survivor of the Phillipines campaign. He lied about his age and joined the Americal Division -- the same division that had become infamous the previous November when news of the My Lai massacre reached the public. He still had copper in his leg where the Army doctors had wired the bone back together. The Japanese killed his brother as they tried to take Alaska. My uncle's bones remain on an icy island somewhere in the Aleutians. I would serve proudly, as they had done.

We were a family of long tradition, tracing our heritage back to the Mexican revolutionary Emilio Zapata. I was baptized Celerino Castillo III after my father, who carried the name for my grandfather. My grandfather brought it from his home in San Luis Potosí, Mexico, when he immigrated in a horse-drawn cart loaded with his carpentry tools. I fully expected to bestow it on my first son.

He began and ended the discussion with his usual directness: "We come from a family that has served our country."

My father drove me to the post office in nearby McAllen, where a bus would take me to San Antonio for my military physical. He had never been one for emotional moments. He clapped my shoulder and offered his best advice. "Everything you do, do it right."

The bus was crowded with fresh-faced recruits and draftees from the Rio Grande Valley. Some were obviously eager for the chance to expand their experience beyond the isolated south tip of Texas. Others stared ahead, looking frightened and ready to get very drunk.

I passed my physical easily. I was lean and wiry from running on the high school track team, 5 feet 10 inches and 130 pounds. From San Antonio, we were immediately flown to the Northwest. As the plane dropped below the clouds, my breath caught in my throat. Mount Ranier jutted up from the earth, shrouded in snow. I had never seen snow except on television. When the first snows covered the base that winter, the other South Texas recruits in my company were as amazed as I was. We dove into the cold white stuff, handling it, tasting it, then instinctively balling it up and hurling it at each other's heads.

We did not have much time to play. The drill sergeants kicked our butts there. Basic training became a whirl of push-ups, bad food, early morning runs and knotted muscles. In the little free time we were given, we haunted Seattle's seamy Pike Street red-light district, explored the local bars, and ducked into the theater to catch *M*A*S*H*, which was still playing in Seattle when I returned to Fort Lewis on my way back to Texas.

The city dazzled me, although I made sure my friends didn't catch me gawking. I was bombarded with new wonders: the overwhelming greenness, the sharp perfume of the pines, the bite of the cold, dry winds.

After basic, the sergeants hounded us through AIT -- advanced infantry training. These were graduate courses for future killing machines: escape and evasion techniques in case we were captured by the enemy; nighttime tactics with live ammunition; advanced hand-to-hand training; delicate lessons on how to plant Claymore mines and booby traps. The 15-hour days and the intense routine left us exhausted, but built our confidence. I left AIT in the spring of 1971 a ball of musclebound endurance, lean and mean. I thought I was ready.

From Fort Lewis, the Army sent me to non-commissioned officer school at Fort Benning, Georgia, where they rushed recruits through the system to get more sergeants to the jungle. They called it "leadership school." We called it "shake and bake." I turned down an offer to go on to Ranger school. I wanted to go to Vietnam. Most of us did -- it was the honorable thing to do. Despite the ugly turn in public opinion after the Tet Offensive in early 1968, my class still believed in patriotism and duty. The public was still deeply divided: that May, thousands of demonstrators, including veterans and construction workers, marched in Washington D.C. in support of the war, less than a month after a group of anti-war veterans hurled their helmets and combat ribbons on the Capitol steps.

I was given a month back home before beginning my tour of duty. My father was visibly proud; Mom was worried sick. Her eyes carried an anguished, hollow expression that followed me throughout Vietnam. The daily body counts and the grisly war footage on the news did not calm her.

* * *

On August 29, 1971, we landed at Cam Ranh Bay, South Vietnam, after 16 hours in the air. The plane's hatch opened. Hot, damp air engulfed us. We looked around at each other, exchanging one last uncertain look before we took our first steps on Vietnamese soil and began the countdown every GI keeps to mark his time in country.

The place was intimidating, with military jets and helicopters swooping in and out like birds of prey. Everything about Cam Ranh spoke of of tension and anticipation. The first things I noticed were gun towers and bunkers studding the white beach, laced with rolling coils of man-shredding concertina wire. Military Police and sentries were everywhere. This was the first stop for thousands of U.S. troops, and a favorite target for the Viet Cong. They had attacked the base during Tet and again in August, 1969, raiding the convalescent hospital with a small commando force.

The troops at Cam Ranh were still shaking their heads about the 1969 raid. The VC killed two Americans and wounded 99, before slipping back into the landscape without a single casualty. A few weeks later, they called again, lobbing mortar shells over the perimeter. The base was on alert again as I arrived: The Communists were attacking civilian targets and U.S. bases in the northern part of South Vietnam, trying to disrupt the scheduled August 29 elections. Everyone seemed to walk a little closer to the buildings and sandbags, ready to dive at the first thump of artillery.

We were all cherries, plopped down among a collection of combat-frazzled soldiers anxiously waiting to be processed out of the country. An old bus, its mottled paint scarred and faded, carried us to the replacement center, a cavernous compound where new recruits were processed into different companies. A captain marched through the ranks with a clipboard, calling out assignments. I was selected to become a sergeant of the guard, one of the three sergeants in charge of base security forces.

I was in charge of dozens of sentries sent to man the bunkers and lookout towers. The captain obviously considered fear the best motivation. He nonchalantly told me some of the guards had been asleep when the Viet Cong sent its commandos through the lines the previous year. "You know what a sapper is, Sergeant Castillo?" he snapped. I didn't. "They're the sneakiest, most fearless enemy you will ever face, sergeant. They'll run straight at you with a bag full of explosives and take bullets until you hit something vital. The ones we've captured and use as guides can pass through razor wire in five seconds without making a sound. Those guards were found slumped at their posts with their throats slit. Now, you have a nice day. Get to work."

I saluted and returned to my bunk to try to catch some sleep before the graveyard shift began at 7 p.m. The gloomy pep talk worked. I was determined to keep everyone on their toes during my shift.

I patrolled 12 hours each night, making the rounds of the towers and bunkers to make sure the guards challenged me when

I approached. I quickly separated them into two categories. The good ones developed their instincts. They could hear me coming no matter how quietly I crept toward them. I would give them the day's code word and move on. The others saw guard duty as a pain in the ass and passed the time by sleeping or getting stoned.

I constantly caught men smoking dope on duty. "OJs" -- marijuana joints soaked in opium -- were popular among the soldiers for their mellow high. They also liked heroin, which came packed in gelatin capsules for easy concealment and use. I found soldiers shooting up heroin in the latrine, taut faces smoothing into oblivion as the drug infested their brains.

I had no tolerance for drugs. Actually, I had scarcely any experience with drugs. A few of my friends smoked pot in high school, but I never had anything stronger than a shot of whiskey or a beer.

I used the "three-strikes-you're-out" system. After two warnings violators were sent to the captain, who gave them the slit throats speech, then court-martialled them. This did not give me popularity points among the slackers. The threats began. A friend came to my tent one night, warning me about a conversation he overheard in the barracks. "They said they were going to zap you between towers four and five and blame it on the VC." I held my M-16 tighter every night after that, watching the shadows, but they never moved.

* * *

Part of the tension filling Cam Ranh came from the growing rift between the black and white soldiers. The blacks were coming into their own in America and in the military, building a new consciousness and nursing a simmering hatred for whites. The sides mingled only when they had to. As a Mexican-American, I moved in the uneasy space between the two poles.

One night, the tension blew. I was walking the grounds when shouting erupted outside the mess hall. About a hundred black soldiers were on the verge of pouncing on an equal force of white soldiers, who glared and shouted back. Some of them were waving their weapons, angry fingers on triggers.

The stark display of hatred stunned me. Prejudice was always an undercurrent in South Texas, but open confrontation was unheard of. Blacks were practically unknown in the Rio Grande Valley, leaving whites and Hispanics to achieve some kind of balance. Custom buried our tensions deep, and young Mexican-Americans learned the subtle dance almost unconsciously. Only the restroom signs I saw as a child separating "White" from "Mexican" at the Enco station spelled out the racial facts of life.

Now, standing in the midst of a boiling black-and-white feud, I felt no loyalty to either side. I locked and loaded a 20-round magazine into my M-16 and rattled it into the air. An almost reverent silence followed. I put on my most menacing face. A sea of eyes behind the dust and smoke bored into me. I wanted to lash at every one of them for eating away at morale while the enemy grew stronger. I wanted to reach into the experiences of my 20 years and produce some profound truth to defuse the tension. Instead, I came off like an anxious teenager with a gun. I screamed: "You guys are all going to LBJ if you don't cut this shit out."

That probably worked better anyway. LBJ was Long Binh Jail, where court-martialled soldiers were sent to finish their military careers caged and humiliated. After some final posturing and parting epithets, the factions melted back into the bustle of the base. The near-riot, I later discovered, started when the black soldiers claimed the white guys were getting more rations in the mess. I wondered if the would turn on each other when the enemy confronted them.

After two months at the base, I was about to find out. I had been assigned to Bravo Company, 1st Battalion, 12th Cavalry in Bien Hoa.

* * *

A chopper dropped me into the monstrous Bien Hoa air base, home to the Air Force's Third Tactical Fighter Wing and the Army's III Corps. This was Saigon's shield from the Viet Cong and the North Vietnamese Army, the closest base to the South Vietnamese capital. As I searched for the commanding officer, weary grunts milled around, eyeing me with nonchalant amusement. A few sat cleaning their rifles, others snored loudly where they dropped. With my fresh uniform and smooth chin, I looked like a kid in his Sunday best in a gang of vagabonds.

I saw no hint of animosity between these soldiers. In fact, I had trouble telling them apart. The jungle, the dank air and the grind of warfare had an equalizing effect. They were all filthy, with no insignia or rank visible on their worn green fatigues. I looked from one face to the next, wondering how long it would take before I would see the dark circles etched around my eyes.

The platoon sergeant had little time to give me the grand tour. Bravo company had seen a lot of action against the Viet Cong, he said, fishing around his fatigues for his lighter. Lost a lot of men. He put me in charge of a squad, then rattled off the rotating schedule we would follow until we were wounded, killed, or sent home: 30 days in the bush, back to base for a few days, then out again for another round of search-and-destroy.

My squad usually had five infantry men, all privates and E4s, plus a machine gunner and a grenadier. But the most valuable member was a black Labrador retriever trained to sniff out booby traps. The lab had earned the men's respect, warning them away from a hundred trip wires and mines. The dog had its own handler, its own doggie C-rations, and an unlimited supply of water, which the troops lugged through the bush to slake its insatiable thirst. The dog was as frazzled as the soldiers, its big square head plopped between its paws as it dozed in the shade of a tent.

There was no time to make myself at home. My squad flew into the jungle the next day, part of a four-platoon rescue effort for an ARVN ranger company losing a skirmish with the Viet Cong. The rest of the squad was grumbling as we boarded the helicopter. Nobody wanted to risk their skin for the Army of the Republic of Vietnam, the "comrades" we were supposedly reinforcing. The men traded ARVN jokes and stories of bumping into retreating South Vietnamese soldiers during firefights.

* * *

As the chopper dropped lower, I could see the tiny hole cut in the foliage. The landing zone. The pilot dropped straight down, hovering nervously for five seconds as we hurled ourselves through the hatch and sprinted for cover.

Suddenly, I was in a war. All the training, the sit-ups, the firing range practice, and hand-to-hand drills suddenly seemed to fly away, leaving me naked and numb. I broke into a running crouch, scanning the treeline for the enemy. Every branch was an AK-47, every knot in a trunk was a human face.

I heard a scream and whirled around, half expecting to feel a bullet slam into me. One of the men had landed on the stub of a small tree. The thin trunk, sharpened into a punji stick, jutted red through his uniform. One of the men scrambled to him, turned to the lieutenant and shook his head. I took a deep breath. I had seen my first combat death.

We regrouped and followed the lieutenant into the brush. We found the ARVN clustered two kilometers away at the edge of a clearing. They looked like prizefighters who knew the knockout punch was coming in the next round. A number of them lay dead or dying as medics buzzed from one wounded man to the next, slapping white field dressings on crimson wounds.

We heard the familiar whump-whump-whump coming for the casualties. The dead and wounded were quickly loaded on the ARVN helicopter. As the skids rose off the ground, a number of the ARVN soldiers suddenly bolted for the hovering chopper. I was bewildered. ''What in the hell are they doing?'' I asked the nearest GI. The disgusted look on his face mirrored the expression of the helicopter's door gunners, who leveled their M-60s at their charging comrades to drive them back. The ARVN did not need reinforcements, I decided. They needed replacements.

* * *

During my first patrol, I learned to hate the OJs and needles as much as I hated the enemy. My anger flashed at the sight of heavy-lidded eyes staring blankly under helmets. Soldiers were doped up all the time -- some of them got high from the minute they woke up. The officers didn't say anything. They were afraid of getting fragged. I held my tongue, but vowed to shoot the first bastard who put me or my men in jeopardy by getting stoned on patrol.

Nothing could have prepared me for the jungle. The heat was suffocating, a damp, rotting blanket covering everything with an oily sheen. Not even the pounding heat of South Texas could compare to the misery of South Vietnam. The rain came like clockwork, soaking the already damp ground until the clouds parted and the sun baked it back into the air.

My rucksack was packed with C-rations, extra fatigues, soap, toothpaste, and letters from home. I draped a towel over the back of my neck to cushion the load. I carried two bandoliers of M-60 ammunition for the machine-gunner, two bandoliers of M-16 ammo, and six full M-16 magazines in two pouches. We each carried sixteen canteens of water for the dog, who stopped every few minutes to slop water from a helmet. The whole load weighed 80 pounds. It was like hiking up a mountain with a 10-year-old on my back.

We began each day at 5 a.m., marching in columns with a man every five yards. I usually volunteered to take the point, leap-frogging with the dog as we picked our way through the jungle, the dog sniffing out a safe path. Nobody had trained the dog to bark when the VC were in the vicinity. Without warning, the trees would erupt with gunfire. We answered back, called in artillery, and watched as the whistling shells erupted, spreading fire through the area.

When I allowed my mind to wander on level ground, I thought about my father and his dimpled scars. The military declared him 100 percent disabled, but Dad brushed off his wounds and went back to high school. He even played tight end on the football team, copper wire and all. He didn't like to talk about the day he was caught in the ambush, but I remembered every detail he told me. It helped me in Vietnam.

The jungle will warn you, he told me. The birds knew the Japanese were there. He got caught in the open, yelling a warning to the batallion as the first bullets zinged past him. The gunner finally found him, knocking him bleeding to the ground. The medics counted six bullet holes in his arms and legs.

He took pride in those wounds. There was never regret in his voice when he talked about the war, even though his bronze star took 50 years to arrive. But he never could shake that ambush. Even decades later, he would become furious for no apparent reason, then act as though nothing had happened. We learned to ride through these emotional storm clouds, hoping they would pass quickly.

This tradition was passed on as well. When I got home from the Vietnam, I could not sleep in a bed for weeks. My family would find me curled up in the corner of the room, my eyes flashing at them as they peeked through the door.

* * *

For the most part, the U.S. Army were inept invaders, fighting nature, fighting our enemies, fighting one another. We marched through countless thatched villages, searching and interrogating. Teenaged girls from the villages would meet us as we approached with rolled bamboo mats slung across their backs. "Beaucoup boom-boom" meant for five bucks, they would take you into the bushes and let you have your way on the mat. For them, it was better than being raped when the soldiers got to the village. They became the entrepreneurs of their families, making a living off the GIs. We all got the clap so many times, the medic refused to let us rotate back to the base without a penicillin shot.

If we found weapons or tunnels, the place burned. Watching platoon sergeants kill civilians suspected of helping the VC became almost a daily event. If they found a cache of weapons, everyone near it died. The lieutenant was nonchalant about the possibility we were shooting innocents. "I don't want to know about it," he told the sergeants. "You do what you gotta do." If the village was clean, we moved on.

The terrain didn't help, especially for somebody like me from a flat, dry place. The marches would have been exhausting enough without also worrying about getting shot. I fought through a maze of branches, muck, and leaves. I needed new boots every six weeks to replace the tattered leather eaten away by miles of mud, water, and clutching branches. I was constantly dehydrated as I marched against the dense air and tangled vegetation. Every day was a grind of salt tablets and mosquitoes, razorgrass and soggy boots, biting ants and leeches.

I hated the leeches. I was convinced they were creatures sent straight from hell or Ho Chi Minh. They waited in the streams and rivers we crossed, attaching themselves to our legs and groins. Like most of the men, I stopped wearing underwear -- it chafed the skin, leaving a sweat-stung rash. We tied bandanas below our knees to keep leeches out of our crotches, but they always found a gap. They were like the Viet Cong, sneaking up quietly, hunting for exposed flesh. You didn't feel them until they drew blood.

Yet I came to love the jungle for its mysterious beauty. It was so different from the flat, dust-whipped earth back home. The jungle swallowed sounds, leaving an ethereal silence broken only by the birds and monkeys, and the lizards that seemed to call out "Fuck you." When I awoke each morning on patrol, I could hear the churchbell in some nearby village. In time, I was at home there, attuned to its noises and dangers.

The VC snipers shadowed us, terrorizing us with exhausting regularity. My knees automatically buckled every time I heard a rifle crack, but the bullet was faster than a man's reflexes.

My first firefight began with a sniper's bullet snapping the back of a GI marching behind me. Everyone dropped to the turf and fired blindly, holding their shuddering rifles over clumps of grass and fallen trees. No wonder we suffered so many friendly-fire casualties, I thought as I peeked over a mound of dirt. I saw a flash of skin as the VC ran into the trees. Then the jungle was silent again.

My friends died, to be replaced by new friends. Officers rotated through, some killed by enemy fire, some by their own men. A fresh lieutenant came in about two months after I joined the company, a short, skinny West Pointer with short-cropped blond hair and a self-assured attitude picked up in the classroom. He had no feel for the jungle. He led us in circles the first time out, completely lost. We slogged through the same stream four times, picking up leeches with each pass. When the more experienced men pleaded with him to turn over the map and admit he was lost, he sternly refused.

That night, after everyone bedded down, one of the men who complained bitterly about the lieutenant's stubborn ignorance crept up to his foxhole and pulled the pin on a grenade. I was in my foxhole doing guard duty on the perimeter when the grenade went off. Somebody yelled "Incoming!" but I had not heard the whistle of a shell.

Of course, nobody had seen anything.

By then, nothing shocked me. I was one of the hollow-eyed mongrels I had seen my first day at the base. Men were dropping around me, as many from heroin as from enemy fire. The mama-sans in the little villages sold it to the American soldiers who passed through hunting for Charlie. They were little contraband convenience stores. Joints came in Lucky Strikes packages. Heroin was packed into Contact capsules and sold in little bags.

At first, I wondered about the thousands of colorful capsules littering the space between the barracks and the sandbagged perimeter at Bien Hoa. It did not take long to solve the puzzle. Men were shooting up in the open. Soldiers would pop open the capsule, tap the powder into a spoon, and add a splash of water or liquor. With a candle or a can of sterno from their C-rations, they would heat up the spoon until the heroin dissolved and bubbled, then let it cool for a moment and draw it into a syringe. Pumping a fist to coax an artery, they would plunge the needle through the skin and surrender.

They wandered the grounds like zombies, suddenly oblivious to the stress and commotion and fear. They were the weak ones, I thought, the boys who could not cope with the insanity and the killing. They were 19 and going mad.

There was an unwritten rule for the dopers: Don't get high on patrol. Nobody cared what anybody did to their brain on the base, but one heroin-addled mind could cost lives in the jungle.

The Viet Cong did not kill the first man I watched die in Vietnam. Heroin did.

He was a well-built private, about my age, with a young wife back home somewhere in the Midwest. He had received a Dear John letter that day, just before we went on patrol. "It don't mean nothin'," he muttered, folding the paper and stuffing it into his pack. Nobody believed him.

Some of the other guys had introduced him to heroin to take the edge off combat. After a few weeks, he was a borderline addict, shooting up whenever the stress overwhelmed him. That night, he hunkered down in his foxhole and cooked his powder into a clear, pure syrup. As he drew the liquid into the syringe, his buddy tried to talk some sense into him. The distraught private looked away and pulled the plunger back further.

The hit was too big, too pure. He started foaming at the mouth, his body stiffening in a morphine seizure. His buddy called for a medic, but he was dead before they could pull him from the hole. He wanted to die, I thought as I watched the zipper close over his face. If he didn't do it now, he would have done it later. It was natural selection, and one of the weak had been eliminated. A chopper came in the next morning and took him home.

He was the first of many I watched fall to the other enemy in Vietnam. Marijuana was a distraction. Heroin was seduction. Some soldiers simply wandered into the jungle and disappeared. We usually found them somewhere beyond the perimeter, their eyes wide and their mouths caked with dried spittle. If the men who discovered the body decided he had been a good soldier, someone would pump a bullet in the body. The family would be told he died a hero's death, Killed In Action. If the consensus was the dead soldier had been an asshole, he would be sent home with nothing more than the needle pricks in his arm.

Every week, we sent another overdose victim home wrapped in a green bag.

I hated the powder more each day. I tried to brush off my anger, to understand why these men preferred numbness to reality. Sometimes as I marched, the face of that private from the Midwest hovered before my eyes, his expression frozen between ecstasy and anguish. His death scene gave me a purpose. If I ever left Vietnam, I would pour my energy into fighting America's drug habit. Law enforcement had always appealed to me, but now I had a cause.

* * *

To the Viet Cong, heroin was a fighting tool.

The sappers used it for suicide missions, pumping themselves full of the stuff and charging into our camps with satchel charges. They would come dashing out of nowhere, tourniquets cutting into their arms and legs to staunch the bleeding when we shot them. Like the Japanese kamikazes of World War II, they were running to a heroic death. If they managed to penetrate our lines, they would zero in on the nearest pack of GIs and explode.

I was on patrol when the front of the column radioed a warning. VC heading our way.

The sapper came straight at my squad like a sprinter off the blocks. He was more boy than man, skinny legs churning, two bandoliers of AK-47 ammunition slapping against his chest. Several figures in black pajamas materialized behind him, racing and ducking through the foliage. They did not see us.

I raised my M-16 and squeezed off a three-round burst at the sapper. His arms cartwheeled as he dropped. The squad opened up on the black figures, taking down two or three more before they disappeared into the undergrowth. My heart was pounding. I wanted to look, to see if I had killed him, but my rooted feet ignored my morbid curiosity. I heard a low moan. Another soldier walked to the fallen boy, nudged him with the toe of his boot, then sprayed him with his M-16.

Standing over him, I felt a sort of sickening satisfaction. This kid and his buddies had been killing my buddies. I thought about the sniper who picked off one of my squad a few weeks before. The thought chilled me. He was in the rear and took a slug in the back. The sniper was patient, waiting for each of us to pass through his sights before squeezing the trigger. My head had probably hovered in his crosshairs for a moment. I could almost see his finger tensing, then relaxing as he waited for the next man. Now I looked into this boy's dead eyes and felt my muscles relax. My anger finally had its sacrifice.

After 30 days in the bush, we would return to base, shower, eat a slab of water buffalo steak, drink a warm beer and collapse. After my first month-long patrol, I slept for several days, drifting in and out of consciousness. And the nightmares came.

The sapper joined the macabre cast acting out their roles night after night. His face was frozen in surprise: high cheek-bones, smooth skin, dark eyes. Each kick from the rifle opened a red hole in his chest. Some nights, I would watch myself die in a firefight. I would wake suddenly, shaking and damp. I was not the only victim of his subconscious. Some men could not sleep without screaming.

If I was lucky, I dreamed of home.

I would snap awake as a mortar landed in the jungle nearby with a muffled thump. "Shit, I'm still in Vietnam," I mumbled to no one. I cried for the first time since I was a child.

* * *

In my letters to my father, I told him to prepare my mother for the worst. He had survived his ambush. With each day, I became more convinced I was going to die in the jungle.

I should have died when the helicopter went down.

The Rangers were getting thumped in a firefight. We were rushing to reinforce them, with too many bodies loaded into six choppers. I was in one of the middle choppers, mingled in with men from two platoons. One was a big black sergeant of about 35 who was flashing a grin, almost relishing the action. He was due to process home in three days, but had decided to fly one last mission with his squad.

The pilots flew at treetop level in a tight formation, hugging the curves of a river. The men shifted with each turn, watching the green canopy slide past the hatch, hoping our altitude and speed would catch the VC gunners before they could get off a shot.

"Grenade!"

The explosion ripped through the men crouched in the center of the compartment, killing several instantly. A rifle muzzle had caught the pin on a grenade and tugged it off the soldier's chest. A shard caught the pilot in the back of the neck. He slumped forward, sending the chopper into a tight downward spin.

The river surged up to meet us. Several men bailed out as the chopper plunged into the water. They were shredded by the splintering rotors. I scrambled over several dead soldiers and hurled myself through the hatch a few seconds before the C4 and grenades erupted and swallowed the helicopter, incinerating the wounded.

The other Hueys circled back to rescue the survivors. There were only two of us. I sloshed from one body to the next, praying for a scream, a twitch. Then I came to the black sergeant, lying on his back at the edge of the river. He looked unhurt. Maybe he's just gone into shock, I thought as I grabbed the front of his fatigues and heaved him out of the coppery water. Suddenly, the nausea came. His face was just a mask - - the back of his head was missing.

* * *

The company assembled in loose formation, wondering why the captain had summoned us from our dens. It was January, 1972, the middle of the monsoon season. We had just concluded another grueling, month-long tour in the bush. Nobody wanted to spend another second in the downpour without a damn good reason. The captain considered us for a moment, then asked for volunteers for special operations in Cambodia. Before anyone could react, he spat out a disclaimer: "If you get caught out there, as far as the Army is concerned, you were never there."

A half dozen of us volunteered. After the helicopter crash, I had prepared myself to accept death, so I charged it head-on.

The VC and NVA used Cambodia as a hideout, knowing we could not pursue them over the border. The Army did it anyway. We were a trained six-man sniper team, picked from different companies. We were sent to kill village organizers and enemy leaders. It was binational cat-and-mouse, with both sides ignoring political boundaries to slash at the other.

My team moved at night. A chopper would drop us across the Cambodian border a few kilometers from the target. Army Intelligence gave us the coordinates of villages helping the VC. We traveled light, humping through the jungle with our M-14 sniper rifles. The target villages were usually surrounded by a thick wall of foliage, providing us the perfect observation nest. I remember watching the villages stir to life with the first rays of day, church bells chiming, livestock yapping and grunting in disagreement.

Now it was my eye framing bodies in the crosshairs. My vigil lasted all day, as I became familiar with the community's rhythms. We were close enough to hear their voices, trilling in a strange tongue. By late afternoon, we knew who issued the orders. Those were the ones who died.

The rifle would kick, the spotter would call out the result, and we would retreat into the jungle's webbed arms as the first shouts echoed through the village. Sometimes we chose two targets, shooting simultaneously when the spotter dropped his arm. We never missed.

The escapes were pure adrenaline. Once we almost barrelled into a company of NVA as they passed down a jungle trail. I did my best to become one with a thick bush, ignoring the ants crawling inside my fatigues for a free meal. The NVA soldiers swaggered by, talking and whistling just 15 yards from us. I could almost make out the color of their eyes. For once, I was glad to be in Cambodia. The NVA were completely at ease here. This was their territory.

Usually we saw no one. After a kilometer or so, we could relax and wait for the night to sweep into the trees. The chopper would return to the designated coordinates to steal us back over the border before daybreak.

Officially, it never happened.

I worked in covert special operations for the remainder of my tour, bobbing in and out of Cambodia at least ten times between January and April, 1972, for the First Cavalry. I learned to obey my instincts. They had to be coaxed to the surface, but they never misled me. A twinge would warn me away from danger.

Strangely, I cannot remember the names of my friends in Vietnam. I recognize the men whose pictures are on my walls and in my photo albums -- one was Panamanian, another was from North Carolina, another a Puerto Rican from the Bronx. We exchanged addresses, but nobody called or wrote. Somewhere between Bien Hoa, Cambodia, and home, my mind erased some of the details and left me with only lingering images. I left it all behind, even the bayonet I had taken off the sapper I killed.

Nixon was bringing home more and more GIs, dropping troop strength in Vietnam below 100,000 for the first time in more than six years. My tour was cut short by four months. As I left the firebase, I took the traditional ''freedom flight,'' perched on the skid of a chopper with a smoke grenade hissing from my boot as the pilot circled the perimeter. My buddies were clapping and cheering. Others looked at me dejectedly. It was April, 1972, eleven years after President Kennedy began sending troops to Vietnam. President Gerald Ford would not declare the conflict finished until three years later.

I was going home. Alive.

Three
Homecoming
Pharr, Texas - 1972

My transition back to civilian life was rooted in silences.

The first was on the plane leaving Vietnam, a taut, ominous quiet as soldiers sat shoulder-to-shoulder in the jet, sharing an unspoken fear. Fingers dug into armrests. The flight crew was somber. There were no jokes, no happy chatter from the uniformed passengers as the engines whined to life and pushed the liner down the tarmac. Everyone on board knew the Viet Cong liked to salute departing GIs by blasting their planes out of the sky. The silence tightened around us as the plane accelerated and lurched into the air.

When we reached 33,000 feet and leveled off, the compartment erupted with cheers and applause. We were safe. "Next stop, the Philippines," the flight attendant chimed. After stops in Hawaii, Washington, and San Antonio, my last flight swooped over the flat, familiar patchwork of home.

Then another, more familiar silence. My father was at the gate in McAllen's tiny airport. As I approached, he searched my eyes, saying nothing for a few moments as we studied one another. Some of the soldiers around us were locked in bearhugs with tearful parents and wives. Not my father and me.

He was always a quiet, simple role model: President of the PTA, a 10-year school board member. He worked hard, as if his next paycheck would have to sustain the family indefinitely. My first memories are of my father in a Pharr Police Department uniform and a badge, patrolling the narrow, pitted streets lined with small frame houses and flat-faced storefronts. He later traded the uniform for a suit and a bigger paycheck, working behind a desk in the county tax assessor's office before finishing his career as an immigration law consultant for a local law firm.

My father greeted me with his usual composure, an old officer afraid to reveal his feelings to his favorite recruit. In my freshly pressed dress uniform, I felt like the little boy he used to dress in a military uniform and play soldier with. If anything, Vietnam had hardened me into a younger version of him: Disciplined, driven toward perfection, frugal with my thoughts and emotions.

Finally, he broke the silence: "Did you see a lot of action?"

"Some."

We walked to the car.

When we pulled into the driveway, the front door opened as I cut through dad's manicured lawn to the house. My mother stood in the doorway with my grinning sisters in a cluster behind her. She looked at me for a warm moment with tear-rimmed eyes, then wrapped her arms around my neck and kissed me. Her perfume enveloped me. I was home.

Diana and Melinda peppered me with questions about Vietnam, most of which I evaded. But San Juanita was the most excited to see me. She bounced and hugged me, squeezing the breath out of me. She had not understood what was happening until I left for Vietnam.

My mother insisted my father drive us straight to "San Judita" -- the St. Jude Thaddeus Shrine in Pharr, where she had maintained a vigil since I left for Vietnam. "She was at San Judita every day you were gone to pray and light candles," Diana whispered to me as we drove. "Sometimes she woke me up in the middle of the night and made me drive her there to pray. She would forget whether she had gone earlier in the day."

We walked silently over the winding brick paths toward the massive open-air altar. I drank in the scent of the magnolias, listened to the whispering palm fronds towering above St. Jude's sculpted gardens. After months in the jungle, the feeling of order and safety enveloping the shrine was almost overwhelming. As we knelt on the worn pews, I saw my picture on the altar, lit by flickering candlelight. There were other photos pasted and taped around it. The serious faces of young men in uniform stared back at me. I said a silent prayer for them.

Our family was always very religious. We were fixtures at St. Margaret's Catholic Church in Pharr, where I attended Catholic school under the sharp eyes of German nuns who seemed to glide over the ground in floor-length habits.

I smiled to myself at the memory. Catholic school. The nuns. The endless prayers. The musty closet where I was once locked up for misbehaving. Catholic school and I never agreed. I made it to the third grade.

I was expelled along with 16 other boys who finally tripped the nuns' trigger tempers for the last time. The nuns declared me a borderline incorrigible years before, branding my misdeeds into my palms with their rulers.

Naturally, the final incident began with a dare. My co-conspirators and I had puzzled over the same mystery Catholic students everywhere were dying to solve: what do they wear under there? Being the borderline incorrigible in the group, I snuck up behind a tall, black figure -- a stern-faced, blue-eyed nun we called Sister Sana -- grabbed the bottom of her habit with both fists and heaved. For a fleeting glimpse of Sister Sana's cotton bloomers, we were banished to public school forever.

Despite this smudge on my record, I was considered a decent kid by most adults. I was a Boy Scout in Lorenzo Garcia's troop 262, an altarboy at St. Margaret's, and a bit actor in school plays. Public school suited me better, anyway. I felt I was actually learning something useful, rather than wasting the day reciting prayers in a squeaky counterpoint to the nuns' devout voices.

Now I was home safe, ready to give thanks. I learned the value of prayer again in the foxholes, longing to join the villagers when their churchbells sang each morning. I was ready to pray now. St. Jude stared down at me placidly, wrapped in his gold-trimmed robes and clutching his staff. The cavernous shrine, a gray stucco arch where thousands of pilgrims had silently rubbed rosary beads, glowed with the muted light of a hundred white candles. We stopped at the pew and kneeled as a family again, bowing our heads. My mother cleared her throat, breaking the spell as she led us in prayer: *"Gracias a Dios, por entregarmelo todo completo."* Thank you, God, for bringing him back to me in one piece.

By the time the waitress slid a huge steak in front of me at the restaurant an hour later, I was convinced I was dreaming. Real beef. Real ice cream. My mother, my father, my sisters talking happily around me. Cloth napkins. At any moment, I expected the whump of a shell to wake me up back in Vietnam, shaking and alone.

* * *

I lived in my old room at home for a year. The family routine had not changed. It was as if I had walked out the front door one day, then come through the back door the next. My mother still cooked flour tortillas every morning, my sisters still wore the dresses she fashioned from the floral-print flour sacks, my father still trooped to the slaughterhouse every Saturday for his grinning cow's head. And that first night home, the 10 o'clock Southern Pacific rattled down the tracks as I pulled the blanket from my bed and tried to find a comfortable spot on the floor.

The bronze star came a few weeks later. It expressed my country's gratitude for some unnamed gallantry performed in the line of duty in March, 1972. I knew it was for something I had done with the sniper team Cambodia. My father refused to believe me when he pressed for details and I responded with a blank look, then replied, "I'm not sure."

* * *

Slowly, my life began to find the well-worn groove I left behind. It never fit perfectly again. That summer, I enrolled in criminology courses at Pan American University in Edinburg, a short drive from home. I looked up a few old friends, but found we no longer had anything in common. I drove around town, looking at the same buildings and streets and faces with new eyes. I dated a few girls, but never got serious. I was 22 years old and had my life before me. I was taking nothing for granted.

I became a loner, seeking out other Vietnam survivors. I joined the Army Reserve, then the National Guard, where fellow vets congregated, sprinkled among young men finishing the six-year stints they started when the shadow of Vietnam loomed over them. For some reason, I had to remain a soldier. It would be four years before I could let go and quit the Guard.

Before long, all my friends were veterans. They were the only people who understood. At home, I brushed off my family's lingering questions about the war with vague answers until they surrendered in frustration. With fellow vets, I could remove the veil and talk about what I had seen through the crosshairs.

I did not consider myself scarred by Vietnam. I was proud to have served my country. I paraded around campus in my fatigues, strutting like a gang member in his colors, my dappled green fatigues blending into a growing throng of student/veterans.

There were hundreds of Vietnam vets on campus, like me, taking advantage of the GI bill. Without it, most of us could never have dreamed of a college degree. With boots and backpacks, we roamed the place like a veterans' mafia.

I joined the veteran's organization at Pan American and became part of its student government ticket. My interest in politics was minimal, but with an eye on a law enforcement career, I ran for the attorney general seat. I won easily. The job was a natural for me. I was the campus election officer, enforcing election codes, making sure the candidates followed the proper procedures, and sitting in on the occassional campus meeting to see that parliamentary procedures were honored. I also threw my limited clout behind student body president Eddie de la Garza, who would later become a state representative, to fight for more student loans and scholarship money.

The anti-war movement never really took hold in the Rio Grande Valley. We read about the protests in Washington and other distant cities with astonishment. The Valley has always sent more than its share of young men to fight for America. When American troops fired shots anywhere in the world, the Valley wore its patriotism on its sleeve.

The most overt anti-war demonstrations came from the brown berets, members of La Raza Unida who gained most of their Chicano power from the farmworkers. They despised virtually anything Uncle Sam did, staging marches to take their case to a largely indifferent public.

I spent that summer rebuilding my life, carving an island of serene sanity for myself as I pushed Vietnam memories to the furthest reaches of my mind. In time, they came only at night. I attended class by day, and at night I worked the 11-to-7 shift as a dispatcher for Edinburg Police Department -- my summer internship.

I worked like a demon and landed a permanent dispatcher job the following summer. I was on a mission. When I was forced to choose between work and school, or sleep, or women, work always won. It was expected.

As a teenager, I became a workaholic in my father's image. If I wanted school clothes or a car, they came out of my pocket. With work scarce for Valley teens, I looked north. Each summer starting in junior high school I boarded a bus to Chicago, where I worked in a restaurant called The Coffee Shop my aunt Bea Cerrato managed in O'Hare Airport. We were up at 4:30 every morning, trudging into the restaurant to the smell of the day's first pot of coffee. I bussed tables, washed dishes, and helped out in the kitchen. During the school year, I worked stocking shelves for minimum wage at the Winn's department store ten miles away in Hidalgo, a little town hugging the Rio Grande.

As 1974 melted into 1975, everything was coming together. I drank in every detail of my criminology lectures, figuring how to apply my lessons to the streets when the time came. I paid particular attention to any mention of drug laws. When I became a federal agent, they would be my weapons.

In January, 1975, after six months as a dispatcher, I jumped to a patrol car. I was 25 years old. Becoming a cop seemed natural after being a soldier. I loved the discipline, the order. My father supported my decision, watching my progress like a man gazing into a time-warped mirror. My mother, as I expected, could not understand why I sought out such a dangerous job after surviving the war. She could also see my father's blood pushing me along his footsteps, and it frightened her.

After training with a veteran officer for a few days, I was alone on the streets, taking the next step toward what I hoped would be a career cracking down on the drug trade.

I bought into the image of a Texas cop: Spit-shined boots, a nickel-plated .357 magnum pistol tucked into a holster on my hip, and a lead foot. I was determined to be the most aggressive cop the department had. I considered it a personal failure if another officer beat me to a crime scene, no matter what part of town. More often than not, the first badge the victim saw was number 122.

There was a reason the older cops took their time. The job quickly became mundane. We worked small town crime: Burglaries, mostly, with a steady flow of auto accidents, speeding tickets, and drunk husbands beating their wives and kids. My Vietnam instincts helped. On burglary in progress calls, I parked a block away from the address and crept toward the house, just as I had done with the guards at Cam Ranh Bay. Running over level ground with nobody shooting at me, it was almost easy. It got to the point where I could catch them in the house, still picking through the valuables.

Still, I enjoyed my work. The Valley was a quiet, conservative farm belt, studded with endless rows of citrus trees, onions, cotton, cabbage and other cash crops thriving on the rich alluvial deposits from the Rio Grande. Gangs, murders and drug abuse were almost unheard of. The sparkling sands of South Padre Island were a short drive to the east, where salty winds swept over the Gulf of Mexico to beat back the relentless heat. My father and I spent many mornings hip-deep in the shallow bay between the island and the mainland, casting for speckled trout and redfish. In the autumn, I pulled on my fatigues and picked through the cactus and mesquite, hunting dove. In the winter, I stalked white-tailed deer. Valley life was nothing exciting, but it was the kind of place where you could raise a family.

The weeks and months blurred into one another. Watergate, the Paris agreement ending the war, and the fall of Saigon in 1975 all slid by like summer clouds, casting a brief shadow before blowing away.

Then I met Noe on a warm night in Reynosa, the sprawling Mexican city across the river from McAllen. When she walked up to me and introduced herself, I recognized her immediately. Noelia Rodriguez worked at the Sonic on University Drive in Edinburg, a drive-up burger stand popular with cops for its cheap burgers and chili dogs. I stopped there occasionally for dinner as my shift started, calling my order into the little speaker, and then watching Noe hop from car to car filling orders. She had a delicate face and beautiful auburn-tinged hair, short and straight, with the creamy brown skin we called "perlada." When we bumped into one another at the Reynosa nightclub, I immediately asked for her phone number. The next day, I called and invited her to the movies.

She was 17 when we started dating. Her parents hated the idea of their daughter dating a cop, but Noe refused to listen. She was a head-strong, take-charge girl. We saw each other every chance we could, catching movies at the Pan Am Drive-In across from campus, lazing on the beach or dancing at The Rose Monaco, a local disco. Before I realized it, I had stopped seeing other women. I was in love for the first time in my life. We were nearly inseparable for the next two years.

* * *

Shortly before I met Noe, the department promoted me to CID -- the criminal investigations division. I became a detective sergeant, with a dramatic increase in my workload to go along with the jump in rank. Patrolmen can go home at the end of a shift; investigators work around the clock. I would arrest someone at midnight, then drag myself into court early the next morning for the arraignment. The criminal would get a few hours sleep in jail. I didn't. Although I missed the instant gratification of patrol, I appreciated the meticulous work of picking apart a crime scene. We were jacks of all trades, experts in fingerprinting, interrogations, photography, and interviewing witnesses.

Even better, the promotion gave me a chance to go after dopers.

Marijuana, cocaine, and heroin -- the big three at the time -- roared through Edinburg every day on their trek north. The city straddled U.S. Highway 281, one of only three routes out of the Valley. It was also the most direct route from the Reynosa, Mexico, area to San Antonio, Dallas, and the rest of America. From time to time, the dispatcher's phone would ring with a tip about another shipment headed from Mexico. We would jot down the license number and the time the load departed and lie in ambush.

If it sounded like a major load, we called in the drug cavalry. The Texas Department of Public Safety and the local Sheriff's office both had effective drug units, but I leaned toward the Drug Enforcment Administration, a relatively new federal agency created specifically to stop the kind of senseless death I had witnessed day after day in Vietnam, and was beginning to see in my hometown as the traffickers fed and expanded their small clique of users.

Whenever I got a tip on a big load, I called Chema Cavazos and Jesse Torrez at the DEA office in McAllen. In exchange, they let me work the case with them. Both were senior agents: Cavazos, a former Customs officer who was now a DEA group supervisor, was light-skinned and heavy-set with thick glasses. Torrez was dark-complected and slim, with short, wavy hair. Both wore *guayaberas*, the open-necked shirts favored by many men in the hot climate, which gave them the look of a border Laurel and Hardy team. They seemed eager to work with a young local police officer who showed an interest in their work. I had more than a passing interest. I wanted to jump to the DEA as soon as possible.

* * *

Working drug cases in Edinburg did not require much creative detective work. There was one major hotel, the Echo, where most of the out-of-town traffickers conducted their business. We spent many nights in the parking lot, watching them come and go as we waited to get enough evidence to pounce. We knew who most of them were, anyway. The drug network in the Rio Grande Valley was small, as were the amounts transported. Two hundred pounds of marijuana or two kilos of cocaine was considered a big seizure. Ten years later, seizures that size would become routine.

By then, I had a good network of informants throughout the community. I spent a lot of time on the street where people could see and talk to me. It was a simple arrangement. They were typically ordinary citizens with knowledge of drug activity, and a strong desire to rid their community of it. When they learned of a shipment, they called me and I arrested the dopers. No money changed hands. I kept my part of the bargain by simply keeping their identities secret.

Working on the border meant dealing with the Mexican police. Cavazos and Torrez were experts. When my informants fed me information about a load coming over the river, they immediately called the Mexican federal police and set up an appointment.

Crossing the bridge into Reynosa left no doubt you were leaving the United States and entering Mexico. The narrow streets of old Reynosa zigged past rows of low-slung stucco and concrete block houses. On the weekends, tourists and teenagers streamed across the river to fill the gift shops, liquor stores, and bars crowding the *Zona Rosa* a few blocks from the bridge. Wherever they went, they attracted a scraggly train of hawkers and children selling gum. They also attracted the police, a largely corrupt network of squads who saw tourists as an easy target for bogus traffic stops and extra cash.

The Mexican *federales* were a bunch of cowboys, no discipline whatsoever. The first time I trailed the DEA agents into the Mexican feds' office, they invited us along on a raid. It was my initiation into their version of border drug enforcement.

The raid was a controlled delivery. The *federales* waited until the load of hashish reached the target house, owned by a customs broker across the bridge in Hidalgo. We burst into the house, the Mexicans forced the seven men inside to the floor at gunpoint. They cracked the top off a wooden crate and removed the hash, smiling to each other.

The *federales* suddenly turned ugly, kicking and punching their captives mercilessly. I looked at Cavazos with an incredulous expression. He held up a silent hand. We were their guests.

One of the *federales* called to a little boy in the street, handed him a rumpled handful of pesos and said "Bring me a six-pack of Topo Chico." The boy looked at him for a moment. I looked at Torrez, wondering why the Mexicans were ordering mineral water in the middle of a bust. He offered no clues.

"Hot or cold?" the boy asked with a quizzical look.

"It doesn't matter. Go!"

By the time the boy returned with the bottles, the suspects' hands and feet were tightly bound. The *federales* led them hopping into the courtyard behind the house, then separated one from the group and positioned him below the ceiling beams jutting from the side of the house. One of the officers heaved a rope over the stout beam, quickly threading the other end through the man's bound feet.

Two of the Mexican officers grabbed the dangling end of the rope and grunted, yanking the squirming prisoner upside down until his head swayed three feet off the ground like a pendulum. I glanced around the group. The captives were wide-eyed and silent. The Mexican police smiled coldly. Nobody in the street could see what was about to happen behind the high walls of the tiny courtyard. The officer who had ordered the water swung the dangling figure toward him, squeezing the man's head between his knees so he could not move. He popped the top off one of the bottles, shook it vigorously with his thumb over the opening, then shot the foaming soda down the suspect's nose, where it burned its way into his sinuses.

The *federales* looked at one another with sardonic smiles as the man choked, writhing in pain. The water ran from his nose and mouth. He moaned, "Please don't kill me."

The questioning began. "Who does the hashish belong to? Who imported it for you? What was its destination?" The hanging captive cooperated fully, as did most of his comrades. The two who decided to keep their mouths shut received the same treatment. They talked too. They were all locals, traffickers who ran hash and marijuana across the border by bribing customs officials at the bridge.

After a few trips to Mexico, I realized torture was standard police procedure with dopers. The unlucky and the uncooperative were hung from a beam, doused with water and jolted with a battery-powered cattle prod, which buzzed menacingly before biting into their damp skin. The police called it "*chicharra*." The cicada.

* * *

I applied for a job with DEA in 1977, almost immediately after receiving my criminology degree from Pan American. The agency had not hired anyone from South Texas in years, I was told, and to make matters worse, the government was in the midst of a hiring freeze.

I had almost forgotten about the application when the call came, nearly three years later. I was told to report to San Antonio to appear before their board for an oral exam. Several hundred applicants were vying for a couple of spots with the agency, I discovered as I sat nervously outside the conference room. About 30 of us had been chosen to take the oral boards, including several other Mexican-Americans. Rumor had it DEA was under pressure to hire more Hispanics. That did not make me feel any better.

I never liked quotas. I just wanted the chance to compete equally with everyone else. Some of the other hopefuls compared notes. I was flying by the seat of my pants, hoping my military and police background would give me an edge.

Chema called a few weeks later, on New Year's Eve, 1979, with the good news. I rushed to his Edinburg office, where he swore me in at his desk. There were no trumpets blaring, no ceremony, but in my mind, my real drug war had begun.

In the weeks before I was to enter DEA school in Washington D.C., I threw myself into my new job, once again trying to be the first cop at the scene. I was quickly given the opportunity to prove my dedication.

One of the agents approached me in the office with a manila folder.

"We've got a case you can help us with. We've been watching a guy from Edinburg for a while. Looks like a trucker-turned-trafficker, and he's getting big. He's been picking up heroin and cocaine in Las Milpas, then taking it to Chicago in his truck."

I was eager to get to work. "What's his name?" I asked.

"Martinez. He's your girlfriend's stepfather."

My stomach lurched. Noe never said a word to me about her stepfather being involved with narcotics.

I confronted Noe the next day. She spilled the entire story, almost relieved to shed her burden. She said her stepfather was freebasing cocaine, becoming more paranoid and abusive. He thought he was being watched, so he pulled Noe, her mother, and her sister into his web, insisting they drive to Victoria, 240 miles away, to pick up bundles of cash. On another trip, he told Noe and her sister to drive to Illinois with a load of contraband. Her sister concealed the package in her clothing until they reached the buyer's house in Peoria.

"Why didn't you come to me?" I asked.

"He said if he was busted he would invent some story and have us thrown in jail too."

I was livid. Noe never even took aspirin for headaches, much less used drugs. Her stepfather had been running heroin and coke for years, she said. His illicit sideline became the family's darkest secret. They were trapped by fear and shame.

I wanted to take him down myself. I could not fathom a father involving his own wife and stepdaughter in trafficking. I called the office to explain the situation.

Although I built the case against Noe's stepfather, my fellow agents insisted on keeping my name out of the reports, explaining DEA rules prohibited agents from working cases involving their loved ones. I was nervous about the whole investigation: I had no intention of getting fired after my first month. My boss reassured me and asked me to keep feeding information to Bobby Clark, the agent in charge of the investigation. Clark continued writing his reports as if he were receiving the information directly. My eagerness would come back to haunt me.

In the end, Elias Martinez was betrayed by the family he betrayed. He was arrested, jumped bail, and became a fugitive, never suspecting Noe and her mother had brought the DEA to his door. In fact, he called them from his hiding place. A few days later, he was arrested in Victoria and delivered to prison.

I was ready to pack my bags for DEA school immediately. The longer I worked in McAllen, the less I liked what I saw.

The McAllen office had fractured into two cliques whose members tolerated each other in good times and refused to speak in bad times. One formed loosely around Chema Cavazos, the other around an agent named Terry Bowen. I was amazed at the depth of the resentment in the office, something I never sensed as an outsider working with the agents.

I was also shocked at some agents' disregard for some of the basic street rules I learned behind a police badge. They frequently burned their informants. I watched in disbelief as agents busted traffickers just minutes after the informant had made the buy, rather than waiting so the doper could not put two and two together and figure out who had snitched on him. Patience was a vital tool in drug busts: Informants were too valuable to burn, and there was always a next time.

Sometimes the operations degenerated into pure comedy.

I was with Cavazos and his group one night as we set up a perimeter around a K-Mart parking lot. Ten of us sat quietly in our vehicles, waiting for the undercover agent to make the buy Cavazos had orchestrated. Everyone was in position, waiting for the doper to arrive when Cavazos jumped out of his car and jogged across the parking lot.

I squinted through the darkness and saw a familiar face. Then two. Three. They were agents from our office, sitting in their vehicles and squinting back at us. I looked around at the other agents in my group, who returned my puzzled expression.

Everyone met in the middle of the parking lot as Cavazos hunted down the other group's supervisor.

"What the hell are you doing here?" the supervisor asked Cavazos.

"Buying. What are you doing?"

"Selling."

We had set each other up for a bust, two groups of DEA agents, ready to arrest one another as dopers.

* * *

DEA school in Washington D.C. was boot camp all over again. Fifteen weeks of running every other day, climbing stairs, shooting at silhouettes on the firing range, boxing, and whacking each other with padded sticks. In the classroom, we crammed like college seniors on federal drug laws, surveillance techniques, report writing, undercover work, and all the minutiae of being a soldier in the escalating drug war.

Some of the instructors wanted me to quit. They never said so directly, but they did not have to. Their eyes and voices revealed their true feelings: I had seen the same lightly masked disdain in the eyes of some of my teachers in the Valley, and again in the Army. I could sometimes overhear the instructors talking among themselves, punctuating their gripes with "goddam Mexicans." There were several other Hispanics in the class, all receiving the same unspoken messages. Extra laps for no apparent reason. Sudden orders to drop and do push-ups. A surly undertone when we were addressed. A couple of them dropped out in disgust.

It didn't bother me. I was in still in good shape, and the Army accustomed me to racist drill sergeants with volatile personalities. A few extra push-ups were a small price to pay for a DEA job. I finished, standing proudly with the class at the graduation ceremony as Kika de la Garza, my hometown Congressman, watched from the audience. I was ready to prove myself.

Just before graduation, my DEA counselor called me into his office. The agency was sending me to New York City for my first assignment. "Are you sure you have the right Castillo?" I asked, thinking he had confused me with the other Castillo in our class. He showed me the papers.

He launched into a speech about what a wonderful opportunity I was receiving from the agency. I was skeptical. There were a dozen places I thought I would be assigned, but New York was nowhere on the list. My counselor smiled, his eyes searching my face for a reaction. I had my marching orders. I shook his hand and swallowed my doubts.

Back in McAllen, I spent every spare moment with Noe, promising her I would come back. I had no intention of letting her go. Just before I left town, one of my informants called with information about a two kilo cocaine deal about to take place at the Hilton. I reached for the phone to call my office, then set it back in the cradle. I did not trust them. I found the number of a DPS narcotics agent I knew would protect my informant.

I hoped things would be better in New York.

Four
The Planet Manhattan
New York City - 1980

I hated New York immediately. After landing at La Guardia Airport, I took a taxi through choking traffic to a hotel in Queens, where I would live until I found my own nook in the concrete canyons. The next morning, my first crowded subway ride took me to 555 West 57th Street, where the DEA office was located in the Ford Building. In less than a day in the big city, I was overwhelmed. Not even in Vietnam had I felt so lost and alone. Nobody seemed to give a damn about anyone else as they elbowed their way through the throng. Every blaring car horn and sour glance reinforced my aversion to the city. I did not want this to work. I wanted to go home.

I had asked to be assigned somewhere with a large Mexican-American community, where I could put my language and cultural knowledge to work. Instead, I was going to be the first Mexican-American in the DEA's New York City Division Office. I was like a lost child, gawking at the towering landscape as I approached the office on the west side of Manhattan, a block from the Hudson River.

The people crammed into the elevator gave me a peculiar look as I pushed my way inside. The men wore shirts and ties, the women skirts and conservative blouses. It was the dawning of the Reagan era: The federal government was Republican territory again. I looked like a Carter holdover in my best boots, a straw cowboy hat, and jeans. I locked my eyes on the doors until they parted.

The receptionist directed me to the office of Jeffrey Hall, the supervisor for Enforcement Group 6. *My new family,* I thought sarcastically. He invited me into his office with a college boy's smile and a firm grip. Hall was a Harvard graduate, a short, baby-faced former collegiate wrestler who looked like he got lost on the way to the dorms. He wore jeans, tennis shoes with no socks, and a maroon Harvard T-shirt with a hole in the side.

I looked around the spartan office for a moment. There were no plaques or photos on the walls. The office contained little more than a desk and window looking out on the city.

Jeff got straight to the point. "The first thing you have to do is get rid of that hat," he said. "The only people who wear cowboy hats here are queers."

Something inside snapped like a brittle twig. I tossed my badge and my gun on his desk. "I'm quitting. I'm going back home."

He cocked his head and studied me for a moment, then rolled his eyes toward the window. "Why?"

"This is New York City. What the hell am I going to do here? I've got no relatives, I've got no friends..."

Jeff squinted at the skyline again. "I'll tell you what. Take off. Go find a place to live, and come back when you're ready to work."

I suddenly felt ridiculous. I sheepishly collected my belongings from his desk. "Shit, you're right. I've come this far. I guess I'll give it a try."

For days, I walked through Queens, trying to find a studio apartment I could afford on my small salary. I finally found a matchbox apartment on the top floor of a brownstone near Shea Stadium. I took it without even inspecting it. It was not a wise decision. I could have fit the entire $600-a-month apartment into a garage and still had room for my car. The kitchen was barely large enough for one person. My legs almost stuck out the bathroom door when I sat on the toilet. I moved in my few belongings: a small twin bed, a small TV, a dining table with four wooden folding chairs, a few dishes, and my clothes.

I immediately called home, longing for a familiar voice. I told my father of my urge to flee the city. He sided with Jeff, using his stern officer's tone. "You worked so hard to become a federal agent, and now you're a federal agent and you're going to quit? You go out there and try, and if you don't like it, then you come home." There was no discussion.

Celerino Castillo III and Dave Harmon

As I hung up, the building shook. I threw open the back window and watched the tail of a Long Island Railroad train disappear down the tracks. I groaned. The trains rocked the room every hour for the rest of the night as I stared at the ceiling, trying to fight my anxiety, trying to sleep.

A week after our first meeting, I knocked on Jeff's door. He studied me with an approving nod. I had swapped my boots for tennis shoes and stuffed my hat in the closet.

"Are you ready to go to work?" he asked with a boyish grin.

"Yeah. I guess I am."

* * *

DEA's New York office was the largest in the country, with nine enforcement groups, an intelligence section to keep us patched in with other parts of the country, and a task force made up of DEA agents, New York Police Department narcotics agents, and state police. I was impressed. We had a seemingly unlimited supply of money for surveillance, undercover work, and busts. We had a huge network of talented informants. Our bosses wanted to prove America was winning the drug war. I wanted to help prove them right.

The 15 or so agents in our group were known as "Jeff's Raiders," a nickname that reflected Hall's reckless abandon. The other group members considered him "an agent's agent," the highest compliment DEA grunts can give a supervisor. They also considered him certifiably nuts, swapping stories of Jeff storming into buildings, taunting drug dealers, and otherwise ignoring good sense. I found him odd at the very least, breaking off a thought in mid-sentence, then glancing around the room as if I had suddenly become invisible. But he was one of the most intelligent people I had ever met. He had a prejudiced streak: Jeff did not like female or minority agents. I think my work ethic impressed him -- we were both workaholics. So we became friends.

It took me six months to get over the culture shock of New York. I spent my first few weekends alone in my apartment, running up the phone bill with lonely calls to my family and to Noe, whose voice magnified my urge to go home. During one late-night conversation, a light clicked on. I realized then I wanted to marry her, as soon as I could. Meanwhile, I was trapped in a tiny box inside a steel maze.

In time, I surrendered to the city. I took my new DEA car exploring. On Sundays, I ate breakfast at some small diner, or treated myself at the Tavern on the Green in Central Park, then basked on the grass with *The New York Times*. After a movie in Manhattan, I would drive home to Queens. As I became more adventurous, I caught Broadway plays, sampled Radio City Music Hall, and watched movie stars flash into theaters for world premieres.

I slowly made friends and developed the love-hate relationship with New York so common among long-time residents. I learned to drive like a predator. I went to cop bars and cop parties with Puerto Rican and Cuban friends from DEA and NYPD. I fell in love with the food: Cuban dishes at Victor's Cafe in Manhattan, Puerto Rican feasts at a hundred little neighborhood cafes, real Chinese food in Chinatown. I went to the same little deli every morning for a fresh ham, egg and cheese bagel sandwich. I even learned to like coffee.

My first partner, Louis Diaz, was famous in New York law enforcement circles for his role in busting Nicky Barnes, Jr., "the black Al Capone." Barnes was the biggest doper in Harlem before Diaz helped send him away for life. Diaz was a jumble of contrasts: He was a gentleman, raised by Spanish parents in a tough Brooklyn neighborhood, who went on to roam the streets armed with a psychology degree and an impressive amateur boxing record. He taught me how to think, talk, and dress like a New York agent. I settled into a rhythm, driving to his house every morning for bagels and eggs with his family before we set out for my next on-the-job lesson.

After a few weeks, when I learned enough to survive on the streets, Jeff's Raiders welcomed me into their fold. I wanted to see if the group fit its swashbuckling nickname. For weeks, the other agents tried to make me squirm, shaking their heads sullenly when they learned I had become a member of Group 6. "I hope you've got good insurance," one agent said with sarcastic drama. "Wear your vest."

Group 6 was the embodiment of the Reagan-style drug war. The new president wanted action, he wanted results, and he wanted them quickly. Drug treatment programs were gutted in favor of more interdiction. Our budget increased. Our DEA chiefs welcomed the largess, but on the street, we were pressured to repay the favor with numbers. I soon discovered why Jeff's Raiders were the most productive unit in the New York office. Quality had become a slave to quantity.

Everything I learned in DEA school went out the window. This was the real thing; lock and load your weapons and go hunting for dopers. We were every drug dealer's nightmare, an angry pack of federal agents wrapped in flak jackets, carrying Smith & Wesson .357 revolvers. Jeff always led the charge, kicking doors open and screaming ''Hit the floor!'' as a river of navy DEA windbreakers poured into the room. We once scared a doper's pet Chow so badly it jumped through a window and dropped six stories to its death.

We operated like a Vietnam platoon, conducting search-and-destroy operations on the streets. More dopers always followed, instantly filling in the gaps. For important cases, we did things by the book. For the minor junkies, traffickers, and dealers, most of them illegal aliens who would not complain about their civil rights, we made their lives hell to shut them down for the night. There were just too many of them and too few of us.

I remember Jeff telling me, ''The system doesn't work. You'll arrest those bastards and they'll be out the next day, back on the streets.'' We made up new rules as we barrelled through the dark streets, crashing into dopers' houses and apartments. We did away with reading their rights. We conducted illegal searches and seizures. We didn't care about prosecutions. We simply tossed them in jail for a night and took another ounce or kilo off the streets.

The internal affairs office was always watching, but we were protected by the cluster of New Yorkers in DEA's Washington headquarters. They were known in the agency as the ''New York Mafia,'' and they made sure no messy internal investigations got in the way of the numbers. We were connected.

Cocaine was king in New York, bursting back from relative obscurity to become yet another lucrative underworld business. It came by land, by sea, by air, spreading ecstasy and anguish and money, so much money. Colombians were bringing it into America any way they could, feeding their new cash cow and milking it for dollars. The powder washed away class distinctions.

We were busting weak, watery-eyed junkies along with the silver spoon set who came to crave coke.

The poorest neighborhoods of New York soon became a sort of coke-crazed Dodge City. Dominican gangs perfected a new technique to deliver more bang for fewer bucks. They mixed powdered cocaine with baking soda or "comeback," a chemical similar to the prescription anesthetic lidocaine, then cooked the mixture until it formed solid, rock-like cocaine crystals. Crack was born. With cocaine now affordable to the masses, the Dominicans, supplied by the Cali cartel in Colombia, conquered block after block with the city's hottest new high.

Everyone wanted a piece of the action, and the neighborhoods where turfs collided became war zones. NYPD drug busts jumped by nearly half my first year in the city. Between 1980 and 1985, the number would triple. It was Prohibition all over again, machine guns blazing from screeching cars and rival gang members bleeding in the streets. The rumrunners of the 1920s would live again in the crack lords of the '80s. The Jamaicans turned the savage cottage industry into a nationwide conquest, sending streetwise entrepreneurs across America to establish crack houses. Thousands of lives would be shredded in the process.

* * *

Cocaine was like an old starlet, making a comeback in trendy clothes. But smack remained New York's darling.

Shortly after I arrived, the agency placed a new emphasis on heroin. In the late '70s, the drug had made a leap out of the ghettos into the trendy disco circuit. Suddenly, DEA wanted heroin numbers. Naturally, Jeff's Raiders became the best damn heroin-busters in town. I thought back to the soldier I watched die, squirming, in a foxhole in Vietnam. I wanted to be the point man again.

We descended on Harlem's heroin network, lining up informants and greasing palms for names and addresses. The heroin dens were easy to spot. Shuffling addicts came in shifts for their fix, sharing needles in back rooms before shuffling back into the street, their hands swollen like balloons from collapsed veins. I saw young runaways with big-city dreams turned into toys for Harlem heroin dealers.

One undercover bust still bothers me. I was about to buy from one of Harlem's typically flashy dealers, a huge black man decked out in gold and silk, when I asked the standard question: "Is this good stuff?" He grinned and tilted his head back, calling to the back room. Two emaciated girls emerged. Neither looked older than 14. "These are the girls who test my stuff," he said, handing them syringes. The girls stripped from the waist down, smiling in anticipation. My jaw went slack as they plunked down in chairs and spread their legs, expertly guiding needles to the large vein in their groins. Their heads lolled dramatically as they testified to the heroin's quality with thick tongues. After I made the buy, I told the other agents what had happened. They took that pusher down hard, taking special pains to leave their mark on him as the girls were carted off to a shelter.

The scene was repeated a dozen times as we rampaged through Harlem. My conscience screamed at me every time we cracked the hinges off another door. I had always done everything by the book. Here they ripped out the pages and stomped on them. I remember Jeff taking me aside one night and saying: "Look, Cele, this is the way we do things. We're a real close-knit group, we keep to ourselves." *This is not right*, I thought. But I didn't question his methods. I had a duty to uphold. I was a rookie, getting the best experience DEA had to offer, absorbing more in a few months than an agent in McAllen would learn in a career. And I was finally wreaking havoc in the narcotics world, making good on the vow I made in Vietnam. I loved it.

* * *

My first big solo case went down on May 1, 1981, when I broke Elvia Garcia's heart. Elvia (not her real name) had become something of a legend among the agents in the task force, who tried to bust her for more than two years. She quietly became the neighborhood pusher, selling cocaine out of her small house in Flushing. Elvia stayed in business with old-fashioned street smarts: She refused to sell to Anglos, blacks, or Puerto Ricans. She knew they could be cops. That left her a healthy pool of customers from other Latin American countries.

In a city where Puerto Ricans, Salvadorans, and just about every other variety of Latin American could be found by the blockful, Mexicans were rare. I asked if I could try to wiggle past her defenses. A South American informant took me to her small row house and introduced me to the grand dame of the neighborhood. She came to the door in a conservative dress, a thin, old woman with pinned gray hair and delicate hands. I felt like I was about to bust my grandmother. She invited me in, leading me to the kitchen as she ran me through a polite cross-examination. In a thick Mexican accent, I told her I was a Mexican businessman traveling through the area. Strictly pleasure, I added with a smile. She relaxed.

Elvia reached into her purse, retrieving a small plastic bag packed with cocaine. The powder had just come in from Colombia, she said. Very high quality. I bought four ounces for $7,500, thanked her, and left. She welcomed me like a lost son when I returned a few weeks later for the big score: two kilos. The coke was waiting for me, neatly wrapped on the kitchen counter like a gift. I almost hated to bust her. I shook off the thought, telling her I needed to run out to my car to get the money. I gave the signal as soon as I reached the yard, disappearing before the task force agents stormed in. I did not want to see her led away in handcuffs. The agents also arrested another elderly woman who handled the books for their cocaine business. My stock rose immediately in the office.

* * *

I had less pity for Romero and Maria Moreno (not their real names), a Puerto Rican couple who ran an international cocaine smuggling operation out of the Bronx. They were the targets of a new DEA technique. Our bosses had explained the "reverse," and we were eager to try it. The reverse turned agents into dealers: Instead of posing as buyers, we began selling drugs to the bad guys, using seized cocaine to lure them into jail. The technique moved us higher up the drug food chain, busting the people who sold larger quantities. I was one of the first DEA agents to pull it off.

A Puerto Rican informant introduced me to the Morenos in the Holiday Inn on West 57th Street, a few blocks from our offices. We found a booth in the bar and got down to business.

They were an attractive couple, a pair who would blend well in Manhattan's art galleries and charity balls. Moreno was the tall-dark-and-handsome type, a friendly man who was written up in the local press for spending $20,000 at a public television auction. The writers called Rosado and his first wife "enthusiastic, streetwise entrepreneurs." They did not know how accurate they were. Now he had a new wife, Maria, who was their maid before he dumped his wife, and a growing cocaine operation.

He started the conversation with a warning. "If you're a cop," he said with a slight grin, "then I'm talking to a dead cop." I smiled. It was a common technique dopers used to measure prospective partners. Maria, an attractive, dark-skinned woman, immediately cut in: "If I don't like you, we don't do business." Now I had two egos to contend with. I turned on the charm, showering her with compliments about her clothes and jewelry. She purred.

Moreno said his organization was strapped for cocaine. His supplier had dried up. He needed a couple of kilos to keep his customers happy. They wanted to buy one kilo at a time, but I insisted on delivering both kilos together. Making two deliveries increased my risks, I argued. I knew two kilos would keep them in business for at least three months. They could cut it with enough sugar to make six kilos, each yielding a thousand one-gram packets they could sell on the street for $100 each.

"If you trust me, you trust me," I said, standing to leave. "If you don't, we don't do business." After a couple more meetings, they agreed to buy two kilos for $100,000.

On June 6, 1981, I drove to their apartment in a low-rent Puerto Rican neighborhood in the Bronx. They obviously wanted to cloak their wealth in the drab high-rise. Inside, the place looked like a Park Avenue penthouse, full of new electronic toys and expensive furniture.

Moreno took me to the bedroom and picked up a stack of documents from the bed. "This is how I stay ahead of the cops," he said, leafing through the papers. They were intelligence reports from the FBI, CIA, and New York Police Department. I clenched my teeth, wondering if he had a mole in DEA and was preparing to kill me. Instead, he asked me to meet him at the Holiday Inn at a quarter to one that afternoon. I stifled a sigh of relief.

They arrived at exactly 12:45 in their blue Datsun. Maria clutched a blue bag containing a scale and a bottle of bleach, which drug runners used to test the purity of cocaine. I was waiting at the bar with our informant, who met the pair outside, took a peek at the money, then returned to his stool. "They only have $50,000," he said. They wanted to sample the coke before they produced the other half of the money.

The rest of Jeff's Raiders were scattered throughout the hotel and on the street, waiting. *Half will have to be good enough this time*, I thought as I gave the signal. After the agents arrested the pair, we searched the car and found

$48,000 in a bag in the trunk, along with a safe deposit box key. Search warrant in hand, we opened the box and found another $49,000. By the time we wrapped up the case, we had seized $131,000 in cash, $21,000 in jewelry, the Datsun, and a loaded revolver Maria was carrying. Romero and Maria went to prison. After this success, the reverse became standard procedure throughout New York.

Everything changed when Jeff got married. He found some sanity and lost his erratic aggressiveness. There were new house rules: He wanted us home with our families if we were not on the street. He also started what we came to call "Federal Fridays." The office was almost deserted on Fridays. Cases were put off until Monday, and everyone was gone by 3 p.m. to beat the traffic. I stayed late anyway. I had nothing to go home to.

* * *

As the Moreno investigation wound down, I began working with Gerald Franciosa, a veteran New York agent who specialized in organized crime. Where Luis epitomized the urbane Latino gentleman, my new partner fit my image of a Mafioso perfectly: a tall, solid Italian with a moustache and dark hair combed straight back toward the collar of his expensive suit.

We became a team. In our street dramas, Gerry was the Italian mobster from out of town looking to buy or sell cocaine. I was his "South American connection." We began working undercover, busting minor Mafia types. Although every don in the city threatened their soldiers with death if they were caught dealing narcotics, neither the dons nor their men obeyed the decree. We had plenty of work. I was the quiet half of the pair, letting Gerry negotiate, stammering in broken English when I was forced to speak. We thought we had our act down perfectly. It would have to be perfect. We were about to perform for a much more discriminating audience.

* * *

After a long stretch in prison Louis Boyce did not want to go back. Boyce emerged from his cell a grizzled old wolf, drooping at the chin and graying at the temples. He had just started dabbling in heroin when we nailed him.

DEA received court permission to tap Boyce's phone, so our agents knew when he planned to pick up his next delivery. They were waiting at the drop spot in Brooklyn when he picked up a brown paper bag with about a half pound of heroin. Faced with what could be his final trip to the penitentiary, the aging gangster decided to talk. He was actually quite pleasant about the whole thing. I expected bitterness and deception. Boyce gave us cheery cooperation.

In law enforcement jargon, Boyce had "flipped." In the tight-lipped underworld, Boyce turned snitch. He helped Gerry infiltrate a major heroin operation run out of East Harlem by two major crime families, the Luccheses and Bonannos. With Boyce paving the way with handshakes, Gerry met two of the operation's main men: Oreste "Ernie Boy" Abbamonte and Joseph "Joe the Crow" Delvecchio.

Boyce also betrayed his source, a Puerto Rican named William "Crazy Willie" Irizarry. He was the main distributor, the man who received the shipments and broke the heroin into kilos, which Ernie Boy and Joe the Crow then sold. DEA rushed to the judge and tapped Crazy Willie's phones immediately, only to hit a brick wall: Nobody could understand a word Crazy Willie said. I was called in to break his code. His messages to his wife, who set up his deals, were an unintelligible jumble, like Spanish poured into a blender. I had never heard anything like it.

Gerry and Boyce did all the undercover work. I was selected to play their driver, steering the big rented Cadillacs while they rode like royalty in the leather back seat. Gerry was going through his courtship, earning the gangsters' trust with each meal and glass of wine, chipping away at their inbred suspicion to cement the deal. Luckily, the gangsters trusted Boyce. They called him several times to make sure Gerry was okay. As we listened through the tapped lines, he reassured them his new connection could deliver.

I kept my mouth shut and drove, waiting in the car most of the time. While Gerry talked, waving his hands, I waited, watching for other mobsters. I studied our prey. I thought Gerry looked more gangster-like, but I knew they were the real item. Delvecchio was 38 and slim, a shade under six feet tall, with brown hair framing the beaked nose which inspired his nickname. His DEA sheet was impressive: 33 files documenting his heroin activities. Abbamonte was five years younger and the smaller of the two, with curly hair and a pronounced Adam's Apple. He was more prolific, with 38 DEA files bearing his name for the same heroin racket.

Ernie Boy and Joe the Crow preferred to do business in the city's best restaurants, high-dollar clubs, or over cards in Atlantic City. I shelled out a good portion of my paycheck to look the part. DEA was willing to pick up the tab for meals, drinks, and small gambling excursions, but we had to buy our own costumes. My mother would have fainted at the sight of me: raccoon fur coat, a thick gold bracelet with "Anthony," my alias, written in diamonds, two cashmere suits, $500 shoes, and hundred-dollar ties.

The investigation began eating more and more of my time. When I was not driving Gerry and Boyce around, I was in the van helping with surveillance or listening to tapes of Crazy Willie's gibberish. I was working around the clock, wobbling in after long nights of surveillance to write my reports, a job Gerry detested. Thomas Cash, the assistant agent in charge, finally grabbed Gerry and literally locked him in his office for two days. He deputized an unsuspecting agent to stand guard, refusing to let Gerry out until he finished his backlogged reports.

The wiretaps brought new leads and more work. Every phone call was analyzed until we had the names and addresses of a heroin network stretching across the metropolitan area. We filled in another vital link in the heroin chain: Lorenzo "Enzo" Di Chiara, who was in frequent contact with Joe the Crow and Ernie Boy. Di Chiara was the trans-Atlantic middleman, who made sure the heroin leaving Sicily reached New York safely.

After weeks of frustration, a Puerto Rican informant helped me break Crazy Willie's maddening code. His suggestion sounded too simple, but after I listened to the tapes again, suddenly, the gibberish untangled itself into clear messages. Crazy Willie was speaking Spanish Pig Latin, cutting off the beginning of each word and slapping it on the end, creating a bizarre but simple code. I translated the tapes and pieced together his role in the operation. Crazy Willie was taking delivery of the heroin at his home, turning it into a warehouse for Joe the Crow and Ernie Boy and their gang of peddlars. Our list of names grew.

The investigation took 18 months. As the information from Gerry's meetings and our wiretaps mounted, we realized we were untangling the biggest heroin ring our eight-year-old agency had seen. By the fall of 1982, it seemed everyone in the office was working on some aspect of this case.

Jeff Hall was transferred to Washington D.C. as the case reached critical mass. He was replaced by John Land, an Arizona supervisor on the eve of retirement. Land had been investigated by DEA's Office of Professional Responsibility, then exiled to New York to serve his last year. OPR, our internal Gestapo, wanted to put him out to pasture. Instead, he was about to leave DEA in a burst of glory.

* * *

On October 20, 1982, Gerry got his first nibble. As I watched from a DEA taxi, posing as a cabbie, Ernie Boy delivered three kilos of heroin in front of a diner, taking $150,000 as a down payment. Gerry promised to deliver the remaining $390,000 soon. Eight days later, they met again in Queens. Gerry asked for more time to pay the balance. Ernie Boy became a little annoyed and refused, claiming he had a man from Buffalo flying in to pick up the money. Gerry pushed, telling him he would get his $390,000 on November 3. Ernie Boy's eyes narrowed. Gerry quickly poured some sugar on the deal. If Ernie Boy could hold out until the third, Gerry would also bring $1.5 million in cash. It was time to close the big deal they had negotiated for months.

Gerry let the image of stacked dollars dangle in front of the gangster, then yanked. Ernie Boy was hooked. He could wait a few more days for payment. On the third, he promised to bring

17 kilos to the Market Diner at 11th Avenue and 43rd Street. He would take the $1.5 million as a partial payment. The heroin would cost $3.06 million.

I could not imagine that much heroin and money in one place. Seventeen kilos. Almost 35 pounds of pure heroin, enough to kill every junkie in New York if you let them at it.

The deal went down November 3 as planned. It started out as planned, anyway. I was in a rental car with another agent, following Gerry's burgundy Cadillac to the diner. Gerry seemed almost at ease. I could feel myself sweating lightly, knowing half of $1.9 million from the U.S. Treasury was locked in a suitcase in the trunk. I looked around to find my bearings and locate the car with the other half of the money. Every move was choreographed earlier, in the DEA conference room. Dozens of agents surrounded us, monitoring every move. I saw familiar faces trying to look nonchalant in rental cars, taxis, and on the sidewalk.

Taking down Ernie Boy and Joe the Crow was the main event. The plan was simple: Gerry would tell them the money was in another car, ready to be called in as soon as he saw the heroin. When they showed him the smack, we would move in and arrest them. Then the money would be rushed back to the office for safekeeping as teams of agents fanned through the New York area to bust the other members of the ring. Everything had to happen quickly, before someone sounded the alarm. If the other members were tipped off to the raid, we would chase shadows the rest of the night.

Abbamonte and Delvecchio shook Gerry's hand as they scooted into a booth. I rolled down the car window. A light breeze stirred the air, carrying the scent of rain. Cold front moving in, I thought absently. I felt the pistol press against the small of my back, then made eye contact with the agents behind me in the rearview window. Everyone was ready, tense.

Suddenly, Ernie Boy and Joe the Crow were jumping back into their Cadillac. Something was wrong. They were moving the deal. Gerry looked at me for a nervous instant and tipped his head. *Follow me.* The gangsters left in a hurry, with Gerry revving his engine behind them. I yelled to one of the agents in a taxi, who tossed me the keys to the cab and jumped into the rental. I floored the accelerator, looking for Gerry's taillights.

In the next 30 seconds, everything broke down. As I maneuvered through traffic and locked a space behind Gerry's Cadillac, the other agents simply vanished. My head whipped around as I tried to keep an eye on Gerry, read the street signs blurring by, and search for the other agents. I could hear them chattering excitedly on the radio, saying they had his Cadillac in sight. *So where the hell are you*, I thought desperately.

The realization hit me hard. They were following the wrong car. Somehow, they had latched onto another burgundy Cadillac.

A horn blared at me as another cab veered into my lane, trying to squeeze past a double-parked car. Gerry was pushing the Caddie faster to keep up with Ernie Boy. *Gerry probably loves this*, I thought as we ran red lights and careened around corners toward the east side. I screamed into my radio, reading off cross streets. By the time I convinced the other agents they had the wrong car, I was halfway across town.

Ernie Boy turned a corner and parked in the middle of a block between two high-rises. I stopped at the corner and read off the intersection, stifling the urge to scream into the radio again. We were in a Puerto Rican neighborhood, a low-rent block I had worked before.

The street was lit up like a stage, yellow streetlights shining off windshields and pouring onto the pavement. Three car doors slammed. Gerry walked slowly toward the gangsters as they popped the Cadillac's trunk. Gerry reached into the space and straightened, hefting two tightly-wrapped packages in his hands. That was the signal.

I searched the street for the tenth time and saw no one. I fumbled for the radio. ''He's giving the goddam signal. Do you want me to take them down?''

A voice crackled over the speaker. ''Stay where you are. We're on our way.'' I waited, the seconds stretching out into infinity.

Joe the Crow walked slowly toward me. The taxi's motor was still idling. He was suspicious. He stopped in the middle of the street, scanning the dark neighborhood like a snake tasting the air for danger. Ernie Boy and Gerry kept talking. Joe the Crow took a few more steps, studying the cab. I leaned backward a few inches, searching for safe darkness. If he recognized me, Gerry would die quickly.

I jerked open the door and found a dark patch of sidewalk between two streetlights, cupping my hands to my mouth. "Carmen, get your ass down here. I'm not going to wait all night," I yelled at the nearest brownstone. I repeated it in Spanish, making a show of exasperation.

A few people on the street looked up for a moment, then dismissed me. Joe the Crow scowled. I paced below the brownstone, trying to keep my back to him.

"What do you want with Carmen?"

I whirled around to face an older woman leaning halfway through a third-floor window. *Just my luck*, I thought, *there's actually a Carmen in the building.*

"I'm waiting for her," I called back. The head disappeared into the dark room.

Joe the Crow looked at the window a moment, then started back toward Gerry and Ernie Boy. I relaxed.

He got halfway there when the commotion began. The cavalry was here.

A human wave swept down the block, surrounding Gerry and Ernie Boy. Joe the Crow's face froze as he whirled to face the onslaught. I pulled my pistol from the small of my back and hurdled the taxi's front fender, catching him from behind. "We're federal agents," I said, pushing the barrel into his face. "You're under arrest. Don't fucking move or I'll kill you."

The shock lasted only a moment, followed by a stony stare of recognition. "I'm going to fucking kill *you*, you fucking spic," he growled. I almost laughed. I was in a damn gangster film, and Joe the Crow hit his line perfectly.

I led him toward the cars, where Gerry was frisking Ernie Boy inside a circle of cocked pistols. "I'm looking at a dead man," he said as Gerry spun him around and cuffed him. It was a threat he would later deny making when it showed up in the papers. Gerry looked almost amused. We searched their car. Inside was $23,000 cash and a loaded .38 revolver.

It was after midnight, but the operation was just beginning. We broke into teams and scattered through the city, rounding up the other targets on our list. Gerry and I arrested five more low-level gangsters in Little Italy, Brooklyn, and Staten Island. By daybreak, 13 members of one of the city's biggest heroin rings were in jail.

The bust hit every major paper in the country. DEA estimated the network was responsible for smuggling as much as 50 pounds of heroin into the city each week, much of it funneled through Sicily. The next day, FBI Director William Webster held a press conference at DEA headquarters in Washington to heap on the praise, calling our bust "a major blow" to narcotics trafficking by organized crime. It was a great public relations image: the mob, heroin, high-speed chases, multiple arrests. And numbers. Wonderful numbers. We took 20 pounds of heroin, worth an estimated $20 million. The DEA avoided comparing the operation to the French Connection in the early '70s, but placed it among the largest busts in recent history.

The 13 were charged with conspiracy to distribute heroin. The agents present at the arraignment silently celebrated as the judge set bail: Crazy Willie, $3 million. Ernie Boy, $1.5 million. Lorenzo Di Chiara, $1 million. Joe the Crow, $1 million. During the arraignment, Ernie Boy swiveled in his chair to search out Gerry. When he found our seats in the back, he cocked his finger, pointed it at Gerry and pulled the trigger. He was later sentenced to 25 years and fined $75,000. Joe the Crow got 20 years and an $80,000 fine. We got our victory. I had a lot to celebrate. Two months after the bust, when Noe flew to New York for a brief visit, I proposed. We immediately set a date for the wedding and began making plans. I was flying.

* * *

Crazy Willie was sent to the federal penitentiary in Terre Haute, Indiana, where he continued running his street operation through the pay phones. We would have never known, but Di Chiara flipped as soon as he reached his jail cell.

Lorenzo, as I soon started calling him, was an overweight, amusing Sicilian in his early 40s. As with many of the aging gangsters I saw, his hair made its retreat over his scalp as his belly charged forward. He left Sicily 15 years earlier after robbing a bank, finding his niche in New York's crime families. His ties to the old country made him the perfect middleman for Crazy Willie's heroin ring. And the perfect informant for us. He was the first Sicilian DEA had ever flipped, which made him something of a treasure. I was assigned to guard Di Chiara and his family at their spacious Brooklyn home while he fed us information about the Bonanno family and the inner workings of the heroin trade. In return, his bail was lowered by a quarter of a million dollars. Later, the judge gave Di Chiara a 15-year suspended sentence and three years probation. The sentence set off alarm bells throughout the underworld.

After a few weeks of round-the-clock duty, I came to like the man. He had a gorgeous wife and two little girls, whom he treasured. I felt bad for them. It seemed almost unreal this tightly-knit family could walk under such ominous clouds. Still, I had trouble listening to him jovially describe his heroin business while my mind played tortured images of people destroyed by his product. "It's what I do for a living," he told me. "We export it like we export olive oil." He was a businessman. Nothing personal.

Di Chiara knew his former partners wanted him dead, but he showed no signs of stress, cracking jokes and showering me with hospitality. We offered to put them in the witness protection program, but Di Chiara's wife stubbornly refused to leave their home. He was not about to argue with her.

We protected him as best we could. When we were forced to pull out a few weeks later, he took his family to the relative safety of their upstate cottage. Gerry and I visited them a few times a week to make sure they were okay. I looked forward to having dinner with his family, sampling bottles from his wine cellar while Di Chiara cooked for us. His daughters began calling us "Uncle Cele" and "Uncle Gerry."

I saw them for the last time in the spring of 1983. The agency was sending me to Terre Haute, Indiana, with about 15 other agents. Armed with reliable information from Di Chiara, we were going to bust Crazy Willie. Again.

* * *

With a local judge's blessing, the prison's public phones were all tapped by the time we arrived, waiting for us to settle into our new home in the Terre Haute post office and slip on our headphones. We monitored the phones 24 hours a day, taking shifts and listening for Crazy Willie's coded messages. Di Chiara was right. Willie was running his heroin operations over the phone, calling East Harlem to make the deals and direct his remaining forces. For the next four months, we listened.

I took a room in the Ramada Inn a couple of miles from the post office. I was always on alert. Nobody else could understand Crazy Willie's Spanish Pig Latin, so the other agents rousted me at all hours when his voice came on the line. I felt like a volunteer firefighter in a town full of arsonists. Curious postal workers followed me with their eyes as I shuffled in and out of the second floor storage room. They knew the feds were up to something, but they didn't know exactly what.

Every day, Willie was on the phone with his wife, who slipped through our first net and contined coordinating his deals. He wasted no time building a miniature syndicate in the penitentiary. We frequently heard the voice of his new lieutenant, a prisoner called Fat Gigi. Other prisoners were recruited to work the phones when he was occupied. We jotted notes in our post office cubby, identifying each suspect by voice. Our intelligence went straight to New York, where other agents tracked down Crazy Willie's East Harlem cronies.

As we closed up shop in Terre Haute that summer, another wave of New York agents arrested more than a dozen of Crazy Willie's heroin runners, this time including his wife. In Indiana, Crazy Willie, Fat Gigi, and their budding prison syndicate were arraigned in jail, where a judge tacked a healthy stretch onto each of their sentences. I wondered if we had finally fulfilled the FBI director's boast and "immobilized" the mob's heroin ring. I began to doubt. The sense of triumph I felt after we arrested Ernie Boy and Joe the Crow had slowly dripped away as I listened to Crazy Willie chatter his twisted orders from prison. Watching him arraigned for a second time, I felt like we were fighting a Medusa, chopping off one head while another slithered around to bite us on the ass.

* * *

Noe and I were married that July in McAllen. We put the wedding together ourselves, watching every dime. The simple ceremony was performed by a justice of the peace in the lobby of the Hilton where Noe worked. None of it mattered when we exchanged our vows. Noe looked beautiful, our families were there to share the moment with us, and Gerry was at my side as my best man. Noe and I had put away as much money as we could for the honeymoon. We spent a week in Cancun, the booming resort town on the tip of Mexico's Yucatan peninsula. For the first time in three years, we had an entire week to ourselves, no worries, no responsibilities. We swam in the Caribbean, toured the ancient ruins nearby, ate, shopped, made love. On the seventh day, we returned to New York.

The agency did not give its blessing. As soon as headquarters heard of our nuptials, they launched an internal investigation on me. OPR decided my relationship with Noe during the investigation of her stepfather constituted ''poor judgment'' on my part. When I explained my difficult position at the time -- a rookie agent eager to please his bosses, who wanted to bend the rules to nab a doper -- they listened patiently, then stuck a warning letter in my personal file. It was a slap on the wrist, but it stung.

The reproach did not bother me for long. I had a new life to build. Noe moved into my studio in the autumn of 1983, filling the place with her energy. We walked for hours through the city as I played tour guide, showing her my favorite haunts. A month later, she came into the room smiling. She was pregnant. I was going to be a father.

I was having trouble just being a husband. I was working too many hours and too many weekends, jumping out of bed at odd hours at the ring of the phone. After a few precious months together as husband and wife, Noe and I agreed she would go home until the baby came. She needed to be with family through her pregnancy. Meanwhile, I put in for a transfer to Peru, where a spot would soon open. I did not want to raise a child in New York.

With Noe gone, the days seemed to crawl. Winter arrived with howling winds and snowdrifts, making me long for Texas again. The luster had faded from the job. Group 6 disintegrated. Gerry transferred to a new post in Italy, departing New York a legend. He was presented the Attorney General's Award for his role in the Lucchese/Bonanno heroin bust. I asked to be assigned to JFK International Airport, searching for a new challenge and a change of scenery. On February 1, 1984, Lorenzo Di Chiara's hogtied body was found in the trunk of his black Mercedes near the Canarsie Pier. He had been strangled.

* * *

Discrimination, subtle and otherwise, came with the job, but I gave it little thought until another Hispanic agent approached me one day with a proposition. Jesus Muniz was leading a legal attack on DEA for barricading us from the better jobs. If I wrote a check, I could join the class action suit.

Every Hispanic agent I knew fell into the same trap. The agency assigned us to surveillance, wiretap monitoring, and translation duty while other agents got the plum assignments required to climb the DEA ladder. We worked long hours helping our Spanish-challenged counterparts build cases against Puerto Ricans and Dominicans, then stood in the shadows while they received the credit and the promotions.

That did not bother me as much as the problems Hispanic agents found when a non-Spanish speaker tried to back us up during an undercover bust. We could go over the plans and the "bust word" a hundred times, but busts never went down as planned, and the language confused Anglo agents trying to pick out a single word from our rolling chatter. Several times I found myself improvising to suspicious dopers after my backup failed to catch the bust word.

I filled out a check and joined the class action suit with about 200 other Hispanic agents. We all agreed it was time to fight the favoritism that gave the paper-pushers the rewards while we put our tails on the line every day. I could hear other agents muttering under their breath, raking me with suddenly hostile glances. Jeff, who put in for a Special Achievement Award for me after the big heroin bust, then resubmitted the form after DEA ignored the first request, was pragmatic: "you guys do what you have to do." He understood.

* * *

I spent the spring of 1984 with the DEA enforcement group at JFK, helping U.S. Customs and immigration officials separate the dopers from the throngs of passengers. We watched the international flights closely, scrutinizing Colombian passengers who fit our profiles of traffickers. Every week we caught someone trying to carry cocaine into the country in their baggage or strapped around their waist. I became an expert in spotting false-bottomed suitcases, studying the lining for signs of tampering. The traffickers, mostly poor people recruited as mules for the growing cartels, preferred tough Samsonite luggage. We kept a small power drill in the office, which we used to poke holes through the hide of the suitcase. More often than not, the bit came out with a stream of white powder. The mules were easy to flip. We staged controlled deliveries, following them to their drop points and arresting anyone who showed up to claim the cocaine.

Some airport employees ran their own ring. The traffickers would put a suitcase full of coke on an Avianca flight, sending it to New York without an owner. After the baggage handlers locked it up in the unclaimed luggage cage, a supervisor would sneak in at night and carry it away for delivery.

They were not the only officials to tap into the river of drug money. For the first time, I witnessed corruption within DEA ranks. The mules were easy targets. Some agents could not resist shaking them down, pocketing jewelry and cash, then warning the frightened captives to keep their mouths shut if they wanted to avoid jail. I gritted my teeth and kept quiet. A few more months and I was out of there.

The job quickly became routine: Coke from Colombia, Nigerians carrying heroin, Jamaicans with marijuana. Once I picked up the smuggler's tricks, I could almost unconsciously spot the mules as they streamed through the gates. I waited for word from headquarters on my transfer, calling Noe constantly to assure her we would be together soon, listening to her describe the tiny life growing inside her.

Crystal Bianca was born April 7, 1984 in a McAllen hospital as I paced nervously in the waiting room. Noe picked Crystal, her favorite character from the TV show *Dynasty*. I chose Bianca, a South American name, as a tribute to our new life together. My transfer to Peru was approved. I was ready to go back to the jungle, where I would be at home. And after four years of wrenching narcotics from the streets of New York, I wanted to attack the source.

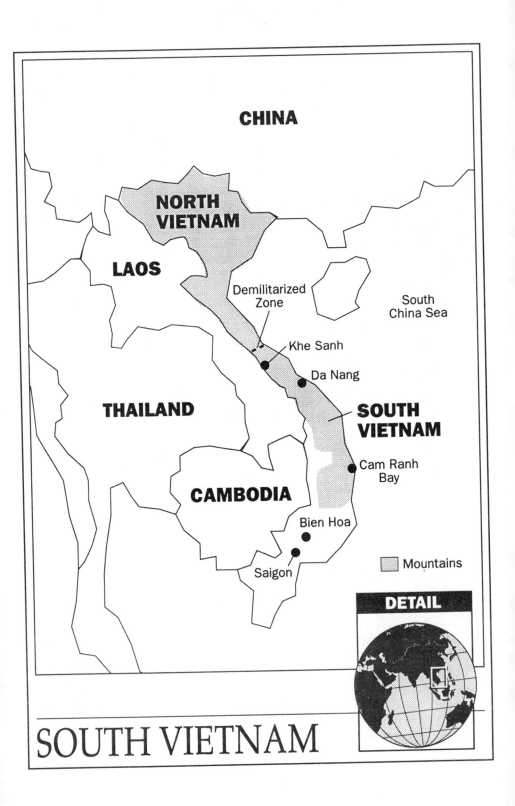

CHINA

NORTH
VIETNAM

LAOS

Demilitarized
Zone

Khe Sanh

Da Nang

South
China Sea

THAILAND

SOUTH
VIETNAM

Cam Ranh
Bay

CAMBODIA

Bien Hoa

Mountains

Saigon

DETAIL

SOUTH VIETNAM

Above: Celerino Castillo in Viet Nam

Left: Celerino Castillo

Below: Cele in brown vest, with Guardia de Hacienda in the Sierra Mountains between Mexico and Guatemala. We lost 6 Guardias in said operation.

IN VIETNAM — Sgt. Celerino Castillo, III, son of Mr. and Mrs. Celerino Castillo Jr. of Pharr, has recently been assigned to the 544th Replacement Co., Guard Force at Cam Ramh Bay, Vietnam. He received his basic training at Fort Lewis, Wash., and graduated from non-commisioned officers school at Fort Benning, Ga. Sgt, Castillo is a 1970 graduate of Pharr-San Juan-Alamo High School.

Above: Celerino Castillo and George Bush. Jan. 14, 1986

Below: Jimmy Carter and Celerino Castillo

Left: Dan Quail in El Salvador 1989

Below: Celerino Castillo in Guate-mala

Above: Military Gear sized from Wally's Residence.

Below: Celerino Castilllo's DEA I.D. with gun and cuffs

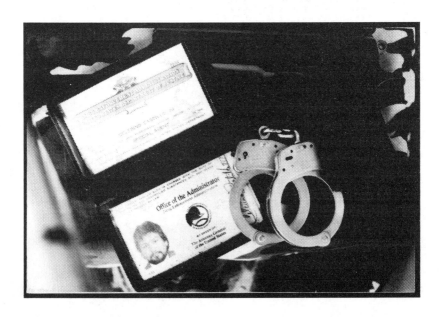

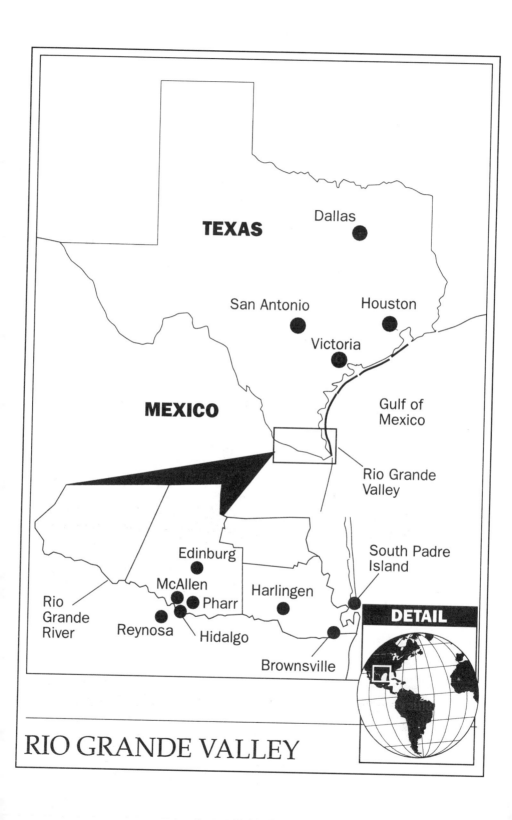

TEXAS

Dallas

San Antonio   Houston

Victoria

MEXICO

Gulf of
Mexico

Rio Grande
Valley

Edinburg

McAllen   Harlingen

Pharr

Rio
Grande
River

Reynosa   Hidalgo

South Padre
Island

DETAIL

Brownsville

RIO GRANDE VALLEY

Five
Riding the Condor
Lima, Peru - August, 1984

My first weeks in Peru were a honeymoon. Noe, Crystal, and I finally became a family. We found a house in El Molino, an upper-crust subdivision clinging to the foothills of the towering Andes mountains. Here, South American suburbanites could live in the undulating hills, blissfully ignorant of the social upheaval in their country. Lima's teeming millions were on the other side of the hills, on a thin strip of coastline sandwiched between the ice-capped 18,000-foot peaks and the Pacific Ocean.

Noe and I unpacked boxes, smiling to each other as Crystal scurried around the house like a cat, inspecting every corner. Our one-story white stucco house was a true hacienda: Red-tiled roof, fireplace, garden, and a backyard swimming pool, all surrounded by a high wall. A maid and a gardener reported for duty as we settled in. The U.S. government paid for everything. I paced the back yard in my bare feet, breathing deeply, feeling the tension from my last months in Manhattan drain away. It was a peaceful island in an uncertain country. For the next two years, this would be home.

I preferred the view of the craggy peaks to the Lima skyline. The sun warmed this side of the mountains, while Lima seemed wrapped in a perpetual blanket of ocean fog, called *garua* by the city's roughly 5 million inhabitants. The mist rolled off the Humboldt Current, a 200-mile wide river of cold antarctic water that acted as a massive air conditioner, moderating Lima's climate as it sliced past the Peruvian coast on its way north. It almost never rained in Lima, but the Humboldt provided ample moisture, pumping its clammy mist into the city's pores.

The fog could not shroud Lima's suffering. The City of Kings, founded by the Spanish conquistador Francisco Pizarro after he vanquished the Incas in 1534, was now the City of Beggars. As Noe and I carried Crystal through the former seat of Spain's New World empire, I could not shake my feeling of melancholy. The proud cathedrals and broad plazas seemed lost in the tide of humanity washing into the capital by the thousands. The city poured over its old boundaries and rotted at the edges, ringed by endless, reeking *barrios*. Like every former Spanish colony in the Americas, Peru's pecking order flowed along bloodlines: The light-skinned descendants of the Spaniards jealously guarded their power, money, and land, while the descendants of the natives worked the earth and filled the slums. The mixed-blood *mestizos* held the middle ground, edging into the ranks of those above and below.

The country teeted between democracy, dictatorship, and chaos: Peru has had all three in the 20th century, as the military and civilians oust one another in a seesaw battle of elections and coups. In 1980, the poor found a fist in *Sendero Luminoso*, or Shining Path, a Maoist guerrilla movement led by Abimael Guzman, a former philosophy professor. A student of Mao Zedong's Chinese cultural revolution, Guzman launched his attacks on the government from the mountains of the Ayacucho district, calling himself the "fourth sword of Marxism," after Marx, Lenin, and Mao.

President Fernando Belaunde Terry beefed up the military's rural outposts to fight the rebels, but generations of animosity between the rich and poor helped *Sendero Luminoso* tighten their ideological grip on the remote villages. From their moutain strongholds, the guerrillas periodically crept into Lima to detonate reminders of their discontent. Every week, another puff of smoke floated above the skyline, followed by the echoes of the blast.

Suddenly, Manhattan seemed like a good neighborhood.

I knew the dangers when I put in for the transfer. DEA assured me living overseas would bring my family under the government's security blanket. In New York, agents and their families faced the same urban hazards everyone else did. Here, we joined the small, privileged diplomatic class, ostensibly protected from Peru's dark side. Our house was surrounded by an eight-foot concrete wall topped with broken bottles embedded in the cement like spikes. Serious-looking security guards, provided by the U.S. Embassy, roamed our small compound 24 hours a day.

I watched Crystal with a mixture of wonder and awe, marveling at how she grew in the months I was away. I felt like a father for the first time. As Noe put the finishing touches on the house, I took Crystal into the backyard pool, supporting her tiny body as she splashed and kicked. She giggled, then coughed out a mouthful of water. It was sink-or-swim time. When I pulled my hands from under her, she sank for a moment, then reflexively closed her mouth and fought her way to the surface.

* * *

The Incas discovered cocaine long before Pizarro discovered the Incas. The coca leaf held a treasured position in Peruvian civilizations for centuries. Peasants chewed it to ward off the symptoms of poverty: fatigue, hunger, depression. The leaves gave them endurance working at high altitudes. The jungle tribes used it to dress wounds. Inca priests and nobles believed chewing the leaves brought them closer to the Sun God. The priests fed it to their human sacrifices, numbing them to the icy winds as they slowly froze to death on some lonely Andean peak.

But when the Spaniards discovered the intoxicating leaves the savages were munching, coca went commercial. When Europeans mixed it with wine, "Vin Mariani" became literally a sensation. Bavarian soldiers used it in the 1880s to fight off fatigue. Sigmund Freud took it as he worked. It was the active ingredient in Coca-Cola when the soft drink debuted in 1886; cocaine gave the drink its stimulating effect until the government cracked down on it and convinced the company to switch formulas in 1906.

In Peru, the government conceded the leaf's ancient place in society. Everywhere I looked, peasants sold and munched legally-grown coca leaves. It seemed the entire adult population walked through life with a wad of green in their mouths, which produced a milder high than snorting powdered coke. For centuries, the Peruvians grew enough coca to satisfy their needs. Then Americans came to crave the powder. Peru would never be the same.

Peru was the world's top producer of coca leaves. A thousand-mile long coca belt stretched along the Andean lowlands through the center of the country, where the Peruvian government estimated peasants illegally grew and harvested about 125,000 acres of the tall, innocent-looking coca plants. The U.S. government's estimate was almost three times higher. In reality, counting Peru's illegal coca fields was as difficult as estimating how many Americans grew marijuana in their closets. No one doubted Peru's position as the king of South America's cocaine crescent, which arced across Colombia, Bolivia, and Peru. From these remote, hostile jungles, some of the world's poorest people grew the world's richest crop. They were mining white gold.

We were sent to stop them.

DEA's Peru office consisted of a cluster of offices in the bowels of the heavily-armored U.S. embassy building in downtown Lima. Guards appeared everywhere you turned, patrolling the tall, iron-barred fence jutting between the American diplomats and the encircling Peruvians. Cement-filled drums squatted at the gate to prevent car bombs from hurtling into the compound. The embassy bore numerous political scars. A mob attacked it in 1925 when Calvin Coolidge tried to arbitrate a border dispute between Peru and its arch-rival, Chile. Now the United States wanted to make war on cocaine, which pumped more than half a billion dollars into Peru's ailing economy, tainting all but the most resolute officals. We were prepared for more violence.

When I joined DEA's Peru office, it was staffed with five agents and an intelligence specialist. Our boss, country attache Peter Rieff, did not pretend to speak the native tongue. Gene Castillo, a short, fortyish agent from New Mexico, spoke a patchy, Americanized Spanish. I wondered how he worked undercover in Lima with such an accent. Another agent, who apparently landed the job through connections in the DEA brass, spoke just enough to order a decent meal. Speaking fluent Spanish obviously was not a prerequisite for the job.

The atmosphere within the department reminded me of McAllen's internal rift. An unspoken tension drifted through the office, carried in the agents' tone of voice and occassionally surfacing in hostile innuendo. Some agents refused to work with others because of personal spats or philosophical differences. The two Spanish-speaking agents already there carried much of the workload, in addition to serving as perpetual translators for the other agents.

To make matters worse, one of the veteran agents refused to work undercover. Fred Villarreal, a cigar-smoking Mexican-American, told me he was finished putting his life on the line for DEA. His attitude shook me. Villarreal started out like me, a young, aggressive Hispanic ready to shake up the narcotics underworld. Over the years, a combination of age, family responsibilities, and a steady diet of slights and abuse from DEA convinced him to leave the dangerous stuff to the younger guys. The more we talked, the more I felt like Ebeneezer Scrooge, receiving a visit from the ghost of Christmas future and wondering if I could change my fate.

After a week in Lima, I kissed Noe goodbye, packed a duffel bag, and flew Air Peru 250 miles northeast to the center of the coca crescent, eager to start my hunt for the clandestine labs and airstrips hidden throughout the forbidding Amazon Basin. Rieff sent me off with instructions to make contact with the *Guardia Civil*, Peru's national guard. DEA could not spare another agent to work the jungle with me. The Guardia would be my backup.

I chose Tingo Maria as my base. The jungle town, hugging a wide spot in the Huallaga River, had charmed generations of tourists with its frontier allure and lush scenery. This was the Huallaga Valley, cupped between low mountain ranges in the eastern lowlands, where the Amazon jungle pawed at the feet of the Andes. Fifteen years before, the valley supported sustenance farming and small villages. Now, in 1984, it was the heart of coca country. The valley alone was believed to produce enough raw coca leaves to feed half of America's cocaine habit. Tingo Maria was its capital, the place known as the "White City."

I found the *Guardia's* headquarters just outside of town, a tall green building ringed by guards. Their commander welcomed me warmly before whisking me to the offices of their U.S.-trained anti-narcotics unit, the *Unidad Movil de Patrullaje Rural* (Mobile Rural Patrol Unit), who patrolled the jungle searching for small cocaine labs. In theory, UMOPAR was to wipe out the valley's processing network, while a government program dubbed "Eradication and Control of Coca Leaf Planting in the Huallaga

Valley'' attacked the fields, whose workers yanking the coca plants out by the roots. I discovered a very different reality.

* * *

The cocaine lab was close. Our informant assured us we would find it soon. The camouflaged figures behind me traded sarcastic comments, their irritation growing with every mile. The sun pulled the sweat through our skin, stinging our exposed, sunburned necks. I glanced at my watch. Four hours of hiking and no lab in sight. The informant sensed my doubt. He checked over his shoulder every few yards, as if expecting us suddenly to turn back. He picked his way through the branches reaching across the faint jungle trails, ducking and weaving like a boxer. Very soon, he said. The lab was just ahead. After only a couple months in Peru, I realized I could spend my entire career pushing through the vines in search of small huts scattered throughout the valley.

I had traded my sneakers and New York street clothes for jungle gear, tucking my jeans into an old pair of boots I kept from Vietnam. It felt good to haul an M-16 through the trees again, covered in camouflage, listening to the jungle speak. My UMOPAR companions carried nasty-looking FAR rifles, unconsciously sweeping the barrels across the path. They swore to themselves quietly, waving away the mosquitoes zeroing in on their exposed necks. For the next kilometer, the only sounds cutting through the damp air were the wet smacks of hands against skin and the warning cries of monkeys and birds announcing our arrival.

Our target, a small coca lab, lay tucked in the far reaches of this green hell the Peruvians called "*la montaña.*" The labs we discovered up to this point followed the same blueprint: Wooden shacks or open-air labs reeking of kerosene, stuffed with cut coca leaves ready for conversion into paste. The peasants who built these crude structures formed the second broad level in the cocaine pyramid. They were the *poseros*, or processors, who purchased piles of coca leaves from the hundreds of *cocaleros*, the peasant growers who converted their small plots into coca farms.

The *poseros* needed more than a hundred pounds of the thumb-sized green leaves to make one kilo of paste, which they sold to Colombian runners in light planes. The system allowed the valley's poor to earn a decent living for the first time in their lives. The rural farmers must have shook their heads in amazement when they discovered the new cash crop. By converting their fields to coca, they could easily double, triple, even quadruple their annual income. The plants matured in a few years, yielded as many as six crops a year, repelled pests naturally, and grew in poor soil. They did not even have to take their crop to market: The Colombians and *poseros* went door-to-door, leaving stacks of dollars in their wake.

The Colombians cartels finished the refining process in scattered clandestine labs, using nearly four kilos of paste to make a kilo of pure, white cocaine hydrochloride for American nostrils. For every dollar they paid Peru's coca farmers and processors, the cartels earned more than twenty dollars from American buyers.

Suddenly, the informant stopped, searching the wall of latticed vegetation for the path. Locating it, he held the branches aside and motioned us ahead. The telltale smell of kerosene led us to the lab, a few dozen yards off the main trail. The Peruvians, young recruits looking for jungle glory with UMOPAR, circled the flimsy structure once before peeking inside. The hut contained the typical *posero*'s starter kit. Several plastic jugs filled with kerosene and other chemicals lined the back of the hut, next to a huge pile of green coca leaves. Two waterproof sacks bulged with finished coca paste ready for delivery.

In front of the shack, a large trench lined with a plastic sheet held a leafy soup of coca and kerosene spiked with sulfuric acid. The *poseros* stirred and mashed the soup constantly, helping the chemicals leach the narcotic from the leaves to produce paste. It had to be the world's most lucrative cottage industry. From these tiny labs sprung Peru's top export.

One of the UMOPAR men pulled out a half-empty jug of kerosene, sloshed it around the base of the hut, then touched his lighter to the damp wood. We stood like boys at a campfire, mesmerized by the climbing flames. When the thin walls buckled in a cloud of sparks, we turned and filed back to the main path, cursing the return trip in advance. Another small victory in the drug war, I mused. Not the dagger to the center of Peru's cocaine heartland I ached to deliver, but another tiny nick to annoy the cartels.

After spending some time in the Huallaga Valley, I learned to measure my progress in small increments. I was a guppy in a piranha tank.

The Colombians owned Tingo Maria. Its quiet farming traditions, its institutions, and its morals crumbled like dry clay as residents jumped into the coca economy. The leaf touched every member of the community, from the adolescent coca paste couriers to the shop owners who suddenly found a market for high-dollar electronics at the edge of the jungle. New pickup trucks rumbled over the dirt streets, clearly identifying villagers on the cartels' payroll. The national currency, the *sol*, was nowhere to be found. The town ran on dollars, attracting cash-hungry bankers from Lima who flew in to buy U.S. currency.

The Colombians knew they had a DEA agent in their midst. When I passed them on the streets, they greeted me with arrogant smiles. If I made too much trouble, they could swat me like a mosquito. Thugs armed with sharp machetes would gladly hunt down a man for pocket change. They obviously did not consider me a threat. Their rule was absolute.

The cartels played both sides by shoveling cash into the jaws of prospective enemies. They purchased the loyalty of Tingo Maria's military officers, who declared a truce with the traffickers. On Sundays, I wandered past the soccer fields and watched Peruvian soldiers playing *fútbol* with the Colombians. Snubbing the government's periodic efforts to wage war on coca, the military insisted its sole reponsibility in the valley was protecting the peasants from Marxist subversives. Cracking down on the local coca farmers and traffickers, they argued, would drive the peasants into the arms of *Sendero Luminoso*.

The military, sent into the valley by President Belaunde to fight the guerrillas, opened their new base in Tingo Maria just a month before I arrived in Peru. It quickly became the most popular post in the country. Most of the soldiers at the base bribed their way into Tingo Maria. It was a small investment, given the payoffs. By the time they rotated home, they could earn enough coca-tainted dollars to retire on. Most of them just blew their money in the cantinas and shops, learning the meaning of conspicuous consumption. Some seemed to do nothing more than cruise the streets in their new Nissan and Toyota pickups, like high school boys angling for girls.

Sendero Luminoso quietly accepted the dollars as well, using the protection money to arm its guerrillas. I laughed at the irony of a Marxist movement selling out to such brazen capitalists. With only the *Guardia* to worry about, the Colombians flew into any one of dozens of clandestine airstrips, picking up loads of coca paste and occasionally returning with AK-47s and other weapons for the rebels.

The *Guardia* and UMOPAR hurled themselves against this wall of corruption, taking me along for the ride as they rolled through the countryside in their four-wheel-drive trucks, hunting for coca. We destroyed the labs we found, dousing them with kerosene and setting them aflame. Any *poseros* caught at the scene went to jail, or what passed for a jail. The *Guardia* warehoused them in a long bank of concrete holding cells with hand-welded bars. The police took their frustration out on the prisoners, tossing hissing sticks of dynamite near the cells and laughing as the prisoners flattened themselves against the bare walls. The shaking peasants were processed, then sent to the tin-topped corral the *Guardia* called a prison.

I never saw a Colombian arrested in the valley. They counted their profits while the peasants swallowed the punishment, paying for their sins with large chunks of their lives.

* * *

I traveled to Tingo Maria every other week, slicing through the jungle for days at a time. A new stress tugged at the back of my mind. I was falling into selfish habits again, throwing myself into the job at the expense of my family. I pushed the guilt aside, promising myself I would spend more time with them. Tomorrow. Next week. But this assignment was too important. I was convinced my tour in Peru would become the highlight of my career. Noe seemed to be adjusting well. The disappearances were part of my job, I explained, more for my own benefit than hers. Noe said she understood. I was not so sure.

When I was home, I spent as much time as I could with Crystal. I took turns with Noe, groaning out of bed in the middle of the night to change diapers, or heat formula on the gas stove, or carry her around the dark house until she cried herself back to sleep. Our guard watched, an amused expression visible over his coffee mug. I wondered if any of us could protect her if the cartels decided I was too deep into their business. I glanced at the broken Coke bottles filled with stagnant water atop the cement wall. I felt vulnerable.

Rieff was no help, grumbling at me every time I walked into the office after another extended absence. He wanted regular phone calls to make sure the cartels had not had me chopped into pieces. There were no phone booths in the jungle, I argued, and the phones at my little hotel in Tingo Maria never worked when it rained. I assured him I could take care of myself.

Rieff seemed to think I could work the Huallaga Valley from Lima, ducking into Tingo Maria once a week to talk to informants, then maybe jump into the trees to look for a lab. I knew better. We depended on the *Guardia Civil* totally. As foreign agents, the Peruvian government had us on a short leash, with no power of arrest, no permission to interrogate, and only an advisory role in anti-narcotics operations. DEA could never make a dent in the valley's coca economy without a constant presence: mine. The cartels' money could quickly wash away any progress we made, buying off our allies and placing our missions at risk.

I got in the habit of presenting my friends at the *Guardia* with small gifts. I picked up liquor and American cigarettes at the U.S. Embassy commissary, or brought them jungle knives, trying to show my appreciation. I presented an old Vietnam flak jacket of mine to a stocky, rawmouthed major who prided himself on his toughness. He immediately pulled it on and ordered one of his men to shoot him. The man grinned. He was not about to pass up the opportunity to plug an officer. He wasted no time, leveling a small-caliber pistol at the major and pulling the trigger.

The stocky major grimaced as the shot spun him sideways, buckling his knees. He removed the vest and pulled the flattened slug from the shoulder, grinning and rubbing what promised to be a world-class bruise. After that, the major wore the 30-pound vest everywhere. I frequently spotted him jogging around the base with it bouncing on his bare chest. ''It's good exercise,'' he said, clapping me on the shoulder.

Many of the *Guardia* resisted the drug money and mounted a real effort to flush the cartels out of their country. We stepped up the patrols, following every lead the informants brought in. The *Guardia* seemed energized when I accompanied them on their raids. My presence gave them a measure of protection. "The military and the Colombians would not think twice about eliminating us if we make too much trouble," an UMOPAR officer told me during one patrol. "With an American, they'll be more careful." I considered that small comfort. With the military and the guerrillas blasting each other across the valley, my death could easily be explained away as an unfortunate attack by the rebels.

Every lab we hit shook the web. More and more peasants complained to the Colombians, who finally took their problem to the military. They wasted no time placing the *Guardia* under de facto house arrest, forbidding any more patrols into the jungle. To justify confining the *Guardia* to their base, the Army claimed the guerrillas now infested the entire valley. Allowing anti-narcotics patrols would be too dangerous, they said. I wondered to whom they referred.

After twiddling their thumbs for a few days, the *Guardia* changed tactics. With a lone Cessna and tips from informants, they pounced on the cartels' airborne couriers skimming the treetops. They took me along on many of these missions, pointing excitedly when they sighted a drug plane. The surprised dopers ignored their orders to land. They assumed the *Guardia* was putting on a show. After all, the bribes were already paid to assure them safe passage to Colombia.

During one airborne chase, our pilot swooped down on the Colombian bird with the sun at his back, broadcasting his orders to land before the cartel pilot realized he had company. We were close enough to see the Colombian flipping us off. We maneuvered on top of the Colombian plane, dropping to within 50 yards of the dopers as they tried to figure out where the invader was. The *Guardia* pilot yelled a suggestion to the UMOPAR members inside, who nodded and raised the side windows. They poked their rifles through the windows and rattled off a dozen rounds at the Colombian plane's wings, puncturing its fuel tanks. We followed the crippled plane until it sputtered and crashed, ripping a scar in the jungle canopy. The UMOPAR gunners returned to their seats with satisfied smiles. It was the first of several one-sided air battles I watched. All ended in the fiery deaths of cartel pilots and runners.

Despite these small victories, I became restless. I felt mired in quicksand, pumping my legs frantically but getting nowhere.

We could burn coca huts and shoot down loads of paste until I retired without crippling the valley's coca trade. Throwing a *cocalero* in jail affected the cartels about as much as arresting a corner pusher in New York. They were replaceable, interchangeable pawns. We needed to attack the Colombians' big investments. The *Guardia* estimated the valley contained 43 clandestine airstrips and a number of major labs. I wanted to know where the hell they were.

The men in UMOPAR feigned ignorance. I turned to informants, who insisted many of the *Guardia* officers were also on the cartels' payroll. It made sense. The Colombians were loading too many planes. There was no way the small-time labs we destroyed could produce enough paste to keep the cartels supplied. The *Guardia* was tossing me bones, guiding me to the *poseros'* tiny kerosene labs while protecting the Colombians' cocaine factories.

The next time I visited the UMOPAR, I tracked down the commander. "Where the hell are the big labs?" I demanded. He shrugged. "We know where they are. But the military won't let us patrol in those areas. They claim those are *Sendero* strongholds, which is their jurisdiction."

I finally called Rieff, explaining my predicament. I hoped we could convince someone in the State Department to convince the Peruvians to intervene and throw the balance more to our favor. He told me to forget it, obviously not wanting to make waves. The Colombians, satisfied after a couple months of quiet, allowed the military to allow the Guardia to resume their patrols. I tagged along, feeling like a damn puppet.

* * *

On February 2, 1985, Noe and I climbed to the top of a low mountain overlooking the city and watched a sea of Peruvians gather below. Hundreds of thousands stood shoulder to shoulder, hoping for a glimpse of Pope John Paul II, who stopped in Lima as part of a 17-city tour of South and Central America. We sat in the sun, holding hands as Peru forgot its horrors for a day.

Four days later, Noe told me she was pregnant again. The warmth spread over me. Crystal had become the center of my world, my greatest treasure. This time, I secretly wished for a boy. I lingered at home for a few days, playing with my daughter and trying to cram a month's worth of attention into a every hour. I began to consider staying in Lima. I could work out of the office; spend more time at home; make hamburgers every Friday. It didn't last. I returned to Tingo Maria the following week.

In mid-February, I ventured into the hills with a column of nine or ten *Guardia* officers. Our informant said he could guide us to a lab he discovered the week before. An hour into our march, we ran across a small camp, a rough assembly of wooden huts topped with palm fronds and aluminum. It looked abandoned. We approached slowly, looking for signs of life. Each hut bore a red hammer and sickle symbol, clearly identifying its owners: *Sendero Luminoso*. The informant looked at me. I looked at the commanding officer. He looked at the huts for a moment, then motioned us to move on. Some of his men clearly wanted to turn back rather than risk stumbling upon a *Sendero* patrol. As we passed, the faces of women and small children appeared like phantoms in the darkened doorways. Everyone checked their weapons.

The smell reached us first, a rancid musk floating on the heavy air. Then the drone of the flies. Something had died.

Then we saw the bodies. An arm reached from the brush. A bloodied leg lay nearby, bent at an unnatural angle. We dragged six of them from the foliage, covering our nostrils with bandanas. Some of the bodies had their arms bound behind them with cord. Others were butchered, their arms neatly hacked off. One was decapitated. Genitals were missing, eyes gouged out, tongues sliced from mouths.

One of the new UMOPAR recruits scrambled away and retched loudly. The informant made the sign of the cross. He was in shock. "That's my uncle," he muttered, motioning to a bloated corpse. He pointed to the next body. "That's my cousin." He continued down the row, identifying all six bodies. All were male relatives of his. They were hanged. The rope left serrated red marks where it chewed into their necks. I hoped they were dead before the mutilation began.

We turned back, forgetting the lab. We knew we were one wrong move from joining the mutilated men we left behind on the trail. The informant could hardly think. He babbled along the trail, wondering aloud if they simply ran into the wrong people at the wrong time, or were butchered as a warning to him.

I thought about my family. After that, I tried to spend more time in Lima, but it was never enough. The guilt struck at odd times, reminding me how many hours I worked, how many nights my wife and baby slept alone, wondering where I was, wondering if I would emerge from the jungle again. Noe commented on how much energy I poured into my work. She did not finish the statement: I was neglecting her and Crystal. She didn't have to. I reminded myself every day. I closed my eyes, trying to purge the image of the mutilated bodies from my mind. I had to get my family out of Peru.

* * *

The news rippled through DEA, carried by phone, cables, and office memos. On March 6, 1985, the bound, broken body of DEA agent Enrique "Kiki" Camarena was discovered wrapped in plastic in Vista Hermosa, Mexico. Four armed men had forced Camarena into a car February 7, after he left the U.S. Consulate in Guadalajara. DEA held its breath for a month as the Mexican police searched for Camarena. They found him just off a road in an area swept earlier by the police. The Mexican drug traffickers decided he had become too much trouble and assassinated him, along with a Mexican pilot who occassionally worked for him. Both were tortured before they died. I felt suddenly empty and paranoid. It could have been me. It could have been a lot of us.

At the end of March, I flew to New York to testify at the trial of one of the minor organized crime figures I helped bust during my tour with Gerry Franciosa. While I was in town, I attended a special mass for Camarena at St. Peter's Cathedral in Manhattan. Camarena's wife and son were there. Somber, uniformed men and women filled the pews. It looked like the entire DEA office and half the New York police force attended. The questions filled my head: Is this "war" worth a man's life? Why are we risking everything and accomplishing so little?

I could see similar questions lingering in the eyes of my old friends as I searched them out after the mass. Everyone was upset about Camarena's death, for the loss of a good man as well as the crossing of some unconscious line. In DEA's small, insular world, Camarena's assassination triggered a roiling anger that coursed through the agency like a current. The consensus among the agents was DEA waited too long to apply the necessary pressure on the Mexicans. From what we heard, the Mexican police could have located and freed Camarena before the traffickers executed him. Camarena warned the DEA brass things were getting dangerous in Guadalajara. The agency ignored him. The story sounded chillingly familiar. On my way back to Lima, I thought of the bodies lying next to the dirt path, hacked and scattered like broken toys. I had a lot in common with Camarena. So did a lot of agents stationed abroad. DEA simply was spread too thin to fulfill its political dreams across the globe. As my plane headed into Lima, I wondered how Camarena's death would change DEA's policies in Peru, Mexico, and a dozen other countries. I also wondered how his death would change me.

After Camarena's murder, Noe was in my thoughts constantly. I wanted to stay in Peru, but this was no place for a pregnant woman. I feared for her safety in Lima, as well as for our unborn baby's. The water was horrible; milk was in short supply; the guerrillas constantly knocked out power to the city. The area shook every few days with faint tremors. My brain played *What If* in a constant loop: What if we could not find a decent doctor? What if *Sendero Luminoso* launched an attack on the suburbs? What if I was abducted?

Noe worried too. Our wealthy Peruvian neighbors traveled with armed bodyguards. She knew if I shook the web too hard, the cartels would take revenge on my family. I could do little to comfort her. That Easter, when we all flew home for a brief vacation, I returned to Lima alone. Noe and Crystal stayed in McAllen without me. It was better that way, I told myself.

In July, 1985, Peruvians elected a new president, 36-year-old populist Alan Garcia. Young and immensely popular, Garcia took a special place in Peruvian history by becoming the first civilian president to succeed another civilian president since 1945. Garcia stoked the nation's hope by vowing to raise wages and play hardball with foreign bankers to defer payments on the country's $13.5 billion debt.

To an outsider, it looked like JFK sweeping into town on inauguration day: A young, charismatic leader claiming the city as his aging predecessor departed. The explosions broke the spell. One bomb, packed inside an orange Volkswagen, erupted two blocks from the U.S. Ambassador's residence on the eve of the inauguration. The military occupied the city for the ceremonies, filling the air with the accumulated noise of helicopters, sirens, and shouting. The guerrillas still wiggled through. They marked the occassion by setting off a series of car bombs across the city. That night, they hit the electrical towers, blacking out entire sections of the city.

It was a particularly violent month in the drug war as well. In Colombia, five gunmen casually walked up to a taxi caught in rush hour traffic and pumped 13 bullets into Judge Manuel Castro, killing him instantly. Castro's execution followed his effort to bring charges against 16 people connected to the drug-related slaying of Rodrigo Lara Bonilla, Colombia's justice minister. On the July 24, a cocaine lab belonging to alleged drug lord Reynaldo Rodriguez Lopez exploded in Lima. The DEA investigation of Rodriguez, which I participated in following the blast, led us to a travel agency he owned. There, we found a stamping machine. For a fee, Rodriguez could stamp your passport with any visa you wanted. Inside his fire-stained mansion, police found an 84-line switchboard with direct connections to the Mexican consulate and the homes of a number of Peruvian police detectives.

The new Peruvian president wanted fast action against the cocaine cartels operating in his country. Immediately after taking office, Garcia approved the operation his predecessor rejected: Operation Condor was on.

* * *

DEA, CIA, and the *Guardia Civil* came up with Condor. After prodding, CIA provided us satellite photos of the jungle to help us spot labs. The Colombian national police told us the remote area concealed a number of cocaine labs.

I flew to Leticia, Colombia, the country's only toehold on the Amazon. A contingent of *Guardia Civil* officers accompanied me, dressed in their best uniforms. We had an appointment with the Colombian national police to plan the first joint anti-narcotics operation ever attempted by the two countries. The Colombians and Peruvians called it *Operación Condor*, in honor of the massive vulture Peruvians adopted as a national symbol. DEA dubbed it *Relampago*, the Spanish word for Lightning.

We met at the Colombian national police headquarters outside Leticia. The two groups took to each other instantly, quickly becoming a unified team. The Peruvians needed the Colombians. Despite Garcia's purges - - he dismissed 37 generals in his first two months in office - - the *Guardia* still received no cooperation from the Peruvian military. The Colombians had the airplanes and equipment the operation would need. They knew cooperation meant more U.S. aid.

Our target was one hour from Leticia, deep in the Peruvian jungle in an area known as Callaru. Satellite photos supplied by the CIA revealed a huge dirt airstrip, more than a mile long. The strip, located near the Rio Tigre, was the hub for the area, where the jungle hid an estimated 110 airstrips and an untold number of clandestine labs. Neither the Peruvians nor DEA had ever worked the area. It was virgin territory. I circled the mile-long airstrip with a red pen. Phase I would begin there.

I became more and more wrapped up in the operation, losing track of the days. Noe and I talked on the phone constantly throughout her pregnancy. I missed her and Crystal terribly. I could not bear to think about Crystal growing up without me. I worked harder, exhausting myself to keep the thoughts from taking hold of my mind.

For several weeks, we exchanged cables with the Colombians and met in Leticia to plan strategy. As a cover story, we told everyone we were conducting joint drug enforcement training. Even the Colombian anti-narcotics unit did not know exactly where we planned to strike. We kept them out of the loop, fearful of cartel spies within their ranks. But Leticia was a traffickers' stronghold. Word leaked out the two countries were planning a big raid. When our informants told us of the leak, we pushed up the timetable. We knew we had to move fast before the dopers could react.

On August 13, 1985, two Bell helicopters filled with adrenaline-pumped Colombian and Peruvian police lifted from Leticia, bound for the target airstrip. I sat in the second chopper, next to Colonel Zarate, the Peruvian officer in charge of the operation. He was one of the most honorable men I met in any uniform, a young, energetic officer from Lima. After this operation, he would become a general. I peered into the eager eyes around me. None of these men had participated in an air assault. I hoped they could keep their heads if the dopers attacked.

The trip brought me back to Vietnam. We flew at treetop level, the skids almost brushing the green carpet. Thousands of macaws, disturbed by the thumping rotors, erupted from the trees and flew below us in a red, blue, and green cloud. They were so close I was tempted to reach through the open hatch to touch one.

After 45 minutes, the strip suddenly appeared below us. It was a beautiful sight, 50 yards wide and a mile long. Five small planes sat at one end of the brown ribbon, next to a low building.

The lead chopper landed at the far end of the runway, dropped off its half-dozen passengers, then lifted and banked for the return trip to Leticia, where the remainder of the force waited.

The shooting started immediately. The traffickers, flushed from the building by the choppers, aimed and fired, too far away to do any damage. The Colombians and Peruvians returned fire. I silently cursed, willing them to hold their trigger fingers until they closed the distance. My chopper banked and circled over the river. We spotted two sleek cigarette boats, one blue, the other red, cutting a foaming wake through the murky water. One dashed straight for the overhanging branches near the bank, disappearing from sight. The other tried to outrun us. We could see three men inside, one at the wheel, the other two watching the approaching helicopter and shouting instructions to the driver. The chopper pilot banked for better angle, tipping us sideways. A *Guardia* officer gripped the edge of the hatch, took careful aim and fired a burst from his assault rifle. Smoke poured from the boat's wounded engine. The driver yanked the wheel violently, pointing the boat toward the shrouded bank.

We broke off our pursuit to back up the first team. Our feet hit the packed dirt a moment after the skids touched. We quickly divided, leap-frogging down the airstrip.

We caught up with the first team at the far end of the runway. The traffickers were gone. They obviously decided against a pitched battle and fled into the trees. I took a quick head count. No one was hit.

With several men posted to watch for the dopers, the rest of us cautiously surrounded the wooden building at the edge of the runway. I spotted a hand painted sign nailed to the wall: *Casa Brava*. Inside, several picnic tables lined the wooden floor, holding half-eaten plates of steak, chicken, and soup. The screened-in front room also held a few rickety cots, a big Sony TV, and a VCR. A large generator hummed behind the building. To the left, a large kitchen contained a deep freezer with enough steak and chicken to feed a platoon. Open-faced shelves held rows of insecticide, canned food, condiments, and burlap sacks of rice. Against the opposite wall, large plastic barrels brimmed with fresh water.

Across the runway from the building, the dopers erected stout posts supporting huge sheets of black plastic. The crude hangars were large enough to shield two planes. Drums of aviation fuel flanked the hangars in neat rows. I tried to imagine how many planeloads of cocaine departed from this compound every day.

By the time the helicopters completed their shuttle service for the night, 30 men milled around the isolated strip, gaping at the traffickers' lair. We spotted a bulldozer and several other buildings, but it was too dark for more than a cursory inspection. As dusk settled over the jungle, we saw figures scurrying across the center of the runway. The dopers were regrouping. We divided into teams and prepared for another assault.

I organized the perimeter, placing a pair of men every 10 yards around the building and up both sides of the runway to form a U-shaped defense line. When they settled in, Colonel Zarate assigned a team of men to cook a meal. The men rotated from their posts to feast on the traffickers' stocks. I passed from one station to the next, urging them to stay alert and sleep in shifts through the night. If the dopers returned with more men, we needed every eye and ear tuned to the trees.

An hour later, we heard a voice crying from the darkness. *"Ayudame, estoy herido."* Help me, I'm wounded.

The perimeter broke into excited chatter. Probably an ambush. I moved toward the treeline, turning to ask for a volunteer. The conversation stopped. Finally, Colonel Zarate drafted one of his men to accompany me. I whispered a few instructions, then we dropped to our knees, crawling through the undergrowth with flashlights and M-16s.

The voice continued, a low moan in the darkness. *"Ayudame, por favor."*

If this is an ambush, they've found a convincing actor, I thought. I whispered to the Peruvian, "Watch out around us for movement." He nodded. We crept the last few yards.

The man lay sprawled on his stomach at the base of a huge tree. The beam of my flashlight played over his prone body. He looked about 25, with a medium build and light complexion. His striped shirt was covered in mud. Blood stained his dress pants a deep crimson. I hissed at him, ordering him to identify himself. He was a pilot, shot in the ass as he fled the assault.

We crawled back toward the airstrip, dragging him behind. I still had not ruled out an ambush. We reached the perimeter, facing a line of gun barrels. Two Peruvians immediately yanked the pilot to his feet and began slapping him around. Then the Colombians joined them. A real show of cooperation, I thought sadly as they aimed kicks at his wound. The pilot was close to tears. He claimed he just arrived at the airstrip and was waiting for his load. He said he did not know anything about the traffickers' operation. The answer brought more fists from the unconvinced police. They assigned two guards to the pilot and made him sit upright in the dirt the rest of the night.

* * *

The shooting started around 9 p.m. First one rifle, then two, then a dozen opened up, muzzles flashing in the darkness as men yelled and branches snapped. I broke into a running crouch, looking for the team who started the shooting. I reached them, screaming a cease fire order for the tenth time. The guns fell quiet. The pair stood shoulder-to-shoulder, squinting at the treeline.

"I saw them," the first man whispered, pointing into the dark jungle. "They're out there," his companion added, nodding vigorously.

"Did they return fire?" I asked.

"No."

"Then don't fire unless you're fired upon," I said sharply. I was annoyed. If one side of the perimeter aimed the same direction as the other, they could kill each other in the crossfire. I trudged back to *Casa Brava*.

An hour later, the perimeter erupted again, rifles chattering into the stillness. The officers insisted someone was out there, but no one could be sure where. I repeated my warning.

At dawn, I crept through the trees around the perimeter until I reached the area where the shooting began. Four bullet-riddled bodies lay scattered among the broken branches. I summoned the men from that section of the perimeter. The pair who started the shooting stared wide-eyed at the bodies. Their buddies burst into fits of laughter.

The monkeys never had a chance.

We spent the morning inspecting the area. The compound was huge, with buildings tucked into the foliage. We followed well-worn footpaths about 50 yards into the jungle and discovered a sign painted with a skull and crossbones: *"Peligro. No fumar."* Danger. No smoking. We had found the lab. The large wooden lab sat at the center of a cluster of buildings, all joined by screened walkways. Blue plastic protected the roof of every building.

The first thing I saw were the vats, huge metal containers straight out of the Frankenstein movies, with gauges and tubes snaking between them. Kilo-size cardboard boxes lay scattered everywhere. Rows of heat lamps suspended from a large board served as cocaine dryers. We found generators, drums of coca chemicals, an electric mixing vat with revolving arms, and testing equipment.

This was no coca paste operation. They were producing cocaine hydrochloride. Col. Zarate looked simultaneously excited and troubled. This was unheard of in Peru. We always assumed Peru made all the paste and Colombian labs churned out the finished product. This place turned the conventional wisdom on its ear. A new, two-story refinery under construction near the lab alarmed the colonel even more. If the traffickers completed it, the new lab contained equipment to make an even stronger, purer product. One-hundred percent pure cocaine.

Next door, a wooden building was labeled "depósito." The lab's cocaine warehouse. It was empty. If there was cocaine here when we landed, they moved it quickly.

Each path ended at another building. We discovered six dormitories stacked with enough bunks to house 600 people. A rough hut sat on the banks of the river, where most of their supplies obviously arrived by boat from Leticia. One shack held nothing but 55-gallon chemical drums. Next to the lab, another shack contained 15 bunks shrouded by mosquito netting. A sign tacked to the wall read *"Guardia."* The lab had its own security force. There was even a rough-cut shrine made of three wide boards nailed into a triangle. The makeshift shelter, mounted atop a thick post, looked like a tiny A-frame house. It shielded a small statue of the *Virgen de Loreto*, the guardian of this sprawling Amazon district. A wooden cross was nailed to the peak of the shrine.

The wounded pilot insisted he knew nothing about the whereabouts of the paste. But he rattled off anything else he could think to tell us. He said *Casa Brava* usually employed about 25 people, who served as the ground crew, cooks, and guards for the busy drug hub. He explained the cartels' rigidly compartmentalized operation. Neither the pilots nor the *Casa Brava* staff were allowed into the rest of the compound, which was run by a different crew. The guards who slept behind the mosquito netting next to the lab would shoot a nosy pilot as quickly as an invading police officer.

We found a number of radios in the guards' shack and clicked them on. Somewhere in the jungle, the traffickers were carrying on a conversation. "They'll never find the stash," one voice reassured another. "It's too well hidden."

We knew they could not have taken the product far, but after a lengthy search of the compound, we were about to give up. Then a shotgun blast ripped through the trees. A Peruvian *Guardia* member aimed and fired again, whooping as he chased a large toucan. The panicked bird hopped from branch to branch, desperately trying to flap a shattered wing. I asked the Peruvian what the hell was going on. He said he wanted to eat the bird. I was not about to question another country's eating habits.

He continued the chase as we watched. The bird stopped, exhausted. The Peruvian crouched, aimed carefully, and pulled the trigger. The shotgun kicked, followed by the sound of splitting wood. The toucan disappeared in a cloud of feathers, which fluttered to the ground as the bird dropped like a stone.

We heard a yell and turned toward the toucan hunter. He was gone. The ground had swallowed him. We rushed to the edge of the hole and peered in. He thrashed about in a puddle of water. All around him lay bulging white sacks covered in leaves and shards of rotten wood. The stash.

* * *

In the days following the raid, the compound became a zoo. General Walter Andrate, the head of the *Guardia Civil,* flew in with Rieff, who suspended his eternal state of distress over my jungle disappearances to congratulate me. Our DEA counterparts from Colombia showed up with a video camera to film the entire area. Peruvian and Colombian officials descended on the site like press-hungry vultures, gesticulating and posturing for the international and local media.

People milled around the compound like ants, oblivious to our gentle requests not to move anything. It was total chaos. The joint leader insisted on unlimited access for the cameras. They wanted the pens to scribble and the shutters to click. It looked good for the United States, which financed the operation. It looked good for the Colombians, who knew they were considered the world's cocaine Wild West. Most of all, it looked good for Peru's new president, who could boast of his country's victory over the traffickers. I avoided the cameras as best I could. For an undercover agent, exposure meant failure. I huddled with my paperwork, writing endless reports and filling dozens of clipboard pages with an inventory of the compound.

A few days later, the South American newspapers published multi-page articles on the raid, repeating the numbers: Four tons of coca paste seized from a lab capable of churning out 500 kilos of pure cocaine a day. The Peruvian government estimated the compound's value at $500 million. It was the biggest cocaine lab capture in South American history.

We seized five planes, three with Colombian registration, one Bolivian, and one American. We never found the wounded cigarette boat or any of the Colombians who fled into the night. We captured assault weapons, military uniforms, boxes of 9mm ammunition, and a firing range with hand-drawn silhouettes, pocked with bullet holes. We later discovered the lab belonged to Arcesio and Omar Ricco, members of the Cali cartel.

For the rest of the week, I supervised phase II of the operation, buzzing over the treetops in search of other buildings and airstrips. We discovered another hut a half mile from the main compound, a communications center jammed with radio equipment. We found six smaller airstrips in the immediate area, one made of cement. The crude compounds, none approaching the size of the first, were dynamited, disappearing in a shower of splinters. We arrested a few young Colombian pilots at the airstrips. They were flown to Colombian jails.

When I wandered into the Lima office a week after the raid, I picked up a local paper left on my desk and almost choked on my coffee. My photo, snapped by a Reuters photographer with a telephoto lens, took up a quarter of the page. Luckily, I was wearing a large pair of sunglasses, but the DEA insignia on my camouflage jacket was unmistakable. A number of other papers published the photo in their spreads on the operation, with headlines screaming *"Contra narcotraffico."* Against narco-trafficking. Wonderful.

After Operation Condor, the dollars flowed into Peru at an unprecedented rate. The Peruvian government rewarded the Guardia by allowing them to use the confiscated planes for their anti-narcotics operations. DEA rewarded the Peru office with a new base in the Huallaga Valley, named Santa Lucia. The agency built a runway and barracks in the jungle, then sent more agents down with three Hueys to increase the pressure on the cartels.

I flew home in late September, arriving just before Noe went into labor. My son was born in the same McAllen hospital where his sister arrived. We named him Celerino Castillo IV. I immediately nicknamed him C4.

Back in Lima, Rieff was irate when he saw my photo in the papers. When I returned from McAllen, he insisted my tour be cut short, claiming my safety could not be guaranteed now that my picture was undoubtedly tacked to the cartels' bulletin boards. I shrugged it off and flew back to Tingo Maria. UMOPAR gave me a much warmer welcome, crowding around to congratulate me on Condor's success. Rieff remained obstinate, muttering I was going to get killed, or, worse, get someone else killed. I was beyond caring anymore. The cartels knew who I was. They surely saw my photo. But after a year in the Huallaga Valley, I knew the jungle better than their men did. I had spun my own small web, connecting strands throughout the valley to warn me of trouble. I trusted my *Guardia* friends, I trusted my informants, and I trusted my instincts.

I was not the only one receiving unwanted media attention. On August 11, 1985, an article appeared in The Washington Post described how the Nicaraguan rebels fighting the Sandinista government were sustained after U.S. funding ran out the previous May. The article exposed the man who held the Contras together almost single-handedly: Lt. Col. Oliver L. North.

Through September, I spent as much time as ever in the valley, running over the trails with UMOPAR. I avoided Tingo Maria, just in case the cartels decided to use me as an example. Ironically, both Rieff and the traffickers feared a repeat of the Camarena tragedy. Rieff knew his career would suffer a major blow if an agent under his command was killed by dopers. The cartels knew the wrath of two governments would descend on them if another DEA agent died in the line of duty. Neither wanted the kind of debacle then playing out in Mexico.

The real reason my boss wanted me out of the country, I thought, was my relationship with the Guardia and UMOPAR. Instead of consulting with Rieff, the generals and colonels came straight to me for advice about anti-narcotics tactics. They knew I spent most of my time in coca country. They trusted my instincts. Rieff resented that.

The word came at the end of September. Rieff called me into his office to tell me I would be transferred to Guatemala on temporary duty, or TDY. In addition, he refused to recommend me for promotion to the next level. I could not believe what I was hearing. When I first arrived in Peru, he told me the promotion was automatic after spending a year in the country. I looked at him, the irritation showing in my eyes. He gave me a half-hearted shrug. I just had not paid my dues, he explained.

Six
Tightrope
Guatemala City, Oct. 10, 1985

As Copa flight 313 droned north over the jungle, I ran down my mental checklist on Central America. Leftist rebels, a permanent fixture in the region, had locked the military governments in Guatemala and El Salvador into bloody wars of attrition, while the poor multitudes in both nations, as usual, absorbed the crossfire. War would complicate my job considerably. To a government fighting for control in its own backyard, everything else becomes a distraction. But Uncle Sam's aid bought hospitality for the State Department's political operatives, a jungle playground for the U.S. Marines, and a tiny beachead for DEA.

In Guatemala, the locals would be hostile. The government carried a lingering bitterness toward the United States since the Carter Administration cried human rights violations and yanked U.S. military aid in 1978. The Israelis quickly moved into the power vacuum to take care of the Guatemalans, training the security forces, financing the war machine, and running covert operations against leftist movements in Nicaragua and other republics. Under Reagan, a trickle of U.S. military aid resumed by 1985, but the Guatemalan government had new friends and was slow to warm to U.S. intelligence and drug agents poking around their jungles. I knew from working with Israeli intelligence in Peru they could give me all the information I needed to sort through the chaos. I made a mental note to look them up as soon as I got settled.

As we moved into Guatemalan airspace, another leadership shuffle was taking place below. The country had a new democratically-elected government, headed by Marco Vinicio Cerezo Arévalo, a Christian Democrat still gloating over his triumph at the ballot boxes. The long-suffering Guatemalans had endured a string of military dictatorships that stretched back, virtually unbroken, to 1954, the year the CIA toppled Jacobo Arbenz Guzmán. Arbenz had the audacity to legalize the local Communist Party and launch an agrarian reform movement, passing out 400,000 acres of uncultivated land to the peasants. Unfortunately for the would-be reformers, some of the idle land belonged to the United Fruit Company. At the time, Senator Joe McCarthy's red-hunting was burning in the public mind, the Soviets had the Bomb, and the CIA was a budding agency looking to connect its first body punch against the Communist threat. The CIA called their pet coup ''Operation Success,'' and declared it a victory over Communism in Uncle Sam's back yard. But Arbenz had helped seal his fate by playing Robin Hood with a U.S. company's land, and the lesson had not been lost on the Guatemalan establishment.

We became the protective uncle in Guatemala, installing Carlos Castillo Armas as president in 1955. Our policy settled into a comfortable, conservative groove. The United States wanted stability in Guatemala, and backed every right-wing regime that came down the power alley, looking the other way as they crushed any opposition and wiped tens of thousands of their people off the face of the earth. Three decades later, not much had changed. Although the Guatemalan Christian Democrats traced their birth to 1955, after Arbenz fell, and carried the banner of moderate reform, the party forged blood bonds with the military as it ascended. Cerezo would assume the presidency in January, but he would need the okay from the men with the medals and the gold braid before he so much as broke wind in his new office.

My ears popped, breaking my train of thought as the plane dropped into its landing pattern. I leaned from my aisle seat to take in the view. In the dusky glow of a dying sun, Guatemala's famous volcanoes filled the landscape, lined up like sentinels along the spine of one of the world's most unstable areas -- the perfect symbol for a land forever erupting, both geologically and politically. The Guatemalans had named two of them *Volcan de Fuego* and *Volcán de Agua* -- fire and water. Steam hissed from the cone of *Volcán de Fuego*. Fire ruled Guatemala's horizon.

The tires yelped against the tarmac, and the airliner taxied into Aurora International Airport, where my new boss would be waiting. I knew Bob Stia, the country attache to Guatemala, from New York, where we had both worked as agents. We never had more than a passing conversation, and I remebered nothing more than general impressions: a tall Italian guy with straight gray hair and a mild personality. My DEA friends told me Stia had connections in Washington who pulled strings to get him the Guatemalan job. I shook my head. It was crazy to send someone like Stia to Central America. He had three strikes against him as soon as he hit Guatemalan soil: he was Anglo, his Spanish was abysmal, and he didn't know the culture. At least he wasn't out in the field trying to build cases. Hell, it's just TDY - - temporary duty, I thought as the center aisle filled with passengers. My job was catching dopers, not puzzling over policy. I reached the gate and picked my way through the crowd, searching the semi-circle of faces. Stia walked up and extended his hand, smiling. "Welcome to Guatemala," he beamed.

The next hand I shook belonged to Russell Reina, a short, stocky Mexican-American with a close-trimmed beard and black hair combed straight back. Everything about Reina cried out for attention. Gold everywhere - - pinky rings, bracelets, and a 50-peso gold medallion hanging around his neck. His money clip, fashioned out of a 20-peso gold piece, probably set him back $300. He favored *guayaberas*, not the familiar Mexican short-sleeved variety, but the Panamanian style with long sleeves, cufflinks and embroidered fronts. He looked like a Class One doper. Reina carried what we called a "fag bag," a satchel Mexican men sometimes carry that looks like an oversized purse. His 9mm automatic would be tucked in there along with everything a man normally carries in his wallet. At first I thought Reina had just come from an undercover assignment and left his doper clothes on, but I soon realized it wasn't an act - - he really dressed that way.

At the time, Reina was the DEA's lone agent in the Guatemala office, which covered four countries: Guatemala, El Salvador, Honduras and Belize. As country attache, Stia performed mostly administrative functions and served as a liaison between the U.S. Federal agencies and local law enforcement authorities. I could not imagine one agent covering four countries, especially when two of them had become major political hot spots. Enrique Camarena's murder in Mexico underscored the need for DEA agents to back up one another in unstable countries, and Guatemala and El Salvador made Mexico look tame. I was only on TDY, but the agency planned to take advantage of the sudden doubling of their manpower. Stia put me in charge of the aerial eradication program: reconnaisance missions over the marijuana fields and the opium poppy plantations spreading across the Guatemalan highlands. Some creative genius had named the operations Olive Oyl and Popeye.

As we walked toward the exit, Stia turned to me and said, "You're in a different world now. I'm going to take you to our local cathouse." I grinned. Temporary duty would be interesting here. I later discovered the bordellos had become a first-day ritual for most U.S. agents setting foot in Guatemala City - - CIA, DEA, State Department, or military. We piled into Stia's brand-new DEA Volvo and drove to the Hotel El Dorado, half a mile from the airport.

The El Dorado carried a five-star rating, and stayed plump from a steady diet of North American businessmen on expense accounts. I checked in at the desk, flashed my diplomatic passport to get the discount rate given to embassy staff, and the clerk handed me a key to a corner room on the sixth floor. I rode the elevator up and turned the lock. A king-sized bed dominated the room, across from the necessities: a desk and cable TV with CNN. Parting the drapes, I took in the view.

By pure luck, the room made the perfect agent's perch. I could read the identification numbers on planes coming and going from the airport, and the large picture windows offered a clear view of the front of the hotel and down one side. I threw my suitcase on the floor and took the elevator down to the lobby where Stia and Reina were waiting.

We drove down *Avenida de las Americas*, the busy thoroughfare that bisected Guatemala City and cut through the wealthier neighborhoods. The four-lane road was split by a broad esplanade dominated by tall trees and landscaped shrubs. The greenery halted at major intersections to leave room for huge statues of Spanish conquistadores and Mayan rulers locked forever in circling traffic. At the end of the *avenida*, we stopped at a large, one-story brick home where a security guard slouched in front of an iron fence. Stia parked in the street, and the guard finally recognized the *norteamericanos* and waved us through the gate. He assured Stia the car would be in good hands while we were inside.

The three of us looked like bit players in a bad detective show - - Reina in his flashy gold, Stia in his conservative suit, and me in my usual boots and jeans. Stia knocked. Right out of that same bad detective show, a small panel slid open in the steel door, and the brown eyes framed in the opening flashed recognition. The little panel clacked shut and the door opened. If those eyes had seen police uniforms, the owner would have made a hasty appearance to inform the officers who they should call to confirm the required bribe, or *mordida*, had been paid. A heavy square lock would hold back anyone trying to throw a shoulder at the door, and inside, a couple of stout sliding bolts would stop any uninvited guests without a battering ram.

The house looked like any cookie-cutter suburban dwelling you would find in the States, except for the nouveau-Graceland decorating. A huge living room to the right held blue and maroon velvet sofas and velvet drapes sweeping down to dark plush carpeting. Paintings of women in provocative poses adorned the walls. Beautiful ladies in evening gowns reclined on the wall-to-wall sofa, awkwardly mimicking the classical poses on the wall. This was Maruja's, named after the madam who ran the place. Stia and Reina told me the house was legendary in Guatemala for its expensive women. As we crossed into their den, the women - - girls, really, none of them looked older than 18 -- sat up expectantly, waiting for a signal to do business. A waiter in black tails sauntered over, a white cloth draped over his cocked left arm, and steered us to the next room. More girls filled the J-shaped bar in calm anticipation. A bartender in a white smoking jacket busily mixed drinks in front of the full-wall mirror.

A couple of the girls immediately joined us for drinks. They asked me to choose a companion, and I pointed to a Chinese girl with long black hair. She quietly joined me at the bar and I ordered drinks. Her black silk dress cut into a low V in front, showing her bare breasts when she leaned forward. In perfect Spanish, she introduced herself as Li. She looked about 16. As we chatted, she told me she had come to Guatemala from Taiwan a few years before, and the cash she earned at the cathouse supported her parents and several brothers and sisters.

We spent a good two hours at the house, making small talk with the girls over drinks. Reina told me I could pay Li for an hour, or spend a little more, about $25, to bring her back to my room for the night. I passed. I had been away from my wife for six months, with no indication the separation would end, but I was too tired for anything but sleep. Stia and Reina wanted me to become familiar with their haunts. Like the hotel, the cathouse held eyes and ears that could be prodded into divulging information we needed. The girls knew we worked for the U.S. Embassy, and they could tell us when Nicaraguans and Colombians hit town. I wondered if the information flowed the other way as well.

Stia and Reina dropped me off at the hotel. I watched the news for a while, flipped through the *Miami Herald*'s Latin American edition, and collapsed into bed. I had a good feeling about Guatemala. The capital throbbed with the energy of milling masses, and after more than a year in Peru, I needed some time away from the jungle. I clicked off the light, and promised myself I would visit the McDonald's I had spotted from the air.

Stia briefed me on Guatemala during breakfast the next morning in the hotel restaurant. The Guatemalan military, he said, was giving up the government on paper, but would always hold the real power in the country. Despite Cerezo's popular election, minister of defense Hector Alejandro Gramajo called the important shots from his position at the center of the Council of Commanders, a tight ring of military leaders whose decisions overshadowed any of the ostensibly democratic decisions made by the president or the congress. The Guatemalans knew they had to put a democratic face on their Draconian system to stay on Washington's good side, and Cerezo had shown no indication he would test his leash. As far as DEA was concerned, we operated at the pleasure of the military.

After breakfast, Stia shuttled me to the DEA offices, located within the U.S. Embassy. I received an embassy I.D. and met Ambassador Alberto Martinez Piedra, a diminutive Cuban-American, for a 10-minute welcome-to-Guatemala briefing. He never mentioned, and seemed completely uninterested in, the DEA's Central American drug program.

Stia guided me through the embassy compound to the cluster of rooms where the United States government masterminded its strategy to rid more than 8,000 square miles of foreign territory of narcotrafficking. My office held a desk, a chair and a file cabinet, with a large window overlooking *Avenida de las Americas*. The thick bulletproof glass had been gouged by a slug. The natives constantly peppered the building with automatic weapons, our elderly secretary explained wearily. The U.S. government had long ago surrounded its diplomats in Guatemala with a stout iron fence anchored in cement, with concrete-filled steel drums ringing the front entrance. If the 55-gallon speedbumps didn't stop the occasional car bomber, the flock of security guards pacing the grounds would open up with automatic weapons. It was just like Peru. The shit was flying, and Americans were on constant alert.

Stia brought me into his office to continue my briefing. He switched to El Salvador, where I would be spending much of my time. The United States had bought and paid for the country. We chose the presidents, scheduling elections when the previous puppet wore out his welcome. This year, Christian Democrat José Napoleón Duarte had beaten Roberto d'Aubisson, who was linked to the country's right-wing death squads. The election should have been a turning point, but the ruling elite and the military had a chokehold on the republic that no mere politician could pry loose.

Despite the ongoing reign of terror against the peasants, the dollars kept coming. A republic the size of Massachusetts absorbed $1.5 million a day in U.S. aid -- more than $100 for every man, woman and child -- yet the military government still could not exterminate the Farabundo Martí National Liberation Front, or FMLN, the leftist guerrillas who pestered them from the suburbs and the mountains. They both hung on, dragging the civil war into its sixth year and making terror and gratuitous violence a part of every Salvadoran's existence.

Three days after my arrival in Central America, Duarte would walk unarmed into the war zone and plead with the guerrillas to release his daughter. The rebels had snatched her a month earlier, hammering home the reality that no one was immune to El Salvador's incestuous enmity. Death squad killings had slowed since Duarte took office, but that was like telling mothers in Florida to take heart because the number of alligator attacks on children had declined.

The military/political storm troopers of both sides continued snatching people from their homes, and while the Salvadoran air force dropped bombs on guerrilla positions, the guerrillas knocked down power lines, mined roads, and kidnapped mayors. Whoever pulled the trigger, ordinary people died. The Guatemalan government harbored some resentment toward the United States, but at least they maintained some measure of control; the only constant in El Salvador was insanity.

DEA had never worked the country, and we were hoping to establish some contacts and land our first seizure. I soon realized they didn't expect much more than recruiting informants and documenting any drug activity their eyes and ears picked up; actually busting a trafficker and grabbing his shipment would be gravy, as far as Stia was concerned. Later, as I leafed through the files, I discovered the drug war in this corner of the globe amounted to piles of reports documenting traffickers' identities and movements, but few seizures and arrests. We were playing traffic cop, taking down the license numbers of speeders, but never writing any tickets. Stia maintained a we're-doing-the-best-we-can attitude. As he continued the briefing, it became obvious that the agency's priorities here mirrored those in Peru. First, stay out of trouble with the locals. Second, don't make the U.S. government look bad. Third, try to make life difficult for the traffickers.

Then Stia nonchalantly brought up the subject that would dominate the remainder of my DEA career: the Contra resupply operation. He described the covert U.S. operation to the Nicaraguan rebels, run out of Ilopango air base near San Salvador by Marine Lt. Colonel Oliver North. Stia said the National Security Council, where North worked, picked up where the CIA left off after our government cut off aid to the Contras.

The third of five Boland Amendments prohibiting U.S. assistance to the rebels had been in effect for a year at this point, and in April, 1985, the House of Representatives had rejected $14 million in non-military aid to the Contras, despite President Reagan's energetic lobbying for his favorite rebels:

> As you know, the Sandinista dictatorship has
> taken absolute control of the government and

the armed forces. It is a Communist dictatorship,
it has done what Communist dictatorships do:
created a repressive state security and secret
police organization assisted by Soviet, East
German and Cuban advisers; harassed and in many
cases expunged the political opposition, and
rendered the democratic freedoms of speech, press
and assembly, punishable by officially sanctioned
harassment, and imprisonment or death.

I truly believe - - the history of this century
forces me to believe - - that to do nothing in
Central America is to give the first Communist
stronghold on the North American continents a
green light to spread its poison throughout this
free and increasingly democratic hemisphere.

Change the nationality of the advisers, and the President's
speech would have described our allies in Guatemala and El
Salvador perfectly. Nicaragua was not about to let its neighbors
show them up, however; the day I arrived in Central America
Nicaraguan President Daniel Ortega Saavedra suspended civil
rights, such as free expression, the right to assemble publicly and
privacy of mail and home. Ortega said "the brutal aggression by
North America and its internal allies has created an extraordinary
situation."

Its "internal allies" were the Contras and their sympathiz-
ers, who made life difficult for the Sandinistas. Under the CIA's
tutelage, these internal allies sabotaged oil facilities at Puerto
Sandino, torched an oil storage facility, and planted magnetic
mines in Nicaraguan ports. The Reagan administration made no
secret of how badly it wanted to thump the Sandinistas.

"Be careful what you do up there," Stia said, referring to
North's covert venture. "Don't interfere in their operation."
Reports of drug smuggling by North's operation had trickled into
our office, but Stia said DEA had not pursued the matter. He
wanted to do his time in Guatemala, then pack up and return to
upstate New York with his wife and kids. He wasn't about to
throw rocks at a hornet's nest.

I had learned a hard lesson in Peru, and I wanted to lay out
my personal philosophy up front. I told Stia, "If I receive

intelligence the Contra operation is trafficking, I'll investigate and report it." Stia laughed. If I tried to take down North's operation, he said, the DEA brass would waste no time finding some excuse to pull me out of the country.

I made up my mind right there I would check out Ilopango. I didn't care who was running dope; if I confirmed they were smuggling, I would move in. Stia assumed I would salute and play the good soldier. From his statements, I could read his logic: I was a Vietnam veteran. I spent eight months in the jungles trying to shoot Communists, and watched my buddies die in the process. In Central America, the Sandinistas gave the Reagan Administration an opportunity to banish the ghosts of Vietnam forever. Reagan, like Kennedy, Johnson and Nixon before him, had used Cold War Communist fears and the domino theory to persuade America we could finally slay the dragon on a small Third World stage. I despised Communism, but I joined the DEA to fight another war, and Stia had no idea how many comrades I watched die in the clutches of heroin in Vietnam.

I fell in love with Guatemala. I ate fresh vegetables, lobster, steaks. The people somehow remained friendly and polite, although their eyes revealed a hard edge honed by war. My only complaint was the weather. Even in October, it felt like springtime, making sweaters a necessity at night. I still preferred pounding heat. I found plenty of U.S. fingerprints on the ancient Mayan homeland. On the crowded streets, old American cars jockeyed for position, many of them bearing Texas plates. The homesick U.S. businessmen from Akron got their fast food fix at McDonald's or Pizza Hut, and Wendy's was opening soon.

My ears picked up the local brand of Spanish on the streets, and I worked on scrubbing the Mexican signature from my speech. My border Spanish would only raise eyebrows here. It didn't take long for me to pick out the differences between the Guatemalan and Salvadoran dialects. The Salvadorans had a sing-song tone, and used very correct Spanish. The Guatemalan elite prided themselves on their correct Spanish, but the poorer people tended to cut the end off their words and spiced their conversation with slang. With each conversation, I took on more of the local vernacular.

My mission was redefined after I found out Stia and Reina had a lock on most of the aerial eradication work. They both wanted to get enough time in the sky to qualify for their pilots' licenses. They were always flying. Nobody was ever on or off duty here. Reina liked zooming over the poppy and pot fields, but face-to-face encounters with the bad guys were not part of his plan. As much as Reina looked the part of a trafficker, he refused to work undercover -- he never had the instincts for it. He just wanted to have fun. Stia always teased him for working "kiddie dope," and rubbed it in by telling him he wasn't shit until he worked New York.

Five days after I arrived in Guatemala, Reina's passion for flight almost got us both killed in the Guatemalan mountains.

Reina and I met early that Tuesday and drove to Aurora for an aerial reconnaisance mission, my first poppy field hunt. Since DEA didn't have its own aircraft and pilots, we used a Bell 212 Turbo helicopter piloted by Pérez, a contract pilot and a good friend of Reina's. Pérez guided the chopper along the ragged spine of the mountains to San Marcos, the westernmost of Guatemala's 22 *departamentos*. We picked up a Guatemalan soldier, a member of the *Guardia de Hacienda*, at Tacana, a little village near the Mexican border -- guerrilla country. He guided us to a spot in the mountains where the poppy fields glowed against the foliage. The poppy fields looked beautiful from the air, red streaks against a green canvas.

Mexicans owned the crops, and taught local farmers how to grow opium poppies for a cash crop more lucrative than anything they could plant. The Mexicans taught the locals how to score the hard pods with a blade, let the white sap ooze out, then scrape it off and knead it into a ball. The sap turned chocolate brown, and in short order became heroin for American junkies. Long streaks of red and white along the mountainside proved how quickly the poppy trade spread. The Guatemalan police generally left them alone. They didn't want to risk running into a guerrilla stronghold while trying to destroy a bunch of flowers. We landed on the side of a mountain, in the middle of a poppy field, and took a few plants as samples.

Ironically, the *Guardia* officer told me, the fields were frequently guarded by the Guatemalan Civilian Self-Defense Patrols, the rural indians organized and armed by the military who were supposed to be keeping the guerrillas busy. When General Efraín Ríos Montt took power in 1982, he organized the patrols to spearhead his counterinsurgency war in the mountains and pressed close to a million civilians into service within two years. Now here they were, guarding the poppies. I could sympathize with them to some extent. They were very poor people who sided with the military for protection.

The Guatemalan guerrillas also fed off the hopelessness of the Indians, who formed the base of what they saw as an inevitable and massive peasant uprising against the ruling elite. They took names like the Guerrilla Army of the Poor and Organization of People in Arms, fighting from the rugged jungles of Huehuetenango and Petén in the northern part of the country. The guerrillas spent most of their energy ambushing army patrols, and the military responded with reflexive thumpings of any village suspected of aiding the guerrillas. I wondered how these simple villagers decided between the military and the rebels, with both sides threatening to kill them if they chose the other. It reminded me of the fable about the lady or the tiger, except the unfortunate indians could count on finding a tiger behind either door.

The *Guardia* officer said he never heard of the civilian patrols shooting a guerrilla. But they were always shooting at the DEA planes and helicopters with their M1 rifles, and the planes frequently returned with bullet holes. Every trip into the mountains was a risk.

Once we had our poppies, we dropped the *Guardia* officer in Tacana and headed north to Huehuetenango for the next leg of the mission. That's when Reina took over the chopper's controls. He wanted to learn how to fly a helicopter, and Pérez just smiled and let go of the stick. Reina didn't have much trouble until we got to Cuilco, the little village where we were going to meet with *Guardia* officials to chart more plantations. But as we reached the point where an experienced pilot would instinctively cut back his airspeed to prepare for landing, Reina continued bearing down.

I waited for Reina to let up on the stick. By the time I said something, it was too late. I yelled to Pérez over the intercom, "We're coming in too fast." Reina yanked on the stick and the helicopter lurched upward until we were looking straight up into the sky. As he tried to bring it back down, I could see a soccer field, a clump of trees, and a school. A hard stone formed in my gut. Drawn by the sound of the rotors cutting the air, the children were streaming out of the tiny adobe and concrete school.

Reina panicked and let go of the controls. "You take it," he yelled to Pérez. Pérez grabbed the stick, but Russ had slammed one of the foot pedals to the steel, sending the chopper into a spin. "I can't control it," Pérez screamed. The Bell spun into the ground, snapping off the left ski before the chopper bounced back off the the turf. As the door on my side flew open, my mind flashed back to Vietnam, to the thump of the grenade exploding through a pack of men, to the chopper blades slicing through panicked soldiers as they tried to escape the wounded bird. I froze. Pérez said, "I've got to lay her down." He nudged the Bell on its side, and dirt showered the metal skin as a blade buried itself in the ground.

In helicopter crashes, usually the next blade slices through the helicopter's body, taking out anyone unlucky enough to be sitting in the wrong place. But somehow, the chopper broke free of the blades, ripping out the transmission and pouring hot fluid all over me. I thought it was blood. We seemed to float for a moment, then the fuselage crumpled into the ground.

I crawled up to the opposite door and pulled myself out, knowing the wreckage could explode if sparks hit the fumes filling my nose. I yanked open the cockpit door and shouted to Russ. He looked at me in a daze over his dangling sunglasses. He glanced down at his lap, where the belts held him at a right angle to the ground, then at Pérez, who was clawing like a caged lion trying to escape a fire. Reina unbuckled his belt and dropped on top of Pérez with a thud. Pérez let out a yell that knocked Russ out of his daze, and the two finally untangled themselves and climbed out of the shattered Bell.

We stood silently near the wreckage, bruised and bleeding from numerous scrapes and cuts, as a mob of children watched from a respectful distance. Class had obviously been dismissed due to a helicopter crash in the soccer field. Russ tried to light a cigarette and failed miserably; his shaking hands couldn't work the lighter. A little wide-eyed Mayan girl walked up with a handful of oranges and said "Eat these, they will calm you down." Reina took an orange and wolfed it down, skin and all. I lit his cigarette for him. Pérez was shaking too, but out of anger rather than fear. The first words out of his mouth were "No fuckin' insurance." He had turned a $500,000 helicopter into a schoolyard scrapheap.

The tiny military post in Cuilco radioed their headquarters in Guatemala City and told them about the crash, and their commander called the U.S. Embassy, who scrambled a helicopter to beat the guerrillas to the school. The CIA pilot who pulled us out swore he thought we were dead when he saw the wreckage. The embassy, he said, went ballistic when someone radioed in that the guerrillas had shot down two DEA agents on a recon mission.

Damage control began immediately, and I got a quick lesson in Guatemalan palm greasing. Pérez stood to lose his license for letting Reina fly the helicopter, so he paid off the FAA investigator, and the heat blew away. Stia instructed me to write a cable explaining the crash, omitting the fact that Reina's hands were on the stick when we lost control, and stating "it has not been determined what caused the malfunction and crash." I didn't like it, but Stia made it clear he didn't want headquarters bringing the hammer down on us for Reina's blunder.

Stia and Reina later accompanied me to San Salvador for the obligatory introductions. We flew into Ilopango, a sprawling air base used by military and civilian aircraft.

In El Salvador, the tension level had been slammed up a few notches. You could feel it, an oppressive mixture of fear, hostility and suspicion that permeated every glance, every movement. The base bristled with security. We drove to the U.S. Embassy, where I met Edwin Corr, the U.S. ambassador to El Salvador. I told Corr we received intelligence about large quantities of narcotics passing through El Salvador, and I would be DEA's point man in his domain. Corr struck me as a mild-mannered, affable guy, and unlike his counterpart in Guatemala, he seemed genuinely interested in assisting the DEA. Over the following months, Corr became one of my strongest allies; the one U.S. official I could count on for support as my investigations pushed into sensitive areas.

After the near miss in the helicopter, I decided to work on the ground for a while, and Stia introduced me to a few of our best informants, the people who would ultimately determine the success or failure of my undercover operations. If they could give me accurate information and introduce me to the right people, we could make a dent in the trafficking. If they turned on me, I could be dead. Stia first introduced me to Luis Aparecio, a heavyset Guatemalan businessman in his 40s the agency knew officially as informant number STG-81-0013 -- meaning he had worked for the DEA since 1981, and was the thirteenth informant signed up in Guatemala that year.

I pegged Aparecio as a con artist the minute I met him. He talked fast and smooth, and could easily lure you into a trap with his bullshit. He spoke perfect English, and had lived in San Francisco for many years, where he headed the Hispanic Lions Club.

In San Salvador, he owned a coffee shop. Four months before I arrived in Guatemala, a group of guerrillas with machine guns had driven by the cafe in two pickup trucks and killed four U.S. Marines as they sat outside. Aparecio told me the guerrillas chased one of the marines inside the restaurant and shot him as he cringed on the floor near the bathroom. It was no big deal to Aparecio; those things happened on San Salvador's streets. The Salvadoran military caught up with the guerrillas and arrested or killed all of them, although rumors spread they had nabbed the wrong men in their rush to placate the U.S. government.

Despite its bloodstained reputation, the cafe still drew Americans, probably because of its prime location in San Salvador's club district, the *Zona Rosa*. By the time I arrived, American servicemen and diplomats had a curfew after which they were not to be in public. But that never stopped the Marines I watched from getting drunk, falling in love with whores, and shooting off their rifles.

Our relationship started on a tense note. I discovered why Aparecio left San Francisco: he was a doper, a fugitive from justice in the United States. In addition to his civic-minded Lions Club activities, Aparecio led an organized crime syndicate in San Francisco, a group of Central Americans running large quantities of cocaine into the United States. The DEA had filed charges against him for CCE, Continuous Criminal Enterprise, and narcotics trafficking under the RICO law. They just couldn't catch him. In San Francisco, he gained a reputation for his guile; DEA reports showed the frustration of agents who tried to tail Aparecio, only to lose him when he suddenly shot the wrong way down a one-way street. Because the United States didn't have an extradition agreement with Guatemala, the DEA couldn't touch him. Aparecio told me later that a DEA agent once called in the Guatemalan police to kidnap him and put him on a plane to the

United States - a popular technique for extraditing criminals from countries with no extradition agreement with the United States. When they busted through the front door, he jumped out the window in his underwear and hid in a neighbor's house. He called his military friends, and they grabbed the agent in Guatemala City and brought him to Aparecio, who politely asked him to back off. The agent probably felt lucky to escape with his life, but they didn't harm him. Aparecio hated violence, and refused to carry a gun in a place where bullets were the ultimate arbitrator in most disputes.

We had a Class One cocaine violator in our sights with RICO warrants out for him and nobody could touch him. I realized then we were sleeping with the enemy. But I had little choice but to use him; he was our top informant in El Salvador, and we wanted to log our first bust there. Like it or not, we were a team. I checked up on him periodically, asking locals I trusted if he had returned to trafficking. They assured me he was out of the business.

He might have been a con artist, but Aparecio proved himself as an excellent informant. He liked my determination, and I learned I could rely on his information. I had the undercover expertise, and he was the guy who showed me around and set up meetings. His contacts consistently amazed me. Aparecio seemed able to go anywhere and speak to anyone in El Salvador. His networking stemmed from his role in the Nationalist Republican Alliance, or ARENA, a union of politicians and military men who seized the country in a 1979 coup. Aparecio endeared himself to ARENA's top echelons through his skills as a mediator and organizer. He could bring the right people together, and with his silver tongue and waving arms, Aparecio could settle most personal and political disputes in short order.

Aperecio married a Canadian, who fled San Francisco with him. Ironically, the wife of the doper became a hopeless junkie, hooked on the product that bought them the trappings of the elite. Disgusted, he shipped her back to Canada. I knew Aparecio was a user and trafficker, and I set down the ground rules immediately. If he started in the business again, I would lock him up. He agreed, probably because we paid him well. The DEA gave him about $1,000 a month, a lot of money in Central America. Plus bonuses of $2,000 to $3,000 if his work led to a big bust. He knew I could see through his facade, and his disposition changed around me.

As we began working El Salvador, my dependence on Aparecio grew. I had no one else to turn to. After Camarena's torture and murder in Mexico, DEA administrator Jack Lawn said no American agent was to travel or work alone in a foreign country. But with two agents to cover four countries, DEA had no choice.

Aparecio had a girlfriend, a very attractive Salvadoran who worked as a prostitute. He had fallen for her after meeting her at one of the local cathouses, and they had lived together off and on ever since. He even opened a boutique for her next to his cafe, and she struggled for a while to sell women's clothes. Meanwhile, she continued her night job and fed Aparecio a lot of information about the Colombians who bounced in and out of San Salvador. I used her as a sub-source, and time after time her information proved reliable. Later, she would provide a few more entries in a growing list on the Contra operation.

I took over the undercover operations and began organizing and training anti-narcotics units, the "Teach a man to fish" approach to interdiction. The State Department had earmarked money for us, and I wanted to put the cash to use. I visited the different police forces in Guatemala, interviewing men and women, talking to their supervisors as I searched for those with the quickest minds and the best street smarts. The country had plenty of security to choose from, thanks to generations of turmoil.

The masses were kept in check by overlapping webs of muscle. The Treasury Police and the *Guardia de Hacienda*, who guarded the National Palace, fell under the 11,000-member national police. The military boasted almost 40,000 troops, with its own sub-groups. I soon learned the members of the different forces refused to work together. They all answered to different chiefs, and openly despised one another, so I had to choose one force and recruit from it exclusively. I started with 25 or 30 members of the national police, then formed a second squad within the *Guardia de Hacienda* within a year.

One security organization I avoided was G2, the intelligence/counter-intelligence unit of the Guatemalan military and the most feared organization in the country. They held the big power, reinforced by a reputation for stone-faced cruelty. More than 1,000 people disappeared each year at the hands of G2, which Guatemalans referred to ominously as *La Dos* -- "the two." *La Dos* ran the death squads, and favored nondescript white vans for their sinister work. Some of the unlucky victims dragged from their homes turned up later as mutilated carcasses, but most simply vanished, joining the legions of *desaparecidos* -- the disappeared. The snatchings were so widespread that relatives of the disappeared formed their own organization, the Mutual Support Group. Of course, that made them subversives as well, and the death squads began making return housecalls on some families.   The G2 goons were experts, trained by United States and Israeli intelligence and fed with American tax dollars. They learned their lessons well, and used techniques I would later see first-hand. Their interrogations always brought results; unlike the CIA, G2 didn't worry about red tape or bureaucrats. They would simply extract the information they wanted, then kill their victim and blame it on "death squads." The vans often took their quivering captives to a bridge close to a neighborhood where all the military brass lived. *La Dos* drove their quarry -- students, opposition party members, professionals, clergy, and peace corps types -- into small sheds under the bridge. People in the area could hear the screams at night.

After a few weeks in Guatemala, I developed a twisted admiration for the local security forces. They got results, while we wallowed in a quagmire of futility. "*El Coyote*" personified our impotence. Luis Montoya earned his nickname by setting up a service to smuggling Cubans who lacked documentation in and out of Central America. He also flew all types of contraband on his trips, including narcotics. He neglected to pay off Bahamian officials during one trip, and they arrested him with a plane full of marijuana. The Colombians had given him cash for bribes, but he kept it, thinking he could sneak past the Bahamians. The Colombians went back and got the load back, which was the only reason they spared his neck.

He flew for Reina as a contract pilot, and as their friendship blossomed, Reina signed him up as an informant. He sucked money out of the DEA, feeding Reina information about the cocaine he flew for the Colombians to Florida and Texas. Reina set up ''controlled deliveries,'' to catch the cartel members on the receiving end. We would help Montoya refuel at small Guatemalan airstrips, then call our DEA offices in the U.S. to bust whoever showed up to collect the powder. In theory, *El Coyote* would be arrested for show, then set free while the bad guys went to jail and the agency weighed the cocaine for the press releases. Or Montoya could give the Columbians directions to a certain parking lot where the coke would be stashed in a DEA van, which would promptly run out of gas and leave the stranded Colombians easy prey for our agents.

But *El Coyote* never landed at the right airstrip. Each time, he explained the Colombians had changed the destination at the last minute, or offered some other excuse for leaving our counterparts brooding in the dark at some barren Florida airstrip. Reina usually asked me to go undercover on these operation, which totalled about 50 flights by the time I quit counting. I posed as a maintenance worker, refueling the Cessnas and Caravans as I checked out the loads. Most flights carried 300 to 500 kilos of cocaine, and I knew Montoya charged them $500 per kilo for delivery, plus expenses. He had a sweet arrangement, taking money from us for information on the cartels, then making as much as a quarter million dollars delivering loads that yielded not a single arrest or seizure. After realizing we were in effect refueling narcotics flights while the trafficker pointed us to the wrong landing strip, I protested to Reina. *El Coyote* had duped us every time, I said. Reina just shrugged. They were friends.

In Guatemala, friendships were everything. If I wanted to make any progress, I would have to work with the military -- despite my disgust with their methods. I met with every military commander I could find, and even paid a courtesy call on the G2 office in the Palace. They seemed eager to work with me. They confided their distaste for the CIA, who supplied them with the high-tech gizmos they loved, but tried to dictate how they worked. After running the country for three decades, the military was not about to take orders from anyone. They saw me as an asset, someone who could melt into the countryside and bring back information on the guerrillas in exchange for their support in the drug war. After a few informal visits, I compiled an extensive list of military contacts, and within a month I sealed their trust with information on Cerezo.

* * *

Corruption had rotted Guatemala from the top down, and my growing network of contacts brought the extent of the decay into focus. I talked to customs agents at Aurora, bartenders and waitresses at the Camino Real and El Dorado hotels, U.S. embassy domestic workers and relatives of government officials. Everyone told the same story. The pilots who worked in Aurora talked about the cocaine shipments that frequently passed through on both private and commercial flights. The bartenders and waitresses had served Guatemalan officials during their meetings with Colombian cartel members. The customs workers occassionally caught government officials smuggling bags onto U.S. commercial flights without going through inspection. They had looked the other way because the men carried government credentials. The officials recruited people in U.S. airports who would pick out the marked bags and take them to a scheduled drop point where cartel runners picked them up.

In short, Guatemala had become a major hub connecting the cartels to their customers in the United States. Back in the office, I began running the names of Cerezo's top lieutenants through our computer, and almost every name came back with a black mark. The list read like a flowchart of the Guatemalan power structure. Among the Guatemalan high command documented as traffickers were the president's brother, Milton Cerezo-Garcia; Claudia Arenas, a top aide; and two members of the Guatemalan congress: former interior minister Alfonso Cabrera-Hidalgo and Carlos Ramiro Garcia de Paz.

I leaned back in my chair, trying to absorb the enormity of what I stumbled upon. Our government had leaned on the Guatemalan military for elections and trumpeted the birth of a government whose top officials were involved in narcotrafficking. Somewhere, our priorities had become skewed, hopelessly mired in the residual shame of Vietnam and Korea while a new monstrosity feasted on our minds and bodies. We spent billions trying to beat down an ideology in Central America, while the cartels rented nations as transit routes.

After fighting both wars, I knew which posed a greater menace to America. Communism had accomplished little within our borders, but drugs were quickly turning our inner cities into war zones and choking our prisons, hospitals and morgues with empty husks. In New York, I watched the drug culture grow, throb, and metastasize to the streets. In South America, economies had surrendered to the most powerful growers the continent had ever seen. Now, I had evidence Guatemala's infant government was addicted to cocaine. Winning our narcotics war in Guatemala would mean taking down a good portion of their government, and that would never fly in Washington.

Warily, I took my information to Stia, who had heard about it already from informants. As usual, he had chosen not to follow up. I held my tongue; Guatemala's high officials didn't seem concerned about hiding their drug activity, so it was only a matter of time before I gathered hard evidence on them.

The Guatemalan military proved a better judge of Cerezo's true character than the Reagan Administration. They had vigorously persecuted Cerezo years before, and one of my informants discovered Cerezo never forgot his trip into exile.

Enrique, a Colombian-born informant who ran a clothing business in Costa Rica, gave me an intimate look at the political side of Cerezo's inner circle. One of Enrique's good friends was a well-placed Guatemalan official, and I asked him to feed me anything he heard about the men on my trafficking list. Enrique's friend took him to a surreptitious meeting in downtown Guatemala City where a high Government official, met with two Cubans, a Russian and several Nicaraguans.

Enrique said they spent the evening discussing how to overthrow the Guatemalan military.

I wrote my report and gave it to Stia and the CIA. The CIA didn't believe me, so I called G2. Two of their officers rushed to my office for a quick briefing. It was hot information, and they were stunned. Captain Fuentes (whose full name I never learned), was clearly impressed. "Someone tipped us about the meeting, but our friends within Cerezo's government could not discover the location in time to act," he said. Fuentes pressed for the name of my source, but I balked. He didn't know how to react. Glaring at me, he told his lieutenant I probably worked for the CIA, and it took me a while to convince him drugs and politics were so intertwined I gathered good political intelligence with almost every drug case I worked. He thought for a few minutes, then dropped his interrogation and thanked me for the tip.

I shut the door behind them, feeling strangely secure. I had their respect.

One of our informants worked for both the Guatemalan government and the Contras, and his loose tongue gave me my first concrete intelligence about the rumors Stia had mentioned. Everyone knew him as Sofi. Socrates Amaury Sofi-Perez was a Bay of Pigs veteran, a short, thin Cuban with a big nose, glasses and a receding hairline. Despite his vague resemblance to Gandi, Sofi had his fingers in every illegal and immoral activity in the region, including the government's death squads. He carried G2 credentials, but essentially worked as a free agent, leading the squads and dabbling in narcotics on the side. Like Cerezo, he surrounded himself with bodyguards, massive men he hand-picked from G2.

Sofi never tried to hide his connections to the death squads. Accountability barely existed in Guatemala, and he had all the connections he needed with the military, the government and the ruling elite. They kept Sofi and his fellow commanders very busy. A British human rights group estimated 100 Guatemalans were killed for practicing the wrong politics each month, and another 10 people disappeared each week. I knew those anonymous white vans could pluck me off the street at any point. I couldn't touch Sofi.

One of his tentacles reached into the Contra operation, and as Sofi bragged about his connections with the rebels, he shed more light on North's shadowy operation. He told me the small Contra air force at Ilopango smuggled drugs as well as war materiel, and drug money helped feed their crusade against the Sandinistas.

"We have to support the Contras fully," Sofi often told me. "Nicaragua must be liberated from the Sandinistas at any cost, and if trafficking provides the means to that end, so be it." Like Stia, he considered me trustworthy because I was a Vietnam veteran, a fellow traveler in his eyes. Like so many Bay of Pigs refugees loitering around Central America, he lived to battle Castro and Communism. By sharing the details of the operation, he wanted my implicit approval of their activities.

Sofi owned a shrimp company in Guatemala City he used to launder narcotics profits for the Contras. He played the role of trafficker and banker, picking up cocaine in Colombia, hiding it in shrimp bound for Miami, then turning over the profits to the rebels. He paid off a U.S. Customs agent who would receive the cocaine/shrimp shipment and hurry it past inspection, arguing it would spoil. I wondered what Bob Stia would say if he found out the cases of frozen shrimp Sofi brought him were part of a smuggling operation.

Sofi told me he had started double-dealing, piggybacking big cocaine loads from Guatemala to Miami for the same Guatemalan government officials I had on my list. I had never met a man so adept at exploiting chaos. Sofi's only loyalty was to himself, but he sold his services simultaneously to Cerezo, the Guatemalan military, DEA, and even the CIA. I later discovered he was double-dealing on the DEA as well, monitoring our activities and reporting to the Contras. He asked too many questions about my intelligence on Ilopango, always pestering me to run computer checks to find out if DEA had opened any files on certain pilots or Contra operatives.

One incident Sofi passed along revealed how badly President Reagan wanted to keep the resistance alive. North had negotiated with the Guatemalan government to receive a shipment of surface-to-air missiles bound for the Contras, in exchange for a generous increase in U.S. aid. On the way to the Contra base, the missiles were seized by the Hondurans. A hasty phone call from Reagan convinced President Roberto Sauzo Cordoba of Honduras to release the shipment, and North later revealed Washington's reward: additional aid. The Guatemalans obviously reaped their own quid pro quo for their part in the transfer; the following year, U.S. military aid to Guatemala increased from $500,000 to $5.4 million.

Sofi maintained his sales pitch for the rebels, but I wasn't buying. I admired the Contras for their tenacity and their ideals, but I suspected Sofi's surrepticious seafood scam was just a sample of their drug involvement. I repeated the pledge I made to Stia -- if I caught them running dope, I was going to report it. Sofi looked as if I had slapped him. His questions persisted, but he stopped volunteering information on his activities for the Contras.

After a month in Guatemala, I shifted to El Salvador to repeat the networking process. I spent a lot of time with Aparecio, drinking in everything he knew about contraband in the country.

He was a walking encyclopedia on everything from Colombian trafficking in El Salvador to the black market baby trade.

I told him what I learned about Sofi's shrimp connection, and he filled in more blanks on the Contras. The military gave them carte blanche use of Ilopango, with the blessing of Juan Rafael Bustillo, head of the Salvadoran air force. Ramiro said they were indeed running narcotics out of Ilopongo. He said a Bay of Pigs veteran named Max Gomez - - which I later discovered was the *nom de guerre* for Felix Rodriguez - - headed the operation and reported to Oliver North.

Ramiro said everybody who spent any time around Ilopango or the Salvadoran military knew about the operation, and the people running the show didn't bother to hide anything. To his air force officer friends, there was nothing covert about the operation. It meant more U.S. aid, and they supported it enthusiastically.

I added Aparecio's statements to my files on the Contra operation, which included careful notes of everything Sofi spilled. As soon as I could accumulate enough intelligence to make a strong case, I planned to drop the hornet's nest in Stia's lap.

* * *

The goal of every investigation was to get the doper out of Central America and into a U.S. court for trial. Unfortunately, we too often turned our handcuffed prizes over to a Byzantine system. Central American justice had a way of misplacing well-connected narcotics violators, or releasing them for lack of evidence. The locals saw the drug trade as a huge cash pipeline that could be tapped into almost at will, and it was standard practice in many countries to hold cartel operatives and their drug loads for ransom. As flawed as American justice might be, the drug lords feared it like nothing else, and we had several techniques for getting otherwise unextraditable offenders into our system. On November 10, Reina called me to back him up on one of these rule-bending busts.

Counterintelligence experts in Belize had maintained a wiretap on Johnny Zabaneh, a DEA fugitive and banana baron living in Orange Walk, Belize. Zabaneh was fat, Lebanese, and the biggest doper in the country. The U.S. government wanted him for conspiracy to import and distribute marijuana. Reina had been trying to bust him for a year. Without an extradition treaty, we had to wait for him to leave the country, and when the Belizian eavesdroppers heard Zabaneh planning a trip to Guatemala to purchase some sort of equipment, they called Reina with the flight number and time. We detained him at Aurora, then asked our friends with the Guatemalan police to kick Zabaneh out of the country as an undesirable. It was a poor substitute for an extradition treaty, but it worked.

The Guatemalans knew the drill, and grinned when they told Zabaneh he would be returning to Belize -- via Houston. I bought two tickets and called DEA in Houston to send someone to collect a fugitive. As the 8:30 a.m. Aviateca flight left Guatemala City, Zabaneh still looked puzzled. The Guatemalans had evicted him, but he was not sure how that translated into a trip to the United States. He figured it out when I read him his rights from the airplane seat as we approached Intercontinental Airport.

''I'm placing you under arrest for narcotics trafficking,'' I said. Zabaneh didn't make a sound as I led him off the plane. My DEA counterparts collected him at the gate, and I turned around and re-boarded the plane for the two-and-a-half hour return flight to Guatemala City. High Times, a famous dopers magazine, wrote about the incident in August, 1986, and I saved a copy for my scrapbook. We had broken rules to nail a trafficker, and he would actually go to prison for his crimes. For the first time since I came to Guatemala, I was proud.

My phone in the El Dorado rang constantly as our eyes and ears at Aurora discovered I would respond in a few minutes when they had a tip. Three days after the Zabaneh bust, one of our informants called when a group of Libyans passed through his security checkpoint. They carried Libyan and Bolivian passports, and the suspicious security team pulled them over for closer scrutiny. They insisted they were tourists, but a search turned up an ominous cache of documents: addresses, phone numbers of contacts, and crude torture diagrams, with the human body's lethal points circled in red.

I pulled on my boots and rushed to the airport. Five minutes later, I confronted the Libyans. They stuck to their tourist story in animated English. If they had landed five months later, when President Reagan ordered the retaliatory bombing of strongman

Muammar al Qaddafi's house, their presence would have sent off warning bells all over the isthmus. I called Manny Brand, a Cuban CIA agent based in Guatemala City, and told him about the group. Manny told me not to get excited - - they were probably trying to come in as illegal aliens, and I should take down all the information I could and call him the next day. They had not broken any laws, so I followed his instructions. The Libyans were released.

I could not drive the red circles out of my mind. As soon as I reached my office the next day, I turned the information over to the FBI's Central American attache, then called Manny with the Libyans' names. Manny called back shortly, panic-stricken. The CIA computer listed them as terrorists. Manny said Jack McCavett, chief of station for the CIA in Guatemala, had previously worked in Libya, and Qaddafi threatened to assassinate him. The ominous tourists were now a hit squad, and Manny was going crazy trying to find them. The CIA wanted every shred of information they could find, and sent a Lear jet from Langley to Panama to catch up with the FBI attache I had briefed.

The next day, the morning traffic into Guatemala City hummed past the bodies of the Libyans. Manny had called *La Dos*, and it took their best predators one day to hunt down the Libyans and kill them.

On November 18, I flew to New Orleans for Zabaneh's hearing. He was furious, claiming we had kidnapped him. I couldn't stifle my smile when the judge said he didn't care how Zabaneh got there, as long as he was arrested when he hit U.S. soil. He was going to jail, and we had another small victory in our futile war.

My euphoria disintegrated when my wife called from McAllen. There had been an accident, and Crystal Bianca was injured. I jumped on the next flight to McAllen, feeling helpless. When I last saw her in October, Crystal didn't want me to leave - - I could see her standing at the airport waving goodbye. I could also picture the accident Noe described, a car coasting through a stop sign and smashing broadside into my wife and daughter. The images swirled through my head until I rushed home and opened the front door. Crystal had a gash on her head, but nothing serious. She smiled at me with her bandaged head, and almost broke my heart. "Daddy, I didn't think you were going to make it."

On my way back to Guatemala, I took advantage of a stopover in Miami to stock up on gifts for my friends. I picked up a bottle of Dom Perignon at a liquor store for the Guatemalan police who evicted Zabaneh. It always paid to reward the people who came through with reliable intelligence. I always brought them bottles of American booze, expensive champagne, and cartons of Marlboros. The men loved giving their girlfriends boxes of candy I brought back for them.

I could afford it; the DEA gave me danger pay for every trip to El Salvador and covered my expenses while I was in the field -- which was almost every day. My personal expenses shriveled to almost nothing, so I could play Santa Claus to my network. Friendships were everything.

By December, I was confident enough in my feel for El Salvador to start working undercover. On December 5, I picked up Sofi in my DEA Volvo and followed Highway 1 through the mountains surrounding Guatemala City before picking up Highway 8 to the Salvadoran border. The two-lane road cut through beautiful rolling farmland, but its reputation for bloody accidents forced me to catch only glimpses of the scenery as I concentrated on the traffic. We stopped at the Las Chimanas checkpoint between the two countries, where Sofi had set up the meeting with Leonel Gaitan-Gaitan, a Salvadoran trafficker who moved large quantities of cocaine for the Medellín cartel.

I didn't trust Sofi, and he became a little annoyed when I repeatedly ran through how I wanted everything done. He never liked being told what to do. I was in no mood to deal with his ego. Working undercover in El Salvador with Sofi as my only backup was plain stupid. If our Salvadoran friend became spooked, I half expected Sofi to scurry under the nearest car, or worse, blow our cover and get us both killed. When I asked Reina to come along, he begged off; he was tied up with his aerial missions in Belize.

We met Gaitan-Gaitan in the parking lot of a restaurant just inside the Guatemalan line. Sofi and I began sweating, only partly out of nervousness; El Salvador was always an oven compared to Guatemala City's cool mountain air. Sofi introduced me as Carlos de Cordova, a Mexican buyer looking for a new supplier. I borrowed the alias from my friend Tony Cordova, a Texas Department of Public Safety trooper. Gaitan-Gaitan was almost as relaxed as he was sloppy. His rumpled slacks and dress shirt hung limply on a short, beefy frame, and he had unbuttoned the top of his shirt to reveal gold ropes Reina would have been proud to own.

My nervousness melted away when Gaitan-Gaitan took the initiative, eagerly chattering about his unique access to the Colombians. He looked and sounded like a used car salesman trying to hit his monthly quota. I told him how many kilos I needed, and promised to call him later to set up the deal.

I smiled as we shook hands. I saw no trace of suspicion in his face, no threatening eyes watching from the perimeter, no signals to hidden associates. Undercover work, the deceptive art of gathering evidence and building a case, simply didn't exist here. The local authorities had no use for it; they grabbed their man, extracted their information, and often decided the punishment on the spot. The idea that I was anyone other than who I claimed had never occurred to Gaitan-Gaitan.

On January 14, Vice President George Bush visited Guatemala City to put the U.S. stamp of approval on Cerezo's inauguration. I met Bush at the obligatory coctail party at the ambassador's residence. Embassy personnel and Guatemalan dignitaries elbowed through the crowd, jockeying for floor space near the Vice President. I was standing alone, watching the steel-faced secret service agents watching everyone else, when Bush approached. He read the tag on my lapel identifying me as a member of the U.S. embassy, and asked what I did. As he shook my hand, someone snapped a photo. I told him I was a DEA agent assigned to Guatemala. He said, ''Well, what do you do?'' I knew it wasn't wise to bring up the Contras - - this man was part of the Administration, and Reagan had even declared himself a Contra.

I just blurted it out. ''There's some funny things going on with the Contras in El Salvador.''

Bush didn't reply. He simply smiled and walked away, seeking another hand to shake. After that exchange, I knew that he knew.

In Washington, the Contra public relations machine continued its mission to scrub the Contras' image in the eyes of Congress and the American public. Years later, Congressional pressure forced the declassification of documents outlining how taxpayer money paid for the Administration's PR campaign on

Capitol Hill. In 1983, National Security Advisor William Clark created the Office of Public Diplomacy for Latin America and the Caribbean (S/LPD). "The President has underscored his concern that we must increase our efforts in the public diplomacy field to deepen the understanding of and support for our policies in Central America," Clark wrote in a July 1, 1983 memo.

By 1985, the public relations firm hired by S/LPD to handle the Contra's image referred to their efforts as a "White Propaganda" operation. In an "eyes only" memo from one spin master to another, Johnathan Miller of International Business Communications alerted Pat Buchanan to several negative news pieces and outlined their media counterstrikes. "I will not attempt in the future to keep you posted on all activities since we have too many balls in the air at any one time and since the work of our operation is ensured by our office's keeping a low profile," Miller wrote.

In the winter of 1985, the blitz even reached McAllen, where retired Gen. John Singlaub appeared at the McAllen Public Library with Mario Calero, brother of United Nicaraguan Opposition leader Adolfo Calero. Singlaub, head of the United States Council for World Freedom, claimed he was raising money from ordinary folks to support the Contras. Later, the truth would come out. I happily noted Singlaub didn't get a dime from the ordinary folks in McAllen -- fundraising was against library rules.

Four days after Singlaub's McAllen visit, the first hint of the Contras' drug connection appeared as a blip in the national news. On December 21, an Associated Press article appeared, quoting unnamed U.S. investigators and American volunteers working with the rebels: "Nicaraguan rebels operating in northern Costa Rica have engaged in cocaine trafficking, in part to help finance their war against Nicaragua's leftist government."

Thirteen months later, another story on the Contra drug connection would appear on the front page of *The New York Times*. Quoting anonymous Administration officials, the story outlined a DEA investigation at Ilopango. It would be the closest my reports ever came to exploding in the White House.

With Bush's visit still echoing in my head, I wrote a report on the Contras based on more than three month's worth of intelligence from Sofi and Aparecio. I gathered up my notes and

wrote the main report, then individual reports under each informant's number to show what information came from whom. I
signed them and dropped them on Stia's desk. He read them
slowly, carefully, shaking his head. His discomfort was obvious,
and for a moment I was afraid he would refuse to sign.

"This is too big, and it's going to come back and bite us in
the ass if we don't report it," I argued. It didn't take long to
convince him; if he didn't sign the reports, I was ready to send a
cable out to the El Paso Intelligence Center, which coordinated
and dissected intelligence from all over the world on narcotics
trafficking. Stia knew he was covering his ass, and scribbled his
name on the reports.

From Stia's desk, they were forwarded to the DEA Latin
American Desk in Washington. If this had been any other operation, I knew our foreign office would cut loose a few intelligence
agents on temporary duty to help out. I waited for a reaction from
Washington. Nothing.

Meanwhile, our appointment with Gaitan-Gaitan arrived,
and I called the Salvadoran national police to help Aparecio and
me make the bust. Sofi's role was finished, and I always tried to
keep my informants from meeting. The police, however, wanted
to beat us to the scene, and they exploded into the filthy San
Salvador house with a gang of men. When Aparecio and I arrived,
the Salvadorans were searching the house as they led their
prisoners outside. When Gaitan-Gaitan emerged, he squinted at
me through a swelling eye and silently shook his head.

His mouth didn't look as though it would function anyway.
The police were energetically knocking them around, screaming
for the location of the hidden cash. With their thumbs tied
together behind their backs, the men groaned helplessly as the
police delivered swift kicks to their midsection and swatted them
across the face with thick San Salvador phone books. Somehow,
they held their tongues.

The police looked about half finished stripping the house of
all valuables. I started to object when the phone rang. I picked up
the receiver and the voice on the other end asked for Leonel. He
said he was calling from Bogota. I switched to my Salvadoran
accent and told him I was Carlos, Leonel's right-hand man.
"He's at the store," I said. "He should be back in a minute."

The line was silent for a moment. Finally, the voice from Bogota decided to believe me. "Tell him our friend is going to arrive tonight with 25 *aparatos*." The word meant apparatus, a good non-specific term for a kilo. He gave me the flight number of a plane arriving in San Salvador that night and said we should make sure our friend arrived without any problems. I assured him I would personally wait for the flight. He described the passenger briefly and hung up.

The mad scramble continued throughout the house, and I could barely control my anger. The Salvadorans picked over the place with greedy fingers, hunting for the still undiscovered cash. The 30 kilos they seized from Gaitan-Gaitan lay forgotten on a table as they hurried to their vehicles with televisions, stereo equipment, and whatever else struck their fancy. On a lucky hunch, I picked up a large stereo speaker as Aparecio reached for its twin. We grunted with the effort -- they were almost too heavy to lift. Aparecio grinned as we tore open the back panels and found them packed with brown paper bags full of cash.

The Salvadorans watched intently as we wrapped the money with tape, marking it to show signs of tampering. I felt better when we arrived at the police station, where I searched out my regular contacts and enlisted about 15 police officers to help count the cash. It came to $800,000 in worn U.S. dollars, which we turned over to their commanders.

From the police station, I drove to El Salvador International Airport to meet our visitor, whom the man on the phone had identified as Nivias. Aparecio had stayed at police headquarters to make sure the money didn't disappear, so I needed some backup for the meeting. I called Victor Rivera, an advisor to the president of El Salvador.

The CIA had hired Rivera as a contract agent and advisor to Duarte, and he and I quickly become good friends. His street skills could help any operation. He was one of a half-dozen Venezuelans training the Salvadoran security police in counterinsurgency techniques. Changing political tides had forced them out of Venezuela, and the Salvadorans generously donated an office in national police headquarters in exchange for their expertise. Sharing grisly techniques had become a thriving cottage industry in El Salvador, and Rivera and his cohorts found cozy positions with both the Salvadoran government and the CIA, who paid Victor a reported $5,000 a month for his work.

Victor met me in front of the airport, and we quickly fanned out among our contacts in customs and immigration so Nivias could bring his apparatus into the country unchallenged. I spotted him waiting at the baggage carousel and introduced myself. He shot me a quizzical look and asked, "Where's Gaitan?" I had rehearsed my excuse: Gaitan was at the house taking care of the money. He relaxed. I asked if he had the stuff, and he picked up the suitcase and handed it to me.

"Are we going to do it like the last time?" he asked. I had no clue what he was talking about, so I blurted, "Yeah, we're just going to take it out the front door." I grunted as I picked up the big Samsonite, and Victor shot me a wry smile. My arm felt like it was being yanked from its socket. I asked Nivias for his passport and handed it to one of my contacts at immigration, who stamped and returned it with a blank stare.

We walked to Victor's Toyota Celica, and Victor plunked the suitcase in the trunk and popped the clasps. The kilos were packed tightly inside, wrapped in brown tape. I turned to Nivias and told him he was under arrest. Victor cuffed him, and a plainclothes Salvadoran national police sergeant took the wheel of the Toyota. Victor and I got in the back seat, cramming Nivias between us. We had a 45-minute drive from the airport to the capital, plenty of time to question our guest. Victor and I played bad cop/bad cop, asking him how many shipments he had delivered to El Salvador, who he paid off at customs, and other details about his smuggling. Nivias refused to answer. "I don't know what you're talking about," he insisted.

After a few failed attempts, Victor snapped. He swiveled in the cramped back seat and lashed at Nivias with a hard-muscled arm. The punch mashed Nivias' chin with a crack and continued through, smacking me in the face. Victor apologized briefly and continued working on our stubborn captive. After another 15 minutes, he lost his patience and told the sergeant to pull onto a side road. Victor grabbed Nivias by the hair, threw him to the ground, and growled, "I'm tired of this bullshit. If you don't cooperate I'll kill you here like a dog." He pulled his Glock 9mm, snapped a round into the chamber, and aimed the barrel at Nivias' head.

Nivias pulled himself to his knees, begging. "Please don't kill me, I have a family." Victor lowered the Glock to Nivias' face and fired. I looked away, convinced he had killed the man. He was that crazy. I began sweating, wondering if Victor would turn the gun on me to eliminate witnesses.

I heard Nivias whimper, then Victor's deep laugh. He had pulled the Glock to the right and fired a round next to Nivias' ear, missing him completely. Victor was laughing, and Nivias remained sprawled on the dirt, breathing in fits with his eyes tightly shut. Between gasps, Nivias said he was ready to talk. We took him to the police department in San Salvador, where he dictated a signed, sworn statement claiming to be a member of the Colombian terrorist group M19. He said the smuggling had gone on for years. The cartels hired him and other gofers to carry cocaine past paid-off officials. The risk, he added, was minimal.

Everybody was excited about the bust. The Salvadorans could point to the bust with one hand and extend the other to Uncle Sam for more anti-narcotics money. In light of Nivias' confession, the Salvadorans tried to paint it as a terrorist organization smuggling narcotics to support the rebels. Naturally, the dollars followed. Later, the State Department released money for an anti-narcotics squad in El Salvador. My workload again doubled, and for a few weeks, the Contras slipped into the back of my mind.

By mid-February, TDY had become permanent duty. I knew the area, had a big bust under my belt, and they needed the help. Stia asked if I wanted the job, and I jumped at it. I returned to Peru to pick up my household goods, and moved into the embassy transit apartments in Guatemala City's zone 10.

About this time, I recruited a Salvadoran who put the hard evidence I needed on the Contras at my fingertips. Hugo Martinez worked at Ilopango, writing flight plans for the private planes streaming in and out of the airport's civilian side. That included my flights in and out of the airport, and we talked frequently as my presence in El Salvador increased. Hugo impressed me with his pro-American and anti-drugs sentiments, and his strategic position at Ilopango made him a perfect candidate for intelligence-gathering. Recruiting him was easy; he had worked for us indirectly for months. Hugo occassionally fed Aparecio information as a sub-source, and he cemented his reputation with a tip that led to a 500-kilo cocaine bust.

During one of my visits to Ilopango's civilian side (I could never get access to the military side where North's operation was based), Hugo confided he had become unhappy with the arrangement. He had originally balked at becoming a documented informant because he feared getting caught. Emboldened by success, he was no longer happy with taking whatever cut Aparecio chose to pass along. His disgust with the drug trade, plus his addiction to the intrigue of spying, had him hooked. I said, "You're giving us this information, you might as well get paid for it." He readily agreed, and I gave him his informant number. From that point on, I paid him about $200 every time he gave me intelligence.

Hugo wanted to prove his value, and uleashed a flood of documentation on narcotics smuggling out of the air base. Suddenly, my reports contained not only the names of traffickers, but their destinations, flight paths, tail numbers, and the date and time of each flight. Hundreds of flights each week delivered cocaine to the buyers and returned with money headed for the great isthmus laundering machine in Panama. I could have started a weekly newsletter: *Ilopango Doper*. Still, our seizures didn't increase much; the traffickers usually airdropped the cocaine before landing in Florida or the Bahamas, swooping low as some poor grunt in the back kicked the bundles out of the cargo hold into the waves below. Waiting speedboats would fish the cocaine out of the water and race to shore undetected.

Many of the loads found their way to the streets through the skills of George Morales, a three-time world champion speedboat racer who smuggled millions of dollars worth of marijuana and cocaine from the Bahamas to Florida before he was caught and convicted in Florida. In his testimony before the U.S. Senate Subcommittee on Terrorism, Narcotics and International Operations, chaired by Sen. John Kerry of Massachusetts, Morales said he paid off Bahamian officials so his powerboats and airplanes could operate unmolested.

When I asked Hugo about the Contras, his eyes lit up, and by the time he finished talking I knew we were in over our heads.

He explained the operation in detail. The Contra planes flew out of hangars four and five, and Hugo could identify their planes by the black cross painted on their tail. The CIA owned one hangar, and the National Security Council ran the other. I knew the CIA, like DEA, had a long history of hiring men with less than stellar reputations. In this case, they were narcotics traffickers. Hugo said the pilots often brought the drugs to Ilopango from either numerous private airstrips in Costa Rica, or the U.S. military base in Panama. They flew weapons, cash, and cocaine from these safe havens, taking the powder to the United States.

Ilopango reminded me of O'Hare Airport in Chicago, bustling at all hours of the day and night. Murga was one of the busiest men on the base, tending to a continuous line of pilots waiting for their flight plans. Like Aparecio, Hugo had no trouble picking up incriminating information; many times pilots told him outright they were taking cocaine to the United States. The CIA had hired them, they boasted, and nobody could touch them. Hugo would quietly jot down their names after they left. Most of the time, Hugo simply poked his balding head into the planes as he made his rounds. When he spotted the tightly wrapped kilos, the pilot's name joined the others on his list.

As Hugo described it, every pilot had his own preferred technique for getting his illegal payload to U.S. soil. Some liked the John Wayne approach, flashing their CIA credentials at Florida airfields and unloading the drugs in plain view. Those who wanted to maintain a lower profile shipped the kilos out in innocuous cargoes like towels, seafood, frozen vegetables or auto parts. Many landed at military bases around the United States, knowing no one would inspect a Contra plane. The air drops were probably the least risky and the most popular, since many of the pilots had plenty of experience dropping bundles in the Bahamas or off the Florida coast.

They returned with cash to Ilopango. Hugo said some of the pilots flew the money to Panama for deposit in the Bank of Credit and Commerce International, later indicted for money laundering and bribery. From Panama, the money was wired to a Costa Rican bank account held by the Contras. They used the money for supplies and arms, completing the cycle.

When I ran Hugo's list of names through the computer, they all came back as narcotics traffickers in DEA files. Little wonder the Contras used them, I thought. Nobody knew the terrain like drug pilots, and their dive-and-dump flying skills perfectly matched the job description for covert operations.

When I realized how deeply Hugo had probed into the Contra's small air force, I increased my presence in El Salvador, checking in with Hugo and Aparecio constantly. The Contra supply operation had clearly become a link in the cartels' smuggling operations, with Ilopango as the main hub between Colombia and the United States.

We began tracking the drug flights out of hangars four and five. I used pages ripped from Hugo's log book to jot down the date, time, flight number, tail number, destination, and the names and passport numbers of each pilot and co-pilot. Finally, I had concrete evidence.

I wrote a string of reports on the Contras through the end of March with the stream of intelligence Hugo and Aparecio generated. As Aparecio zoomed in on our target, his air force contacts in Ilopango shared their knowledge on the activities in hangars four and five. He had access to the military section of the airport, and he would visit with his military buddies every time he needed booze for his restaurant. The military had a monopoly on El Salvador's liquor sales, so they were the only source for all of the bars and restaurants in the country. Aparecio would go in every week to buy his whiskey and tequila and shoot the bull with the air force brass. They talked openly about the Contra operation. I updated my reports after every trip to El Salvador.

By this point, I was in El Salvador at least every other week, meeting with Aparecio and Hugo in my room at the Sheraton. Stia kept shaking his head and signing the reports. He figured the deed was done, and they couldn't come down on him too hard. He was just doing his job.

On March 16, 1986, President Reagan took another shot at the Sandinistas in a speech televised nationally. As Congress prepared for another vote on Contra aid, Reagan accused the Sandinistas of drug running. "I know that every American parent concerned about the drug problem will be outraged to learn that top Nicaraguan government officials are deeply involved in drug trafficking," Reagan said, then showed hidden camera footage of several men loading cocaine onto Barry Seal's plane near Managua in April, 1984. Seal, a burly Louisianan who headed the Medellín cartel's shipping operations, had become a DEA informant and was helping the agency infiltrate the cartel. One of the men loading the bundles onto Seal's C-123 cargo plane was Federico Vaughan, who the President said was a top aide to Nicaraguan interior minister Tomas Borge. Seal's cover was blown the previous summer when his mission into Nicaragua was leaked to the press.

Before his name hit the papers, Seal planned to carry $1.5 million in drug money to Managua, where the cartel kingpins waited. Oliver North wanted it. On July 28, 1988, DEA officials told the House Subcommittee on Crime North had suggested the Sandinista drug money be diverted to the Contras. North did not get the money. Seal was murdered in Louisiana by two gunmen in February, 1986.

Despite his willingness to solicit for drug money, North, of course, dismissed any possibility of a connection between his Contras and the drug trade. In his autobiography, North tried to put the allegations to rest. After special investigator Lawrence Walsh spent millions of dollars in his probe, "If there was even a grain of truth to these stories, it surely would have come out."

Hints of the truth surfaced in 1987 and 1988 as Kerry's subcommittee interviewed 27 witnesses and subpoenaed documents -- including North's personal notebooks. The notebooks arrived heavily censored, but scores of references to narcotics or terrorism remained. One of the entries, for July 12, 1985, read "$14 million to finance came from drugs."

Morales, given a day pass from federal prison to testify before Kerry's subcommittee, revealed his involvement with the Contras. Marta Healey, ex-wife of Contra southern front military commander Adolfo Popo Chamorro, approached Morales in 1984 after his second arrest for smuggling and arranged a meeting with Chamorro and two other Contra leaders, Southern group air force chief Marcos Aguado and political head Octaviano Cesar. Aguado and Cesar told Morales they were CIA agents and asked for financial and military assistance.

As far as the Contras were concerned, whatever Morales lacked in scruples, he made up for in money and planes. In return, they promised to use their "personal knowledge" of Washington to help him with his indictment. The Contras needed to fly fabric for uniforms and 40,000 lbs of weapons out of Miami; Morales needed well-connected friends, and quickly. It was a perfect match.

That summer, Gary Betzner, Morales' best pilot, took off from Executive International Airport in Fort Lauderdale with a load of weapons Morales bought at a gunshop in southwest Miami. He landed in Costa Rica, where the weapons were unloaded and, as Morales testified, Betzner picked up a different cargo:

Senator Kerry: What were you expecting to have come back?

Mr. Morales: About 400 or so kilograms of cocaine.

Senator Kerry: Did you know where he was going to pick up   those kilograms of cocaine?

Mr. Morales: It had been arranged. He had the map and the   *coordinates, and the airstrip appears on the Costa Rican* air   *map. It is an american rancher's.*

About two weeks later, Morales cleaned out the inventory at another Miami gunshop, and Betzner pushed his Panther off the runway at Opa-locka Airport with another load for the rebels. Again, he returned with cocaine.

As far as Morales could tell, the Contras fulfilled their end of the bargain. He was told the DEA and FBI offices in Miami knew of his involvement with the Contras, yet the flights continued. After one of Morales' deliveries to the Contras in 1985, an associate told Morales he overheard a conversation between a U.S. agent and an informant, outlining the details of an earlier shipment. "This is one of the reasons which has led me to believe that I was very well protected," Morales testified. "Otherwise, one of these agencies would have intervened."

Morales rewarded the Contras handsomely, starting with $400,000 in cash and checks in October, 1984. By the end of 1985, the speedboat smuggler's cash contributions to the Contras totalled, by his estimate, $4 million or $5 million. Kerry asked him twice, just to make sure:

Senator Kerry: My question to you is, Was the majority of that money mostly drug money that you delivered to the Contras?

Mr. Morales: I would say that about 100 percent.

Senator Kerry: Except for the $100,000 or so that came from your company?

Mr. Morales: Exactly.

Senator Kerry: The rest was illegal profits?

Mr. Morales: Yes, sir.

Kerry's committee also talked to the Contras, with Kerry flying to Costa Rica for depositions of Aguado, Cesar, and Karol Prado, who was Southern front commander Eden Pastora's second in command. The Contras corroborated Morales' story, and Cesar said when he told CIA officials at Ilopango about their relationship with Morales, they condoned it ''as long as you don't deal in the powder.'' The Contras said they loathed taking money from a drug trafficker and using his airplanes to transport supplies, but with the CIA money gone, their troops in southern Nicaragua slowly ran out of boots, clothes, medicine, and ammunition. ''I'm not proud of having had this type of relationship,'' Cesar told Kerry during the deposition on Halloween, 1987.

Back in Guatemala, I was preparing for a long tenure. I returned to McAllen for Easter and helped my family pack for the move to Guatemala. Thankfully, the kids were too young to know what was happening. Crystal was two, and C4 was eight months and crawling enthusiastically. Although it meant leaving her family, Noe actually looked forward to the move. I was relieved; she was learning about the life of a diplomat's wife.

In mid-April, a cable arrived from Bobby Nieves, the agent in charge of our Costa Rican office. Nieves advised me to check hangars four and five at Ilopango; a very reliable informant gave them intelligence about large quanities of cocaine being smuggled from Costa Rica to El Salvador. The cable named two Costa Rican pilots who had been flying into Ilopango. It ended with a line that jumped off the page: *We believe the Contras are involved in narcotics trafficking.*

When I get back to San Salvador and tell Hugo and Aparecio, this will make their day, I thought. Word was getting around.

I immediately called Nieves and briefed him on everything I knew about Ilopango and the connection between the hangars and North's Contra operation. ''That's what I thought,'' Nieves said. The same shit is going on in Costa Rica at a large private ranch, he said, with dope shuttling from the airstrips to Ilopango. We agreed to keep in touch, and share any new information we received.

I bolted from the office and jumped into the Volvo. I set a new personal speed record on Highway 8 to San Salvador, then burst into Aparecio's cafe with a copy of the cable in my fist. I asked him to drop by Ilopango and ask Hugo to check the pilots' names. He came back after sifting through the log books and handed me a list detailing each pilot's flights into Ilopango, along with their tail numbers. The pilots were flying out of hangars four and five.

The next day, I went to the U.S. Embassy in El Salvador and met with Robert Chavez, the counselor general for the U.S. State Deparment -- and the man who issued all visas from the embassy. Chavez told me the CIA had just requested a visa for Carlos Alberto Amador, a Nicaraguan pilot documented in the computer as a narcotics trafficker. Chavez said he thought Amador flew for the Contras. I checked with Hugo, who confirmed it. That added more fuel to the fire. Why would the CIA give a known trafficker a visa? Chavez was concerned. He knew approving the visa could come back to haunt him, and he asked me to do something about it.

I closed myself in my office and began forming a mental list of the people I needed to visit over the next few days. My reports on the Contras seemed to be falling into some sort of faceless, bureaucratic black hole. I wanted someone to look me in the eye and respond to the evidence.

It was time to get noisy.

Seven
Conspiracy of Denial
Guatemala City - April 1986

Moving provided a much-needed break, and rejoining my family washed away much of the stress that chewed at me since Noe and Crystal's car accident. We made a family trip of it, driving our Jeep Wagoneer from McAllen to Guatemala City and stopping wherever the urge struck during the three-day trek. We spent a night in Veracruz, along the Mexican Gulf coast. When we took our luggage to the car the next morning, Crystal stopped my heart, dashing ahead of us toward the street. Luggage clattered against the sidewalk as I chased after her. To this day I can see the brown taxi bearing down on her, the driver's jaw clenched as the old Chevy's tires locked. The taxi squealed to a halt five feet from Crystal, who stared in frozen dismay at the front bumper. She turned and gave me a helpless look, and I lifted her off the street as the taxi driver screamed at me to take better care of my kid.

He was right. That was the whole idea of moving to Guatemala -- to take better care of my family, to soothe the pangs of guilt, to try to bridge the growing space between Noe and myself. Now, the doubts creeped back. Just one day out of McAllen, and Crystal had almost been run down. I thought about Duarte's daughter, kidnapped by the rebels in El Salvador. The president had traded a captured guerrilla leader for his child. I wondered if I could protect my kids from the chaos in Guatemala; and if someone snatched them, what did I have to offer the captors?

After driving through some of the world's worst human deprivation, our new home seemed like a palace. The two-story brick house was in zone 13, an upper-crust section of Guatemala

City. Our neighbors were the big landowners, business tycoons, government officials, and others at the top of the Guatemalan food chain. The mayor's residence was a few doors down, the most prestigious link in an unbroken row of connected dwellings.

Noe and the kids fell in love with the house the moment I unlocked the massive wooden double doors. The floors were paved with Italian tile, and a big fireplace separated the sunken living room from the dining room. Ceiling-to-floor glass doors overlooked a kidney-shaped pool fringed by tropical plants. A wooden spiral staircase dominated the vaulted entryway, and diffused sunshine streamed in through a glass dome in the roof. We hung stuffed tropical birds, including a huge peacock, in this airy space - - and constantly worried about the kids crawling over the low partition above and falling. After more than six months in a cramped hotel room, I felt like a kid on Christmas morning when we unpacked our belongings in this sparkling house. Unfortunately, the place lacked a heater, and I cursed the cold every morning as I left the warm bed and tiptoed over the frigid tiles to the bathroom.

I was receiving a lot of hazard pay and travel money for my field work, so we had enough to hire domestic help. We started with two housekeepers. Maria, a short, wiry woman in her 50s, arrived first and annexed the kitchen. She had neither a husband nor children, which probably made her somewhat of an oddity in the tiny coastal village where she grew up. Maria had worked in Guatemala City for several years, finding a special niche working for embassy employees. We gave her a room on the first floor, which she later shared with the second housekeeper, Ana. Maria quickly became like a live-in grandmother. I remember chasing C4, ready to give him a whipping for some indiscretion, when she pulled him to her chest and glared at me. ''You are not going to spank him,'' she boomed, and marched to her room with him nestled in her bosom.

Ana was in her early 20s, and watched over the kids with a tomboy's energy. Somehow she kept up with C4, who had perfected his crawling skills and scrambled around the house on a perpetual Easter egg hunt. Ana had a mother's instincts for looming danger, and as a Guatemalan mother, her radar was amplified several times. Ana saved little Cele's life twice: once catching him as he chugged over the lip of the pool, and later, snatching him off the ground as an errant Fourth of July rocket zoomed between her legs.

Ana was from a poor Indian village in the mountains, and to her, death was a cold hand seeking an opportune moment to close around the innocent and the unprepared. The guerrillas killed her brother, and her parents stubbornly remained in the free-fire zone while she and her three children sought a better life in the city. Ana usually brought them with her to work. I think she actually enjoyed the knee-high pandemonium.

We also hired a handyman/gardener, Don Chavelo, to do odd jobs and care for the landscaping. He lived in the filthy ring of wood and tin squatters' camps around the city. The lost souls in these squalid settlements often lived literally on top of the city's garbage. People were continually picking through the rancid piles like ants. Don Chavelo knew the owner of our house, and when he appeared at our door looking for work, I hired him on the spot. He was a quiet, thick-muscled six-footer -- incredibly tall for a Guatemalan -- with an old man's grizzled face and snowy hair. I never knew whether to judge his age by the etched lines around his eyes or his powerful grip. He was a tireless worker. He reached the house by catching one of the mini-buses, called *micros*, before sunrise each morning, then walking the remaining half mile to our neighborhood. By the time I finished my shower each day, Don Chavelo had washed the Jeep inside and out.

The neighborhood was both a haven and a target. Police patrolled the area constantly, yet people lived amid bodyguards and guns. We benefitted from our proximity to the mayor, but the house was still armed with an expensive security system. Both Ana and Don Chavelo carried devices to trigger the screeching alarms. We all knew what happened in these neighborhoods to the innocent and the unprepared: thugs from both sides of the conflict often kidnapped members of wealthy families for ransom. The cycle fed upon itself, with the rich worried about their safety, the right wing worried about threats to its ideology, and the poor worried about surviving another day. Nobody slept soundly in Guatemala.

The chasm between opulence and indigence glared at me from every corner of the city. On my way to work each morning, a little barefoot Indian girl sat on the corner selling newspapers. She was a happy kid, maybe four years old, hawking papers as her mother squatted nearby in numb silence. I bought a paper every day, and she learned to watch for me at the busy stoplight. She always rewarded me with a toothy smile, her perfect teeth clashing with the tattered skirt and blouse she wore every day.

* * *

In early June, I drove to San Salvador, where Hugo waited with with more intelligence from Ilopango. He had been watching hangars 4 and 5 closely, and gave me a detailed list of Contra planes and pilots hauling narcotics. He named Carlos Amador -- the man for whom the CIA was seeking a U.S. visa -- as well as three other pilots who carried cocaine payloads. Another name caught my interest: Carlos Armando Llamos, El Salvador's honorary ambassador to Panama. Hugo had watched Llamos for a long time, and in November, 1985, Hugo said the Ambassador proudly showed him cardboard boxes containing $4.5 million in cash he was taking to banks in Panama, for laundering. Reading from his log book, Hugo ticked off corresponding tail numbers: TIANO, YS265 and N-308P.

Hugo also dug up more information on Transportes Aereos El Salvador, an Ilopango-based air transport company owned by two brothers named Gutierrez. Aparecio, always with the best connections, told me weeks earlier the brothers were trafficking. The DEA computer once again proved him right. Hugo said they had begun chartering planes to the Contra pilots, who used them to run dope and money. I took down another tail number, N-82161.

As the names, dates and eyewitness reports accumulated, I collected my notes for another Contra report. When I had enough new intelligence, I planned to go office-hopping. I wanted to know if any of the bureaucrats would break ranks to help me take this information beyond the conspiracy of denial which seemed to include every U.S. official in El Salvador.

* * *

Early one Wednesday morning, the phone rattled me awake. Hugo's excited voice sent my feet to the cold floor immediately. Chico Guirola was making a run to the Bahamas. Hugo had watched Francisco Rodrigo Guirola-Beeche for weeks, hoping to help me bust one of the Contras' busiest pilots. Guirola's planes frequently carried dope and cash, so we made him a priority target. Like most Contra pilots, Guirola carried air force credentials signed by General Bustillo, making him an instant VIP in the Salvadoran air force. He was also one of the Gutierrez brothers' better customers, frequently renting planes from them.

Hugo went to great lengths to make friends with Guirola. He talked shop with "Chico" enough to gather plenty of incriminating information on his new buddy. When I ran Guirola's name in the computer, it popped up in 11 DEA files, detailing his South America-to-United States cocaine, arms, and money laundering activities. Business was obviously booming: In 1985, law enforcement officers in South Texas arrested Guirola with $5.5 million in cash.

"Guirola left for the Bahamas a few minutes ago with a load of cash," Hugo said with an excited edge in his voice. I looked at my watch; it was just after 7:45 a.m. Hugo hung up, and I quickly dialed the DEA office in the Bahamas. Just as I feared, the receiver buzzed in my ear. The Bahamian office did not open until 9 a.m. Nobody would be at the landing stip to meet Guirola. Not from our agency, anyway. As usual, the dopers got up a little earlier than we did.

We tried again a few days later. Aparecio and I set up surveillance on Guirola at Ilopango, watching him from the civilian section of the airport. He landed on the nearby runway, loaded several boxes into a red compact car, and raced off. Aparecio and I waited for the signal from Hugo. If Guirola was carrying narcotics or cash, Hugo was supposed to appear at the window and give us the thumbs-up sign. As Guirola zoomed away, we stared at the window. No signal. When I asked Hugo what happened, he threw up his hands. "Now Chico has credentials from President Christiani, identifying him as a presidential advisor." Aparecio and I exchanged a grim look. Our best target joined the ranks of the untouchables.

I began to wonder if we would ever bust a pilot. The national police didn't want anything to do with a sting at Ilopango because the pilots carried Bustillo's air force credentials. If I could somehow convince someone to arrest a pilot, Bustillo would undoubtedly drop the charges for lack of evidence, then scream to Corr about my "illegal investigation."

I wasn't sure how Corr would react if I slapped an arrest report on his desk. Every time I visited his office in El Salvador, the Ambassador showed a genuine interest in my operations, and offered his encouragement. Corr served as U.S. ambassador to Bolivia about the same time I was in Peru. He saw firsthand the kind of power drug organizations wielded across the Western Hemisphere. Corr obviously knew about North's resupply operation, and supported it as a matter of policy, but I had the feeling he did not agree with his methods.

* * *

On June 24, I wrote another Contra report, based largely on Hugo's detailed observations of the previous two weeks. The report went through the usual channels, to be filed in the usual places with the usual results. Eventually, it landed in Washington with nary a ripple.

I was reaching my frustration threshold. The rules of the game here prevented me, or any DEA agent, from searching pilots and planes. We could not arrest, interrogate, or initiate an investigation without a member of the local police present. Later, when we organized an anti-narcotics group in El Salvador, even our recruits from the National Guard could not help me with the Contras; they needed official approval to snoop around Ilopango's military side. Bustillo would never allow it.

Ambushing pilots when they landed proved fruitless as well. Knowing their flight plans didn't help. Like El Coyote, they never emerged at the right place at the right time, and most airdropped their cargo, then landed with nothing more incriminating than a sly grin.

* * *

I collected my notes and returned to El Salvador to begin building a Salvadoran anti-narco unit -- and visit a few officials with my Contra evidence. Every time I worked in El Salvador, I was supposed to check in with the embassy to inform them of my plans. This time, I had a motherlode of information on the Contras. I was eager to see how they would react. I checked into the Sheraton, planning to stay a week.

Aparecio and I began our recruiting immediately, selecting about 15 energetic young conservatives from the national guard and other security forces. The process moved along much smoother than in Guatemala: the Salvadorans kept a tighter rein on their security forces, and tolerated no infighting. We called the task force FUCA, the Spanish acronym for United Anti-narcotics Force. I placed Aparecio in charge as the group's chief adviser. I resisted the urge to ask Aparecio if he saw the irony in placing a drug fugitive in charge of an anti-narcotics squad.

Money from the State Department, the Department of Defense and the CIA paid for training the group. FUCA's training consisted of lectures on the cartels, on narcotics trafficking techniques and investigations, and U.S.-style weapons training. Aparecio took center stage, transfixing the recruits with real-life tales from both sides of the drug war.

On May 27, Lt. Col. Alberto Adame, a U.S. military advisor to El Salvador and a fellow Texan, recommended one of his friends as a firearms instructor. When he introduced the short, middle-aged man, the name clicked in my head immediately. Dr. Hector Antonio Regalado, a San Salvador dentist, was a household name in the country's power corridors. I was shaking hands with "Dr. Death," as he was known in U.S. political circles, the man reputed to be the Salvadoran death squads' most feared interrogator. In El Salvador, he was known simply as "El Doctor." Regalado's prestige among the right wing stemmed from his ability to extract teeth -- and information -- without anesthesia.

I wanted no part of *El Doctor*. I asked Adame if the embassy had approved Regalado as an adviser. He said Col. James Steele, the U.S. Military Group commander in El Salvador, gave Regalado his blessing. The military obviously wanted this man aboard, human rights abuses and all. Regalado was hired, and we began spending a lot of time together. I saw him almost every time I visited the National Police headquarters, where the Salvadorans donated a group of dingy second-floor offices as classrooms for FUCA.

On the surface, Regalado was a friendly, genteel man. Underneath his gentle demeanor, though, he was the type who would shoot a man, then spit on him to make sure the point got across. He always carried a hair-trigger .45 pistol holstered at his side. *El Doctor* harbored a boiling hatred for anything associated with Communism or revolutionaries, and showed particular disdain for the clergy, who sympathized with the peasants.

Regalado was good. He could draw either of his two holstered pistols in an instant. One moment, you would be looking into his eyes. Suddenly, they were replaced by the cold, black eye of his .45. When I asked him how he did it, he looked around theatrically, as if about to reveal a coveted secret. "I oil the holsters, then rub wax inside so the gun slips out like a feather."

He passed his tricks down to his teenage daughter, who sometimes accompanied him. She was almost as fast and accurate with a gun as her father. I tried to picture her when she was Crystal's age. She obviously had wasted little of her childhood playing dress-up and collecting dolls. Feminine innocence was a luxury she could not afford: her family was in constant danger from the FMLN, who wanted to perform their own crude surgery on her father, and end his bloodline if possible.

Regalado loved guns, which made him the perfect firearms instructor. He taught the recruits how to squeeze a trigger without jerking the weapon, and supplemented shooting practice with briefings on how to react in a life-or-death situation. "Can you kill someone? Can you actually pull the trigger if your life depended on it?" he asked, stalking between the rows. Most of the males immediately assured him they would have no problem. But looking at the recruits, who averaged about 22 years old, I could tell some would not know until the time came. El Salvador had bled as much as Vietnam, but unlike the war-hardened Vietnamese, these young men and women came from a privileged class shielded from the crossfire.

The FUCA recruits regarded Regalado with something bordering hero worship. When he entered the room, they fell silent and leaned into his soft voice. When he lectured, they furiously scribbled down every word. He treated the classroom like a stage, casting himself as a sort of squat James Bond. Early in their training, the recruits learned a new trick from the old predator. Veering from his discussion on how to kill efficiently, Regalado repeated the mongoose maxim: The prey can always turn on you. "Never hesitate," he said. "If you feel someone is after you, you have to move. You have to learn to run and shoot at the same time."

Regalado pulled his .45 from its waxed nest, removed the clip, and smiled at the eager faces around him. Without saying a word, he ran straight at the wall, his eyes fixed on an imaginary assailant to his left. The click-click-click of the empty .45 echoed in the room as Regalado ran up the wall and snapped into perfect backflip, landing on his feet. The recruits looked at each other, grinning. El Doctor knew how to get his point across.

Later that summer, *El Doctor* used us to send a message to the guerrillas. Col. Adame called one Sunday morning to ask me to accompany him and Regalado on a mission. When I met them at Adame's home in San Salvador, Ramiro had been summoned as well, and greeted me with a quizzical look as several men from the anti-narco group piled into jeeps. Regalado explained we were to drive into the mountains and check out reports of a marijuana plantation hidden in the jungle. With *El Doctor* leading the charge, we rattled over winding dirt trails in the afternoon heat, only to abandon the jeeps when the road ended at the base of a mountain.

The operation made me nervous. We were in guerrilla territory, traveling on foot, in civilian clothes, with M16s slung over our shoulders. Any government troops in the area would undoubtedly mistake us for a rebel patrol and open fire. If the rebels happened upon us, one look at our American-made rifles and police gear would bring a barrage of AK-47 fire.

After a few hours, the plantation was nowhere to be found. "What the hell is going on?" I yelled. Regalado simply smiled and marched ahead. Finally, the trail opened onto a decrepit ranch carved out of the jungle. Regalado owned the ranch, Adame explained, and wanted to make a show of force to warn the rebels away. I didn't say anything to Regalado. It was part of the game, with everyone trying to use everyone else and avoid being used. And after everything I had seen, I wanted to keep *El Doctor* on my side.

Privately, Regalado told me the death squads were necessary to stop the spread of Communism in El Salvador. "Everything for the country" was his favorite saying: *Todo por la patria.* The elite and the country, of course, being one and the same.

Regalado painted a vivid picture of the death squads' modus operandi. After watching their intended victims for a few days to learn their movements, a dozen men in two vans would move in for the abduction. They preferred to strike away from the victim's home, bolting through sliding doors on both sides of the van and yanking the person off the street. As the torture began, they wrote down every name their victim cried out. Regalado practiced his impromptu dentistry on the unfortunate captives with a pair of pliers.

I could see these doomed, bleeding men, screaming names with the faint hope their pain would end if they fed their captors enough future victims. The pain usually ended with a bullet or the edge of a blade.

Regalado said he didn't do interrogations often, but when the death teams caught a particularly notable insurgent, *El Doctor* was in. I felt truly sorry for the men who drew Regalado from his lair.

Regalado was convinced the clergy were Communist infiltrators, trained in Cuba to undermine El Salvador. He considered them cowards, hiding behind the cloth as they spread their diseased doctrine to the peasants he loathed. He spoke of personally directing the deaths of several outspoken priests.

Archbishop Oscar Arnulfo Romero was the symbol of the church's new solidarity with the downtrodden. A conservative when he became archbishop, Romero rebuked the elite after witnessing the persecution of workers and peasants. In an act of high treason against the Salvadoran oligarchy, Romero called on President Carter to halt military aid to El Salvador. The right unleashed its fury on March 25, 1980, when a single bullet ripped through Romero's heart as he lifted the chalice in the chapel of San Salvador's Divine Providence Hospital. The following day, dozens of bombs rocked the capital as his supporters erupted in anonymous rage.

I learned Regalado was part of the assassination team from Aparecio, his good friend. Ramiro once told me about Regalado's role in the archbishop's killing. I didn't really believe him until I brought up the subject with Regalado and he did not deny the charge. After one training session, I casually mentioned Romero, and Regalado's eyes flashed with rancor. He spit the archbishop's name, calling him *hijo de puta* -- son of a whore.

"Did you kill him?" I asked. He looked at me with a faint smile. "What do you think?"

Deep down, *El Doctor* was afraid -- more for his family than for himself. Regalado said if the guerrillas caught him, he would accept his fate. Ironically, nothing scared the orchestrator of so many deaths more than the thought of a similar fate befalling his family. The prey could always strike back.

Inevitably, I met Regalado's superior, Roberto D'Aubisson, the most visible leader of the Nationalist Republican Alliance (ARENA), and the driving force behind the Salvadoran death squads. We met at the downtown San Salvador home of D'Aubisson's right-hand man, who I knew only as *El Negro*. Aparecio and I requested the meeting with D'Aubisson, to confront him with intelligence linking him with drug trafficking. He denied it. Because we lacked the proof to make a case, we let the matter drop. The accusation did not rattle him a bit, and D'Aubisson spent the next 45 minutes sharing his political dogma with us.

D'Aubisson had vowed to deliver El Salvador from Communism. His right-wing enforcers carried out the vow for him with a deadly blend of McCarthyism and Nazism: Root out the Communists, then slaughter them. As one ARENA official told the *Albuquerque Journal*, "If you investigate people like we did, you find everybody has some Communist ties if you look for them hard enough."

D'Aubisson's flamboyant personality was the polar opposite of Regalado's. D'Aubisson was bitter about the U.S. government "stealing the election" away from him. With Duarte in office, he planned to continue his purges until he could run for president again. He did not seem to realize his ties to the death squads made him a political leper in Washington, and his prospects were not likely to improve so long as he flaunted his human rights record. D'Aubisson told me he was proud of his involvement in ridding the country of insurgents. Everyone the squads killed, in his mind, deserved to die.

* * *

Shortly after I turned in my Contra report, Hugo briefed me on another Contra pilot, an American named William Brasher. He was ostensibly in Central America as a representative of a U.S. company selling night vision equipment to the military, but Hugo had uncovered his real vocation. Hugo reported Brasher was in charge of money, equipment, and training for the Contra operation. Brown had impressive connections with the embassy and the Salvadoran military. Like Guirola, he carried credentials signed by Bustillo. Hugo said Brasher regularly flew crates of weapons from the United States into Ilopango, which violated laws in both countries. But like the other pilots, he flew under the military's protective umbrella.

When I returned to Guatemala City, I typed Brasher's name into the computer. He was documented in seven DEA files for flying drugs and arms from South America to the United States via Ilopango. I called Aparecio and told him to grab a pen. We had a new special project.

* * *

That summer in Washington, North's "Project Democracy" hit the newspapers as reporters lapped up numerous leaks, and raced to put the details together first. Spurred by the publicity, members of Congress launched inquiries into the Administration's activities in Central America. They came back frustrated. North and his superiors threw disinformation at Congress to shake them off the trail, with apparent success: On June 25, 1986, the House of Representatives approved $100 million in lethal and non-lethal aid to the Contras, a stunning victory for the Reagan Administration.

By October 30, the legislation placing the rebels back under Uncle Sam's overt protection would become law. Before that, North was looking forward to retiring from the operation, and took inventory of Project Democracy's assets. He recommended they be turned over to the CIA when the time came. North did not know it, but the operation was about to explode in his face.

* * *

I began checking on Brasher during subsequent trips to El Salvador. I started with Adame, who was now part of my team. He knew Aparecio well, and often left his official quarters to stay at Aparecio's house when he was in the mood to carouse. Adame told me he was working with Brasher on the side, using his military contacts to help Brasher sell night-vision equipment to the Salvadorans. Adame also confirmed the link between Brasher and North. Like every other U.S. official in the area, he saw North's operation as a heroic gesture against Communism. He listened patiently to my concerns about their drug involvement, but clearly considered narcotics a subordinate issue. When I mentioned Brasher's name, he assured me "Willy" was a good guy. After all, he was helping the Contras.

I brought Adame with me July 28, 1986, for a meeting with the State Department's political officer in El Salvador, Janis Elmore. We sat down in her tiny office in the embassy, and Elmore listened as I rattled off the intelligence I had accumulated linking the Contra's Ilopango operation with narcotics smuggling. She knew most of it already: She approved all DEA cables relating to El Salvador before they were forwarded to Washington.

I wasn't surprised when she replied with the party line: *That's a covert operation, and you should stay away from it.* Elmore prided herself in having the best intelligence in El Salvador, which she usually did. Elmore said she knew the Contras were running drugs, but had to follow her own advice to keep her nose out of North's resupply operation. The pressure came from Washington. Elmore obviously didn't like it. She resented North giving the Ambassador orders, strutting around like he owned the place. Before we left her office, Elmore, too, confirmed Brasher worked for Oliver North. I wondered aloud who else may have Brasher on the payroll. "Cele, Willy doesn't work for the embassy," she said. I wasn't convinced, and I told Elmore she would see Brasher's name on my next Contra report.

The next day, I took the Contra intelligence report to Robert Chavez, counselor general for the U.S. Embassy in El Salvador. Chavez looked at the list of names, and checked them against his computer database. They were hits -- his computer also listed the pilots as documented drug traffickers. Our computers carried much of the same information, but I wanted to make sure Chavez knew these pilots were traffickers, so he could block future visa requests. Chavez told me then that he knew about North's operation, and knew they were smuggling dope. As hard as he tried to stay out of it, the CIA's visa request for Amador drew him into the mess. Chavez did not want his name linked to this imbroglio. Instead of refusing the CIA's request personally, he wanted to use me as the bad guy: *Hey, it wasn't me, Castillo nixed Amador because he's a trafficker.* I knew Chavez would not back me up if I tried to expose the Contras' drug-running. Elmore, although more outspoken, would probably back away as well.

* * *

In August, one of my Guatemalan informants introduced me to a businessman named Bobby Castillo, whose family owned a brewery and the Coca-Cola factory in Guatemala City. He supplemented his income from Coke with a thriving side business in coke. The informant said Bobby was one of Guatemala's biggest cocaine connections, and probably the least cautious. I started working undercover on him, hoping for a break to turn my luck around. Booby and I talked by phone at first, and after several conversations, and a few lunch meetings at the Camino Real, I arranged to buy 200 kilos of cocaine from him, starting with a ten-kilo sample.

After arranging the meeting, I called our Guatemalan anti-narco unit to help with surveillance. Up to this point, they helped me with several busts, never netting more than a few kilos from the small-time Colombians and Guatemalans they arrested. This could lead to their biggest haul yet. We planned a simple buy-bust: As soon as I saw the cocaine, the squad would move in to arrest Booby. They met me at the airport, then melted into the street, watching discreetly as they did their best impressions of passers-by.

Booby pulled up shortly in a Jeep Wagoneer, trailed by a Mercedes flanked closely by two more Jeeps. Booby's taste in clothing leaned toward casual American yuppie. As he walked up to me, he looked like one of those smiling, dark-haired models straight out of a department store catalog. Booby's smile quickly faded. "I don't want to talk here," he said. "Let's meet at the Camino Real." I agreed, then motioned to the Mercedes. "Who's that?" I asked. Booby said he would explain when we got to the hotel. When their caravan pulled out of sight, I found the officer leading the anti-narcotics squad and explained the situation.

At the hotel, Booby was much more relaxed, greeting me with a hug. "I want you to meet my partner," he said, nodding to an older, heavyset man waiting a few paces away. As I shook his hand, Booby introduced him as *el diputado* Carlos Ramiro Garcia de Paz.

I froze. This was the Guatemalan congressman listed in DEA files as a drug trafficker. De Paz saw the shock in my eyes and smiled, pulling out his diplomatic credentials. "Don't worry, there's no DEA here," he said. "And if you are with the police, you cannot arrest me. I have diplomatic immunity." I heard myself tell him not to worry, as my stomach churned and my palms turned clammy. De Paz grabbed my arm and started to lead me to his Mercedes - - he wanted to do business right there in front of the hotel.

I stole a look down the street, searching for my backup. Obviously, they had seen the congressman and scattered. Good.

I changed tactics, explaining to the congressman I didn't do business out in the open. He patted me on the back, handing me his calling card. "Here's my address. Meet me at 2 o'clock at my residence, and we'll do business there. Nobody is going to rip anybody off." As I walked him to the Mercedes, I told him I needed to notify my people in California of the change.

As they drove off, the squad commander appeared. He looked worried after seeing De Paz, and seemed relieved the bust was cancelled. I hurried to the embassy and called Julio Caballeros, chief of the Guatemalan National Police, to ask if it was possible to arrest a member of congress. It was, he assured me, but only if he was caught with the cocaine in his possession. "Do you want to set it up?" I asked. Caballeros paused a moment. "No, thank you."

I walked to Stia's office, where he was chatting with Reina, and told them about De Paz. The anti-narcotics unit wanted no part of the operation, I said. Caballeros would not cooperate, either. The Ambassador and his deputy in charge of missions were out of the country, so Stia called Larry Thompson, the third-ranking State Department official at the embassy, to ask how I should proceed. Stia returned with Thompson's instructions: Drop the pursuit. We were not here to embarrass the Guatemalan government, he said. We were here to help them.

There was no time to argue. I called Booby to explain the deal was off -- my superiors in California feared I would get ripped off if I did business with a government official. I apologized, but Booby said he understood. Orders were orders.

A wave of depression washed over me. I slumped in my chair. All my work building narcotics squads, all the cultivating and coaxing of informants; all the groundwork we laid to strike at the top of the drug structure had come together beautifully. Finally, a big catch, only to watch our own leaders cut the line.

* * *

My losing streak continued. On August 15, I met with Jack McCavett, the mild-mannered CIA station chief in El Salvador. Again, I repeated my evidence against the Contras. McCavett denied any connection between the CIA and the Ilopango operation. As far as Brasher was concerned, McCavett said "He doesn't work for me. He works for the Contras and Ollie North, and we have nothing to do with that operation."

Three days later, McCavett called me into his office and pulled $45,000 in cash out of his desk drawer. "I've got money left over from my budget I need to spend," he said. "Take this for your anti-narcotics group. Go buy them some cars." McCavett didn't mention the Contras, but I suspected he was trying to buy me off. The CIA, to my knowledge, had never given the DEA this kind of gift. I wrote out a receipt and handed it to him, took the stack of bills, and gave it to Adame and Aparecio. They bought three much-needed vehicles for FUCA.

Near the end of August, I met with Ambassador Corr to brief him on the CIA's attempt to secure a U.S. visa for Amador. I told him what I had learned about Amador's connection to the Contras, as well as my information about Brasher. He knew about Brasher's ties to North's operation, and listened intently to the new evidence my informants had collected. I was desperate. After repeating the Contra speech over and over to many bureaucrats, Corr was the one U.S. official I thought would understand, and maybe give the investigation a push.

I'll never forget Corr's response. "It's a White House operation, Cele. Stay away from it."

Despite my disappointment, I understood his predicament. Corr was part of the administration. Despite Reagan's "Just say no" rhetoric, supporting the Contras would dominate every other U.S. initiative in Central America until the Sandinistas were crushed -- or until someone convinced Reagan the cartel chieftains were Communists.

I left Corr's office, and called Aparecio. He and some of the FUCA team had been watching Brasher carefully. I told him to move in when they had enough evidence to merit a raid. If my superiors would not support an investigation of the Contras, my only option was to bust a member of the resupply operation. If we could prove Brasher was smuggling drugs for the Contras, the bureaucracy would have trouble suppressing my investigation at Ilopango. Brasher's ties to North were well established, but so far, every U.S. agency in El Salvador denied any affiliation with Brasher. He was the bastard child nobody wanted.

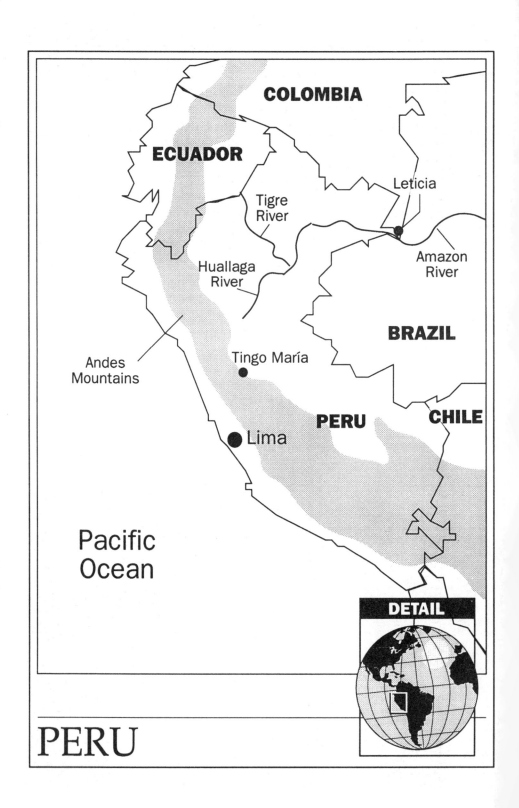

COLOMBIA

ECUADOR

Leticia

Tigre
River

Huallaga
River

Amazon
River

BRAZIL

Andes
Mountains

Tingo María

PERU

CHILE

Lima

Pacific
Ocean

DETAIL

PERU

Above and Below: Operation Condor in Peru

Above and Below: Operation Condor in Peru

Above: Coca plantations in Peru

Below: Celerino Castillo with 300 kilos of Cocaine in Guatemala

Cnel. Adolfo O. Blondón
Jefe

Above: Wally Grasheim Salvadoran Military I.D. He was only a civilian. He was Oliver North's right hand man in El Salvador.

Centre: Joseph Delvecchio "Joe the Crow" New York mobster arrested after the delivery of several kilos of Heroin

Bottom: Castillo undercover in San Francisco.

Above and Below: Colombian Pilots who were killed by Guatemala G2 during operation. 300 kilos of cocaine were seized

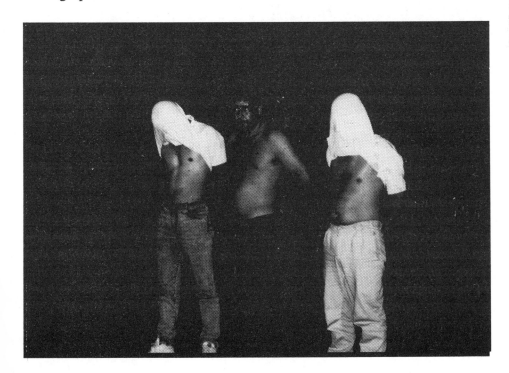

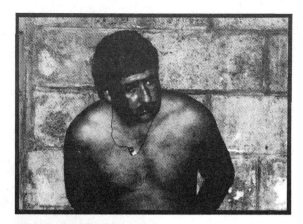

Above: Colombian pilot who was killed by Guatemala G2 during operation. 300 kilos of Cocaine were seized.

Left: Carlos Ramirez member of the Medellín Cartel in Guatemala murdered by G2.

Below: DEA and Guatemalan G2 agents before the arrest of the 300 kilos of Cocaine.

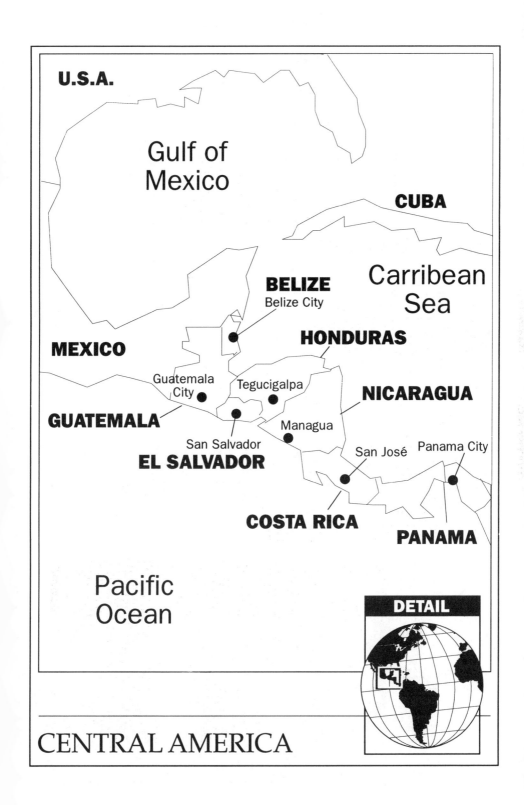

U.S.A.

Gulf of
Mexico

CUBA

Carribean
Sea

BELIZE
Belize City

HONDURAS

MEXICO

Guatemala
City

Tegucigalpa

NICARAGUA

GUATEMALA

Managua

San Salvador

San José

Panama City

EL SALVADOR

COSTA RICA

PANAMA

Pacific
Ocean

DETAIL

CENTRAL AMERICA

Above: Illopango Military Base Office where flight plans were made by the Contras. Castillo's informant worked there.

Below: Illopango Military Base for the Contras.

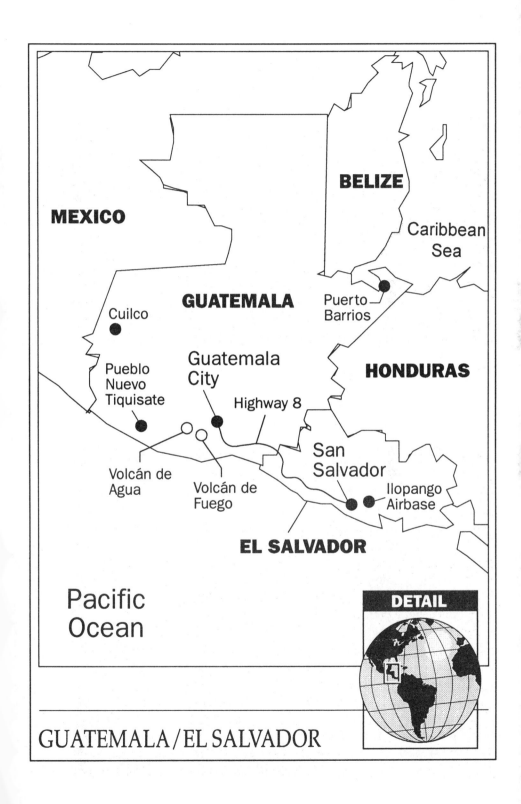

MEXICO

BELIZE

Caribbean
Sea

GUATEMALA

Cuilco

Puerto
Barrios

HONDURAS

Guatemala
City

Pueblo
Nuevo
Tiquisate

Highway 8

San
Salvador

Ilopango
Airbase

Volcán de
Agua

Volcán de
Fuego

EL SALVADOR

Pacific
Ocean

DETAIL

GUATEMALA / EL SALVADOR

Eight
Contraband
San Salvador, September 1, 1986

William Brasher was in New York City when Aparecio and ten FUCA soldiers surged into his Salvadoran residence and blew open a link in the contra connection nobody thought we would touch.

FUCA had watched the house in the Lomas de San Francisco neighborhood for a week, while Aparecio drilled the squad on every phase of the raid. The intensity of the preparations told the recruits they were preparing for their first big bust. They pounced, bursting into the living room like a football team on fourth-and-goal. Brasher's stunned guards didn't have time to react or argue. This was El Salvador: the "state of seige" dating back to 1980 meant the police could enter a home with all the subtlety of a fist between the eyes. No search warrant, no perfunctory Miranda recitals, just a stream of uniforms and your face against a wall.

I was in my office that Monday at 5 p.m. when Aparecio called. "We just hit Willy's place, and we found a whole bunch of shit. I think I might have put you in trouble with the embassy," he said, spitting the words in his hybrid English/Spanish. "You better get your ass down here *now.*"

The flight from Guatemala City to San Salvador left at 7:30 the next morning. A few suddenly-serious FUCA recruits met me at the airport. "Where's Aparecio?" I asked the soldier at the wheel.

"He's waiting at Brasher's house, guarding our seizure," he said, jerking the wheel and screeching into traffic. When we pulled into Brasher's driveway, Aparecio yanked open the car door and led me into the house. The recruits milled around outside, young faces etched with uncertainty.

The house was a mess, with clothes, dishes, and junk strewn everywhere. I poked my head into several rooms. Bunk beds. *No way these people are military*, I thought. The place looked like a barracks for a pack of teenagers.

"Any drugs?" I asked Aparecio.

"Marijuana," he replied. "It looks like personal use. There's a few plants growing out back, and we found more than a pound wrapped in a brown paper bag. It's in the kitchen."

"So what's all the excitement about?" I asked. He brought me running from Guatemala for *this*? Aparecio pointed toward the back of the house.

"Follow me."

He guided me through an enclosed patio and stood at the threshold of a side room, watching my face for reaction as I entered.

Holy shit.

No wonder the recruits looked so distraught. Aparecio had mentioned finding some military hardware in the house, but I was not expecting the arsenal piled before me. The room was filled with enough firepower to arm a platoon. *We've intercepted a Contra military shipment*, I thought, as my eyes roamed the stacks of weapons. A sniper rifle caught my eye first. It looked like a .50 caliber, with a scope big enough to peek into a window half way across town. U.S. military field radios sat atop cases of grenades and neatly packed C4 explosives. There was night vision equipment; M16s; helicopter helmets; Gerber combat knives; grenade launchers; compasses.

As we sorted through the piles, Aparecio held up boxes of M16 and M60 ammunition with a grim look. I ran my fingers over a bundle of mottled green uniforms -- U.S. jungle fatigues.

"Somebody could do a lot of damage with this," I said, hefting an RPG. The shoulder-fired rocket launcher somehow found its way from the Soviet bloc to William Brasher's back room.

We saved the file cabinets for last. Each folder was neatly labeled. I leafed through letters listing payoffs to Salvadoran generals, colonels, and other high-ranking officers. Brasher certainly had connections. One letter promised a general a paid trip for two to New York, and suggested the general pick up a complimentary fur for his wife while he was there. Brasher was obviously making sure he remained on their good side. *Not a bad idea*, I thought, *I've heard about their bad side*. In ten minutes, we found enough documents to prove Brasher's link to the Salvadoran military, the U.S. MilGroup and, as expected, the Contra operation. Col. Adame's business with Brasher was documented as well, with receipts of sales the colonel had secured for him.

I pulled a file bearing the name of Eden Pastora, head of the Contra's Southern Front in Costa Rica. The cables inside contained lists of military supplies, with corresponding delivery dates, times, and locations. I handed one to Aparecio. "That's probably where this cache was headed," I said.

The FUCA unit loaded everything into trucks and hauled it to National Police headquarters, where word of the seizure raced through the building. I saw curious faces poking around office doors as we walked the halls. The police had always regarded the unit as more of a concession to the *norteamericanos* than a serious investigative force. The triumphant FUCA team strutted through the corridors, back-slapping each other like the Bad News Bears of the drug war.

When Aparecio spread out the arsenal for inventory, the procession began. Curious visitors filtered through our offices to gawk at our catch, and listen to the FUCA members recount every detail of the raid. Nobody could get any work done with all the traffic, so we set up tables in the hallway and laid out our haul like a deadly buffet table. The recruits took turns jealously guarding their prizes. Aparecio was not about to burst their balloon by revealing the two guards and the female housekeeper had surrendered without the hint of resistance.

One of Brasher's bodyguards later took a job with Aparecio in his cafe. He and his buddy confirmed Brasher used the house as a barracks for Contra pilots, and as a storehouse for U.S. military hardware bound for the Contras.

The FUCA group didn't yet realize the magnitude of the seizure. With Brasher's trafficking history, anyone we could link to the weapons would have to explain how their goodies had come into the possession of a known smuggler. As Aparecio and I began tracing the gear, we discovered one of the M16s belonged to Col. Steele, who had so emphatically denied any connection to Brasher. The connections were forming like the spokes of a wheel, with

Brasher at the center. I had already drawn mental lines to Oliver North, Col. Adame, and Eden Pastora. Now Steele joined the circle.

The next name should not have surprised me. Aparecio ran a check on the license plates from Brasher's Jeeps. They came back registered to the U.S. Embassy.

Corr. I thought back to our last conversation. *It's a White House operation.* I switched on one of the confiscated radios. It was tuned to the embassy frequency, and U.S. personnel chattered back and forth in English. *Damn,* I thought, *they all looked me right in the eye and flat-out lied.*

We needed help tracing the rest of the weapons. They were U.S. military issue. The serial numbers stenciled on the crates would guide us to their point of origin. I called Richard Rivera, a U.S. Customs agent in Mexico City. Col. Hugo Francisco Moran-Carranza, director of the president's anti-corruption unit, recommended Rivera after they worked a case together. Moran was impressed. "If anyone can find out where those weapons came from, it's Rivera," he said. When I explained our situation over the phone, Rivera agreed to fly to El Salvador as soon as he could get free. I thanked him and hung up.

Good. After thrashing around in the darkness for so long, I could see a pinprick of light ahead. When the inventory was complete, we planned to call a press conference. An arrest warrant had been issued for Brasher, and I wanted to give him a big surprise when he returned from the States. I could see the cameras flashing as the police cuffed him and drove him to jail. As soon as the reporters scribbled down the details from the police, they would surely descend on the U.S. embassy and lie in ambush at the gate. *Col. Steele, what connection does the U.S. Military Group have to Mr. Brasher? Where did a civilian obtain such a large cache of U.S. weapons?*

I was still savoring the image when the FUCA lieutenant rapped on the door frame. His eyes spoke before he did. Something was wrong. "Col. Revelo just told me he received orders not to release the information to the press."

A long minute ticked away on the wall clock as I rocked in my chair. I felt I had been drilled in the chest with an icicle. Someone high in the chain of command had ordered Revelo, the chief of the national police, to cancel the press conference. The lieutenant drummed his fingers against the wood, waiting for instructions.

"What should we do?" he asked finally. It was more a challenge than a question. His brow dug a deep groove between his eyes. I suddenly felt sorry for him, for all of them. They knew nothing about the political storm their raid had unleashed, and I couldn't warn them. My initial shock congealed into a slow, rolling anger.

"Have someone bring a car around to the front. I'm going to talk to Corr."

The CIA had already briefed the ambassador about the raid. I briefed him again, studying his face when I came to the part about embassy license plates gracing Brasher's Jeeps. Corr stared at me, the muscles in his jaw flexing.

"You just hit the Contra operation," he said flatly.

"I told you I was going to hit Brasher," I shot back. "Explain to me what the hell a U.S. civilian in El Salvador is doing with this stuff. I told you this guy's a documented trafficker. He could be arrested as a terrorist."

Corr paused. The jaw flexed again.

"Cele, it's a *covert* operation," he said, holding his palms out.

That didn't answer my question. I played my last card; Corr had always insisted North's orders came straight from the White House, the embassy had no involvement. He had just admitted Brasher worked with the Contras. I knew the license plates and radios we had seized could tie this mess around Corr's neck like an albatross.

I didn't want to back the ambassador into a corner, but a shadowy paranoia was crawling around the corners of my mind. Undercover agents live in a world of delicately woven deceit, the office - - in my case, the embassy - - is the one place they can peel off their underworld identities and confide in people they trust. Everything was being turned upside down; I was beginning to trust my informants more than my superiors. I wanted desperately to trust Corr. I needed answers.

"Why did he have U.S. Embassy radios? Why did he have embassy plates on his Jeeps?" I was close to losing my composure. "If you don't claim him, and Steele doesn't claim him, and Janis Elmore doesn't claim him, where did he get all this shit?"

The jaw clenched again. "We were ordered to give them all the cooperation they needed," Corr said, rising from his chair. The conversation was over.

* * *

If our raid had somehow slipped past the diplomatic radar and hit the U.S. papers that September, Oliver North's cover might have evaporated sooner. U.S.-sponsored drug smuggling might have joined the list of deceptions later known as the Iran-Contra Affair. While we wrestled against our strait jacket, a security breach in Costa Rica later that month pushed the National Security Council's disinformation apparatus into overdrive.

On September 26, the Costa Rican Security Minister held a press conference that revealed the U.S. government's use of the Santa Elena airstrip in Costa Rica to supply the Contras. North shot off a top secret memo to his boss, National Security Advisor John Poindexter: "The airfield at Santa Elena has been a vital element in supporting the resistance. Built by a Project Democracy proprietary (Udall Corporation, S.A. -- a Panamanian company), the field was initially used for direct resupply efforts." North went on to recommend Oval Office visits for Cerezo and Duarte to shore up their support for the Reagan Administration in Guatemala and El Salvador. Preventive damage control. A short photo opportunity could buy them political insurance against future leaks. Referring to Duarte, North wrote: "Given the active support for the Nicaraguan democratic resistance provided by El Salvador, such a brief meeting is highly appropriate."

He included a press guidance sheet with the memo, instructing the agency's spin doctors to say "no U.S. Government funds were allocated or used in connection with this site nor were any U.S. Government personnel involved in its construction."

It was just a day's drive away, but Costa Rica might have well been on the other side of the world. Its government relatively stable, its citizens relatively peaceful and prosperous, and its leaders were more likely to test Washington's grip than the Guatemalans or Salvadorans. They were tired of Uncle Sam using their country for its undeclared war against the Sandinistas. The press conference about the airstrip drove the point home. With El

Salvador in firm U.S. control, we had no chance of finding a disgruntled official who would expose simultaneous arms- and drug-running by U.S. operatives in his country.

* * *

Two days after the raid, I returned to Guatemala City to write my report. As I copied down serial numbers, Aparecio called. "Some people from the embassy just walked in and claimed the radios and license plates," he said. "They took Col. Steele's M16 too."

At that moment, I knew the Brasher investigation was doomed. We were out of allies. The only reward the FUCA men would receive would be a bottle of good American booze after my next trip to the States. But we had to finish out the ride, like a stunt driver who realizes in mid-air he added one car too many to the jump. Richard Rivera flew down from Mexico City, photographed the seized weapons, and took a list of serial numbers back with him. He promised to call as soon as he found something.

Over the next month, Rivera made several more trips to El Salvador, talking to people, checking leads, trying to use the serial numbers on the weapons to find the thread that would unravel the veil of secrecy over Brasher's activities. I didn't tell him he was our last hope.

I threw myself into other investigations, trying to push the raid to the back of my mind. I had a few new leads on the Guatemalan narco-politicians, I desperately wanted another chance at exposing their activities. But the image of the stacked weapons and U.S. fatigues tugged at my thoughts like a impatient child. All the elements were lined up: Brasher's connection to the Contras and Oliver North was well established in the tight diplomatic loop in Central America; his drug exploits were documented in the DEA computer; we had caught him with marijuana and a huge cache of weapons. Yet every U.S. diplomat in sight was protecting Brasher, even though they clearly disliked the man. I decided to keep pushing. Something had to give.

* * *

When I returned to San Salvador, I dropped in on Steele and asked about the rifle. "I thought Brasher wasn't working for you," I said. Steele brushed the question away, claiming he gave Brasher the M16 a long time ago, before they had clashed - - over something he wouldn't discuss. He no longer talked to Brasher, Steele declared. End of discussion.

Later, as the Iran-Contra scandal unfolded, Steele's role was illuminated by Rafael "Chi-Chi" Quintero, a Cuban exile and Bay of Pigs veteran who had worked for the CIA as a Central American intelligence officer. When North recruited retired Air Force Major General Richard Secord to help run the Contra operation, Secord hired Quintero to ship arms to the rebels.

During North's 1989 trial for his role in the Iran-Contra affair, Quintero testified that North told him two men were responsible for decisions about weapons drops: in Costa Rica, CIA station chief Joe Fernandez; in El Salvador, he was to report to Col. James Steele.

As we chatted, Steele clearly wanted to distance himself from Brasher. "You know I'm going to have to include this in my report," I said. In fact, it was already in the report, which had been sent up the line before I left Guatemala. Steele nodded, apparently unconcerned. I left, heading for Janis Elmore's office.

Elmore greeted my briefing with an I-told-you-so look. "Nothing's going to happen," she said. "Willy works for Oliver North."

On my way out, I stopped to chat with a Salvadoran secretary working for Adame. I wanted to find out what had thrown Brasher and Steele's relationship on the rocks. She and I had lunch occasionally in the embassy cafeteria. Like secretaries everywhere, she knew more about the goings-on in the office than her boss. She often supplemented the intelligence I obtained elsewhere with her own fly-on-the-wall insights. She had rest-less ears and an eye for detail. She knew Brasher too.

"He's an asshole," she said bluntly. I asked her what she knew about Brasher's other activities. "He's been running guns and drugs for the Contras," she said. *Yeah, no kidding,* I thought as I rapped on Adame's door.

Adame told me Brasher had challenged Steele's authority in the Contra resupply mission. Brasher was trying to run the operation, but Steele had quashed his power play. I mentioned the incriminating documents in Brasher's file cabinets listing Adame's extra-governmental sales activities with Willy. I was hoping to wring more information about Brasher out of him, but the colonel threw me a reassuring smile and said his arrangment with Brasher was purely business. Adame said he planned to make some real money while he was in Central America, and his association with Brasher had done the trick. The thought that someone might consider this immoral or illegal apparently never entered his mind.

Not that anyone worried about the rules anymore. The CIA, which had ostensibly turned over the Contras' lethal supply line to North and his network, remained an active part of the operation. Rumors of this violation of the Boland Amendment whispered through the system for months, until it became so obvious the agency could no longer avoid action. By January, Joe Fernandez, the CIA Costa Rican station chief, was recalled when the rumors turned into allegations.

* * *

I had become good friends with Randy Kapasar, a CIA agent in Guatemala with whom I shared countless flights between Guatemala and El Salvador. He was an ex-Marine, balding and bearded, whose hands twitched and waved as if his body had chosen them to let off its excess energy. His career took him throughout Latin America; he was an expert in covert operations and demolition. We partied together from time to time, and when he transferred to Miami, we threw Randy a huge going-away party.

He knew I was investigating the Contras, I knew he was helping them. I expected him to deny my evidence of the Contras' narcotrafficking, but he followed Sofi's reasoning: "Cele, how do you think the Contras are gonna make money? They've got to run dope, that's the only way we can finance this operation."

"Arrogant bastard," said the DEA agent in Panama when I asked him about Brasher. The DEA computer mentioned a recent Brasher appearance at the DEA office in Panama. Yes, the agent said, Brasher had paid them a visit, demanding information on certain traffickers. "He strutted in like he ran he place. We asked him for identification. He had credentials from DEA and CIA. He even had FBI credentials," he said. While Brasher waited, they ran his name through the computer. When they discovered his illustrious trafficking record, they happily bounced him out of the embassy. "Be careful with this guy," the agent said. "He's a little nuts."

* * *

On October 7, as I pored over paperwork in Guatemala City, a burly midwesterner was led before a pack of reporters in Managua. I caught the news conference on CNN at the office, and my jaw dropped. The prisoner looked haggard, dressed in filthy jeans and a denim shirt. His Nicaraguan captors allowed him to make a single statement: "My name is Gene Hasenfus. I come from Marinette, Wisconsin. I was captured yesterday in southern Nicaragua."

Hasenfus and three other crew members -- Americans Wallace Blaine Sawyer and William J. Cooper, plus an unidentified Contra operative -- had lumbered off a runway at Ilopango on Sunday, October 5, with a load of munitions for the Contras. They flew south, skirting the Nicaraguan coastline before veering into Costa Rica, then looped north into Nicaragua. A few minutes later, as they approached San Carlos, a surface-to-air missile slammed into the plane and sent it hurtling to earth. Hasenfus was the only one with a parachute. As his comrades braced for their death, the lone survivor floated into history.

The unraveling had begun.

I recognized Hasenfus' name immediately. Aparecio's prostitute girlfriend, had mentioned him as one of the regulars at the Contra pilots' lair in the hills. They constantly invited her to the house, and I had written reports based on her accounts of her encounters with the pilots. She described their parties, where cocaine, marijuana, and sex swirled around the house, punctuated by the rattle of automatic weapons fired into the air by juiced-up pilots. She knew Hasenfus, Oliver North, Felix Rodriguez -- the Cuban-American who helped North with the Contra operation -- and virtually every pilot who flew for Project Democracy out of Ilopango.

When he heard about Hasenfus, Aparecio headed straight to the house with a FUCA team, looking for evidence. He called

30 minutes later. "It was cleaned out completely," he said dejectedly.

The Nicaraguans recovered rifles, grenades, boots and 50,000 rounds of ammunition from the shattered C-123. They also seized an I.D. card identifying Hasenfus as a U.S. adviser to the Salvadoran Air Force. I thought about the documents in Brasher's files listing weapons and delivery dates for the Contras' Southern Front. Had the cargo on that C-123 been stored at Brasher's place? Had Eugene Hasenfus ever slept in one of the bunks in that filthy house?

The hornet's nest had broken open, and everyone was ducking for cover. Oliver North hurried back to Washington from Frankfurt, Germany, where he had been negotiating with the Iranians for the release of the American hostages held in Beirut. He immediately began shredding the paper trail connecting him to the Contras.

By then, Congress had approved $100 million in aid for the Contras, allowing North to shut down his operation to prepare for the CIA's return to the war. Hasenfus said he thought the CIA ran the operation; the Administration began circling the wagons. Secretary of State George Shultz issued a flat denial: "They had no connection with the U.S. government at all."

It was the first of a long string of lies.

The Reagan Administration tried to pin responsibility on Gen. Singlaub, the Contra cheerleader whose fund-raising had been prohibited in the McAllen Library. Singlaub also denied any knowledge of the flight or its mission. Officials later admitted he had been used as a scapegoat.

As more details bubbled to the surface, the President lauded the efforts of the private American citizens who chose to risk their lives to fight the Sandinista regime in their spare time. The Contras played their part in the farce: spokesman Bosco Matamoros assured the world the U.S. government had no connection to the downed C-123. In response, the Sandinistas marched Hasenfus before the cameras and upped the ante. "Two Cuban naturalized Americans that work for the CIA did most of the coordination for the flights and oversaw all of our housing, transportation, also refueling and some flight plans," Hasenfus said.

* * *

As their role in the fiasco came to light, the first political tremors rumbled through the Salvadoran government. But they were dwarfed by the terror that struck five days after Hasenfus was captured. At 11:49 a.m., October 10, every living resident of San Salvador was united for an instant, their minds frozen in a flash of horror as the city lurched beneath them.

The earthquake measured 7.5 on the Richter scale. When the Cocos Plate slipped another notch under the isthmus, the long scar stretching through the city ripped open and claimed its victims. The city's landmarks crumpled: The Gran Hotel, the Ministry of Planning, and the 5-story Ruben Dario office building, where the moans and cries of more than 300 trapped workers echoed through the twisted steel beams. More than three dozen children died in the San Jacinto neighborhood when Santa Catalina Elementary School shuddered and fell. As the day faded, the searchers and the stunned survivors milled over the remains of the city, their silhouettes black against the searchlights and flames.

In Nicaragua, Hasenfus named the two Cuban-Americans who helped run the supply operation. One of them was Max Gomez. Vice President George Bush immediately hailed Gomez as "a patriot," and in a slip of the tongue, called him "Felix Gomez." Gomez, of course, was Felix Rodriguez.

The residents of San Salvador worked through the night, pulling the dead and near-dead from the rubble, praying they could reach the living in time. Sudden thunderstorms doused them as they clawed through the wreckage. In the shantytowns, refugees who had lost loved ones in the crossfire called out the names of relatives they would never see alive again.

The following day, the earthquake and Hasenfus dueled for space on the front pages. Elliott Abrams, the senior State Department official in charge of Latin America, appeared on CNN to repeat the party line on the Evans and Novak show:

Evans: Mr. Secretary, can you give me categorical assurance that Hasenfus was not under the control, the guidance, the direction, or what have you, of anybody connected with the American government?

Abrams: Absolutely. That would be illegal. We are barred from doing that, and we are not doing it. This was not in any sense a U.S. government operation. None.

Novak: Now, when you say, gave categorical assurance, we're not playing word games that are so common in Washington. You're not talking about the N[SC] or something else?

Abrams: I am not playing word games.

Novak: National Security Council?

Abrams: No government agencies, none.

They never thought the truth would wiggle out of their fists.

Only one of San Salvador's hospitals escaped damage, so wounded Salvadorans fought for medical attention as U.S. transport planes swooped into Ilopango with relief supplies and rescue teams. They brought dogs to sniff out the living, and tools to cut through the wreckage, now reeking from hundreds of damp, decomposing bodies. President Duarte estimated the death toll at 890, with 10,000 injured and 150,000 homeless. The American Embassy was a total loss: moments after Ambassador Corr stepped across the hall, the ceiling in his office collapsed.

Bush denied any connection to Max Gomez, or Felix Rodriguez, or Felix Gomez (depending on who you asked), but on October 12 he admitted Donald Gregg, his national security adviser, had some dealings with his favorite Contra patriot.

Hugo called from Ilopango: the pilots were scrambling out of the country, almost bumping into the reporters swarming into the air base. Not that the pilots had anything to fly anymore. The Contras' small air force at Ilopango was quietly flown to a remote airstrip and destroyed.

* * *

The earthquake's aftershocks hit October 13, three days after the initial devastation, sending most of the city scurrying outdoors. Some remained in the streets hours after the last tremor. The death toll reached 976.

In the following days, the Salvadorans began laboriously reconstructing their capital, while America's most popular presidency in decades staggered with each new revelation. The Sandinistas discovered a business card on the C-123 belonging to Robert Owen, North's main intermediary between himself and the Contras (according to Kerry's subcommittee probe, Owen's name was later discovered in an address book found on a DC-4 controlled by Frank Moss, a pilot who flew Contra missions and was investigated, but never indicted, by 10 different law enforcement agencies for narcotics offenses). And as Secretary of State George Schultz picked his way through San Salvador with Duarte, a dozen House Democrats asked the Justice Department to appoint a special prosecutor to investigate whether the White House had violated the Boland Amendment.

On October 21, I filed a follow-up cable on the Brasher raid, this one more detailed than the report I sent from El Salvador. The suits in Washington still had not responded to my first cable. By then I doubted the memo existed anymore.

John Martsh, head of the DEA's Latin American Section, surprised me with a call a week later. He had read my latest report, and he was not pleased. He insisted I use ''allegedly'' more when I described my investigation of the Contras and Brasher. ''Headquarters is pretty upset about this,'' he said. ''Don't step on other people's toes, it could come back to haunt you. If DEA doesn't like your reports, they might reject your re-up.'' The shit was obviously hitting the fan, so now Washington was telling me to back off.

Despite the setbacks, I planned to put in for another two years overseas. I wanted to finish what I had started in Guatemala. Noe agreed to stay for another tour. She enjoyed the cocktail party atmosphere of the embassy social scene. She also landed a job as assistant manager in the embassy commissary. Now Martsh was telling me I might be yanked back to the States if I made headquarters squirm too much.

I scheduled an appointment with Gen. Bustillo, the ranking Salvadoran air force officer at Ilopango, to ask him why he allowed Brasher to run dope. It was a bluff, but Bustillo bit. The general said he was only following orders to help North's operation. He was confused. ''I don't understand your government,'' he said. ''North comes down here and tells us he needs our help with his covert operation. Now *you* tell me what they're doing is illegal.'' As far as he knew, Oliver North represented the White House. That was all the reassurance he needed.

I met with Corr at his residence on November 13. It had survived the earthquake, but the ambassador looked a little shaken when I arrived. ''Guess who just left?'' he said, then filled in the blank. ''William Brasher.'' Brasher had returned from the

States in a rage. Corr told me Brasher had stormed in and threatened him: *If I go down, you and half the MilGroup go down with me*. He wanted his weapons back.

Corr advised him to get his ass out of town while he still could, then confiscated his embassy credentials as he left. Brasher would never get his guns back. We had donated the cache to the national police, who happily distributed it through the ranks; anything left at the house had been picked clean by the CIA. But Brasher would not go to jail, either. Officers at the national police told me they could not arrest him - - their superiors ordered them to leave him alone.

Corr wearily said he was taking heat from Washington because of my reports. "You're not the only one," I replied. The DEA had sent a man from Washington to investigate my reports on Brasher. He repeated the orders to use "allegedly." Then he scolded me for poor grammar in my cables. *Poor grammar?* That was a first.

A few days later, Brasher called me. He apparently had taken Corr's advice to leave the country. He was calling from Miami.

"You and I need to sit down over a cup of coffee. I want to meet you and find out who you are," Brasher said. "I need to straighten you out." He was angry. I had messed up his operation, and he claimed my reports were false. I was in no mood for his abuse. By then, Brasher had threatened every diplomat in El Salvador, using North's name to throw weight behind his wrath. He repeated the threat to each one: If I go down, the whole show goes down.

The Contra operation was collapsing in a heap without Brasher, like the flimsy shantytowns in San Salvador during the earthquake. Across America, the shock of learning Reagan's staff was negotiating with the Iranians for the release of the hostages was followed by the inevitable aftershocks: North overcharged the Iranians to buy guns for a war we were no longer supposed to be supporting. If the Contra-drug connection had been added to the list of sins, it might have leveled anyone left standing. Instead, my own agency was trying to intimidate me, and this asshole was harassing me.

I thought back to his unceremonious eviction from the DEA office in Panama, despite his ample credentials. "Hey, you still have those FBI credentials?" I asked sarcastically. Brasher fumed. I hung up.

Nine
Death Squad Dance
San Salvador - January 16, 1987

It should have been just another brief flight from Guatemala City to San Salvador. The pilot adjusted the flaps, dropping the jet smoothly into its landing pattern. The whining engines competed with the murmur of passengers in the half-filled Copa jet. I sat in the front row, skimming over my work notes from the previous week, a bottle of scotch for the FUCA commander tucked under my seat.

Suddenly, the plane lurched upward, pulling my stomach down to my belt. As the jet roared past the control tower, I peered through the oval window and spotted a white-shirted figure in the tower waving his arms back and forth, like a baseball umpire signalling "safe." His grave expression indicated otherwise. Something was wrong. Flight 317 banked sharply, aiming toward the Pacific.

A flight attendant appeared, her face drawn and nervous. She clicked the intercom and delivered the bad news with a halting voice: The front landing gear was stuck halfway down. After jettisoning most of the fuel over the ocean, the crew planned to attempt a crash landing.

The woman across the aisle, a Nicaraguan who looked about eight months pregnant, prayed out loud, ignoring the effect of her display on the two terrified little girls in the seat next to her. The flight crew instructed the passengers to move to the rear of the plane, but the pregnant woman refused, afraid to leave her seat. The flight attendant frowned for a moment, then patted her shoulder and joined the others in the rear.

I remained in the front with her and her daughters. Muttering my own quiet prayer, I pulled off my wedding band and locked it in my attache case, then jotted a quick note to my wife in my planner:

Noe, I love you and the kids. Guide them. I'm proud of you and I am sorry. Be brave. Tell my family I love them. Cele, 10:45.

I closed the book and cursed to myself, thinking of all the things I should have done. Always too busy. Too much work. Too much stress. It should have been different.

The pilot's voice cracked over the intercom: "The front landing gear is still jammed. Prepare for a very hard impact when the back wheels touch down. We're going to try to jar it loose when we land." A minute later, the plane dropped toward the runway, tail first. The rear landing gear smashed into the pavement, bouncing us in our seats like puppets. After a few terrifying moments, we heard a screech as the gear touched again. I closed my eyes, waiting for the sound of twisting metal. The airbrakes hammered on, dragging the jet to a slow stop. We were safe.

I pried my fingers from the armrests, said a quick word of thanks to Saint Jude, then walked into the sunlight.

* * *

I had little time to dwell on the near miss. At the end of January, articles linking the Contra resupply operation with narcotics smuggling hit the U.S. media. The third secret was out.

The story surfaced in turbulent waters. Iran-Contra was a household word by the beginning of 1987, with new revelations smacking the public in the face every few days. When the Administration ran out of lies, it searched for scapegoats. President Reagan fired Oliver North and accepted the resignation of his boss, Vice Admiral John Poindexter, on November 25, 1986. The first bodies had dropped.

In December, during his weekly radio address to the nation, Reagan admitted "mistakes were made." He would change this comment to "serious mistakes were made" a month later. On December 4, the House and Senate agreed to form a select committee to probe deeper into those "mistakes." On December 19, U.S. Attorney General Edwin Meese named Lawrence Walsh

Celerino Castillo III and Dave Harmon

independent counsel to investigate the now-famous Iran-Contra Affair.

The third secret surfaced in *The New York Times* on January 20. Under the headline, "Contra Arms Crews Said to Smuggle Drugs," reporter Joel Brinkley wrote:

> Federal drug investigators uncovered evidence last fall that the American flight crews covertly ferrying arms to the Nicaraguan rebels were smuggling cocaine and other drugs on their return trips to the United States, Administration officials said today.
>
> When the crew members, based in El Salvador, learned that Drug Enforcement Administration agents were investigating their activities, one of them warned that they had White House protection, the officials said.

The Times then quoted an anonymous U.S. official who said the crew member's warning, which came after DEA searched his San Salvador house for drugs, caused "quite a stir" at Ilopango.

Brasher. Who else could it be? *Someone at DEA leaked details of my investigation to The Times,* I thought when I finally saw the article. The story described it in amazing detail.

Then, in Newsweek's January 26, 1987, issue, a headline asked "Is There a Contra Drug Connection?" The magazine quoted three drug smugglers: George Morales, the champion speedboat racer-turned-trafficker; Gary Betzner, one of Morales' pilots; and an unnamed "FBI witness" who claimed to have seen contra planes loaded with cocaine in Colombia in 1985. Morales and Betzner, both interviewed in federal prison in Miami, accused the Contras of running drugs, claims they would repeat under oath before Sen. Kerry's subcommittee in 1988. The "FBI witness," who passed a lie detector test, said cocaine was packed aboard a Southern Air Transport plane in Barranquilla, Colombia, where other aircraft from North's supply network often landed.

"Southern Air Transport is the shadowy company that has been implicated in Oliver North's network to supply arms to the contras, using funds from the Iranian arms deal. It also provided the Hasenfus plane, shot down by the Sandinistas on a contra airdrop run," the author wrote.

Then, another connection.

The *Times* article mentioned Southern Air Transport as well, saying "Colonel North had told the Federal Bureau of Investigation last October to stop investigating Southern Air Transport ... At that time, Colonel North told the F.B.I. that the investigation would jeapordize negotiations for the release of the American hostages in Lebanon."

An anonymous former federal official - nobody wanted to talk about this on the record - told The *Times* reporter some senior government officials were "very, very worried that Ollie really had stopped that investigation, and this would be the next big scandal."

From my vantage point, it was obvious the government did not want the drug issue to turn the scandal into the Iran-Contra-Cocaine Affair. First, Rivera's weapons investigation was quietly snuffed.

Before the weapons could be traced, Rivera called, distraught. Customs suddenly decided to switch jurisdiction for Central America from Mexico City to their Panama office. His bosses ordered Rivera to pack up his investigations from Central America, particularly anything related to the Iran-Contra Affair, and ship them to headquarters, marked "Classified." Rivera boxed his files and sent them to Washington. We never learned what, if anything, happened to the Brasher investigation.

Then, two weeks after the *Times* article appeared, DEA sent a two-person team to Guatemala to investigate my Contra reports. *Finally, someone is listening.* Or so I thought. I did not know about the increasing publicity the Contras' drug connection was receiving.

I was in El Salvador when the intelligence team arrived. I hurried back, expecting a couple of grizzled veterans. Instead, Stia introduced me to a young, casually dressed man named Doug. His partner, a short woman with straight, shoulder-length dark hair, was a DEA rookie. She was also a diplomat brat whose parents, she said proudly, worked in the U.S. Embassy in Costa Rica. I wondered why the agency would send an inexperienced analyst to investigate such a sensitive topic. *She's probably the only Spanish speaker in her entire office*, I thought.

After a brief meeting with the pair, I ducked into Stia's office, eager to discover what kind of questions they were asking.

Stia said when they interviewed him the previous day, he let them flip through my reports from Ilopango. He assured me he backed up everything in my reports. I nodded. I was going to need plenty of support.

On February 9, the analysts and I filed into Janis Elmore's office. Col. Adame was already there, sitting quietly with an eager-to-please look on his face. I pulled up a chair, wondering if Elmore and Adame would verify my reports. I had my doubts.

The woman started by asking Elmore about the relationship between DEA and the State Department in Guatemala: Were there any problems Elmore would like to air now? No, Janis said, the offices maintained an amicable relationship. She threw me a quick, puzzled glance. I shifted uncomfortably in my chair, which suddenly became cold and hard. The questions continued, edging closer to my actions in Central America. They seemed more interested in searching out criticism of my performance than learning the truth about the Contras. By the time they got around to asking about the Contras -- Doug seemed afraid to say the word, instead asking "What's going on at Ilopango?" -- Elmore seemed thoroughly irritated with their fishing expedition.

Elmore dodged the question, telling them everything at Ilopango was normal. She avoided the Contras altogether. Adame chimed in with his own reassurances: Nothing unusual to report at the airbase. Rumors had surfaced about some Contra pilots smuggling narcotics, he said, but he could assure them if the rumors were true, no U.S. personnel were involved. The woman nodded without looking up from her notebook.

When the female investigator asked to meet with Elmore in private, Elmore shook her head. "Anything you want to ask me, you can ask in front of them," she said. The woman stalked out with her teammate in tow. Elmore leaned toward me. "Be careful. This girl is looking for something to nail you guys on." I nodded and walked out.

Any slim hope I harbored of Elmore and Adame verifying my Contra reports vanished as I left the office. I could not bring myself to be angry. They were avoiding turbulent water. Adame and Brasher, after all, were friends and business partners. He was not about to stab Brasher in the back, or admit the MilGroup allowed a U.S.-sponsored operation to haul boxes of cocaine into the United States.

And whether or not Elmore knew it, the State Department shared some of the reponsibility for placing the drug traffickers on the government payroll. The year before, the State Department awarded contracts to four companies owned or operated by drug traffickers: SETCO Air, founded by a Honduran trafficker; DIACSA, an air freight company that doubled as the Miami headquarters for two convicted smugglers; VORTEX, an airplane leasing company whose vice president was a trafficker-turned-DEA informant; and Frigorificos de Puntarenas, a Costa Rican seafood company owned and operated by two convicted traffickers. Between January and August, 1986, the State Department paid the companies more than $800,000 to provide services to the Contras.

During the same period, the State Department calmly assured Congress that a government probe into Contra drug smuggling revealed only a "limited number of incidents in which known drug traffickers tried to establish connections with Nicaraguan resistance groups." Individual members of the resistance may have dabbled in narcotics smuggling, the department stated, but they did so without the knowledge of Contra leaders. DEA's investigation was equally superficial, and like the State Department's probe, came in the wake of news accounts linking the Contras to narcotics.

On January 10, the investigators headed to El Salvador. They paid a courtesy visit to Corr, but had not planned to interview him. When they told Corr the purpose of their visit, he hurried to assure them everything El Salvador was running smoothly.

Then, the main event: An interview with the two informants who made the investigation possible. We walked into Aparecio's cafe, where Aparecio and Hugo waited. I made the introductions. When everyone settled into their chairs, the female investigator flipped to a fresh page and leaned toward Hugo. She asked him if my reports from Ilopango were accurate. Hugo took a deep breath and rattled off everything he witnessed at Ilopango throughout the previous year. For the next hour, he recounted every detail: The cocaine, the cash, the pilots, even the black X on the tails of the Contra planes. She chatted with him in rapid-fire Spanish, stopping every few minutes to translate for Doug.

She interrupted Hugo several times during his narrative to ask if I was taking good care of him, paying him good money. The insinuations woven through her questions tested my patience, but Hugo came to my rescue. Yes, he was happy with our relationship. Aparecio spoke next, filling in the gaps from his own experience with the Contras and the Brasher raid. I held back the satisfied smile that wanted to spread across my face. *Finally, the truth.* Their accounts confirmed everything in my reports.

The analysts seemed unimpressed. The woman became excited only when Hugo revealed a shady airplane rental deal between Stia and Pérez, who almost got me killed with his helicopter stunt in Cuilco. Hugo said Stia chipped in $5,000 to buy a plane with Pérez. Then the pair turned around and rented it to DEA, charging three times what we normally paid to lease planes from the Piper company. The woman furiously copied down every word. When Hugo returned to the Contras, her pen slowed to a crawl.

After three very similar days in Central America, the analysts returned to Washington and filed their report. Naturally, it echoed the government's well-rehearsed conclusions: Any narcotics trafficking by the Contras was the work of a few unorganized individuals, who snuck the contraband into the United States behind their leaders' backs. An angry Stia dropped the report on my desk, cursing to himself. Despite his initial reluctance to pursue the investigation, Stia dutifully signed all my reports on the Contras. His signature meant he considered my reports valid; his reputation was tied to this investigation as well. He shot off an angry cable to headquarters, asking them how the hell two investigators could reach conclusions about such a expansive subject after only a few days in Central America. He never got a reply.

I read the analysts' report slowly and sighed. My feeling of abandonment and betrayal was total. Once again, when the drug war hit politically sensitive targets, DEA blinked. Confirming my reports meant heaping more embarrassment on the Reagan Administration and making their ''Just Say No'' platitudes sound as completely hypocritical as they were. So DEA let me twist in the political winds. For the first time, I was ashamed of my own agency.

* * *

Shortly after the analysts left, Stia called me into his office to tell me the embassy wanted me to stay away from El Salvador. Stia said my Contra reports were stirring the waters in Washington. With Corr frequently out of the country as Iran-Contra sucked him into high-level Washington meetings, David Dlouhy, the deputy chief of mission, stepped in to declare El Salvador off limits to me. The country was too hot, with reporters nosing around everywhere asking about the Contras.

That was fine with me. With North's Contra base dismantled, my investigation was in limbo anyway. I could turn my attention back to Guatemala. I fished through my desk drawer, plucked out a manila folder, and spread the documents on my desk. My file on the Guatemalan government's drug ring was officially re-opened.

I needed a new angle on the case. Any hope of busting the drug-dealing *diputado*, Carlos Ramiro Garcia de Paz, vanished a few weeks earlier at a party thrown by the national police. When I walked into their headquarters, flanked by a group of embassy employees, Garcia de Paz's face jumped out at me from the huge crowd.

He sat at the front table next to Julio Caballeros, director of the national police. Garcia de Paz spotted me instantly and stared for a moment, puzzled, before wrapping an arm around Caballeros' shoulders and whispering a question into his ear. Caballeros glanced at me, then steered Garcia de Paz to a corner of the room for private consultation. I hoped Caballeros would not blow my cover. Then I watched the shock register on the *diputado's* face as Caballeros spoke. He scowled at me. I pointed my index finger at him like a gun barrel and pulled the trigger. The scowl deepened. I threw him my best cavalier smile. It was all I could think to do. My cover was blown.

In March, the investigation found a new breath of life when Col. Moran, the Guatemalan officer in charge of President Cerezo's anti-corruption force, agreed to help. Short, slim, and balding, Moran could have starred in any of those cheesy banana republic movies as the ramrod military dictator. But Moran was connected. Unlike the conservatives in the military, Moran was loyal to Cerezo. I prayed he was not part of the government's drug conspiracy as well. I had to trust him until he proved he could not be trusted. With the president's weight behind him, Moran would be my hammer. Now we needed a wedge.

We found it in Derek Mata, a man with an interesting set of alliances. According to intelligence I received from G2 and their ubiquitous wiretaps, Mata frequently flew drug missions for the Medellín cartel. He worked for Garcia de Paz. And he was the half brother of Gen. Roberto Enrique Mata-Galvez, the Guatemalan military's chief of staff and the head of security at the presidential palace.

Our first attempt to scare Mata into flipping to our side flopped. Mata agreed to meet with us in Moran's office, but when Moran and I tried to shake him with our knowledge of his criminal activities, he told us to go screw ourselves: His brother was the president's right hand man. Moran started to raise his voice, then thought better of it. He looked at me and shrugged. We needed a new approach.

Before I could gather any momentum, Stia and I came under DEA's internal affairs microscope. Less than a month before the Iran-Contra hearings began, John Martsh, our Latin American chief, flew down from Washington on April 7, 1987 to conduct an OPR investigation of the Guatemala office. We expected an experience akin to a rectal exam. After grilling Stia about his questionable dealings with an informant, Martsh turned the microscope on me. Stia called me into his office soon after Martsh left: "Cele, they're coming after you because of the Contra thing and the reports you wrote. They're trying to get rid of you, but they're going to do it very discreetly."

Martsh was on a mission. He talked to Hugo. He interviewed Aparecio. He spent a day poking around the El Dorado Hotel, where one of my informants, a woman who worked at the desk, told me Martsh asked if we were having an affair. She blushed when she repeated his questions later, but assured me everyone I worked with in the hotel told Martsh I was clean. Her encouraging smile did not erase the ominous overtones of Martsh's visit. My head was on the chopping block. Sooner or later, I would duck too slowly slow to avoid the blade.

Martsh returned to Stia's office and dug through the files, asking if I ever paid Aparecio out of my personal funds. It was a calculated question. Paying informants out of pocket violated DEA policy, but the rule was routinely ignored on the front lines.

Out of sheer necessity, agents frequently opened their own wallets for informants. DEA funds came in quarterly installments. The money usually dried up in October, and sometimes it was December or January before the next infusion. When the cash ran out, agents dug into their own pockets.

By the time Martsh got around to interviewing me, I knew what to expect. I answered each question knowing suspicious eyes in Washington would inspect every word later. Martsh looked like a disheveled high school teacher late for class, a heavy-set man wrapped in sloppy clothes peering through dark-rimmed glasses. He spoke with a cocky edge I instantly resented. He ticked off my misdeeds, passed along to him by the female analyst who visited two months earlier. Martsh said the female investigator was concerned with my relationship with Aparecio. He reminded me the line in the DEA manual stating "social or business contacts are expressly prohibited."

I know the damn manual, I thought bitterly. I wanted to grab Martsh by his thick neck and explain the realities of working alone in a hostile country. I swallowed my anger and answered: Yes, Aparecio and I were friends. With no other agents available, I explained, Aparecio served as my backup. In the process, we developed what DEA considered a prohibited relationship.

Martsh shifted his weight and changed topics. He wanted to know about Stia's involvement with the plane.

"As far as I know, the plane is under Pérez's name," I said. The day before my meeting with Martsh, Stia asked me not to say anything about the $5,000 check he handed Pérez to buy the plane. I promised to keep my mouth shut. My answer was truthful. Stia made sure the plane was registered in Pérez's name. I told Martsh I heard rumors about Stia writing a check for the plane, but I never saw the check. Also true.

Martsh frowned.

"Have you been paying Luis Aparecio out of your own pocket?" he asked, studying me over the top of his glasses.

I paused. "I know it's against the rules, but every agent has to do it," I said.

Martsh puckered his lips as he jotted the answer. He cocked his head again, like a teacher about to discipline a disruptive student. "You should be more careful about how you conduct yourself with informants," he said.

''Well, then you need to send us more agents. The rules also say you're supposed to have two agents present every time you pay an informant. That's impossible in El Salvador. There's nobody but me.''

Three weeks later, Martsh ordered me to fly to Washington. He spread the written statements out before me and handed me a pen. I studied the neatly typed summary of our conversation, then signed. A warning light flashed, but I overruled it. I had nothing to hide. Before I left, Martsh repeated his question about Stia's interest in the plane. I stuck to my previous answers. That seemed to trip his temper. He warned me again about my Contra reports. Reporters were asking questions, he said. I should keep my mouth shut.

* * *

In May, 1987, as the Iran-Contra hearings began flickering across American television sets, I retreated to the jungle, searching out opium fields anchored in the mountains.

With help from the *Guardia de Hacienda*, I began feeling productive again. Squirting herbicides on opium plants was concrete and satisfying. You find the poppies, you spray them, they die. For a while, it did not even matter that the mountain peasants replaced their crops as quickly as we could spray. I was doing *something*.

When weather and crosswinds permitted, we sprayed the poppies from the air. When flying was impossible, we called the *Guardia de Hacienda* and humped up the mountains on foot to knock down the fragile plants with sticks and machetes. The risk increased every kilometer we climbed. The mountain villagers in Guatemala were switching to poppies as rapidly as their counterparts in Peru switched to coca. In Peru, the military and *Sendero Luminoso* swatted away anti-narcotics efforts. Here, they used the Civilian Self-Defense Patrols, the paramilitary groups forcibly recruited from the villages as counterrevolutionaries.

Oscar Diaz's blood pressure rose so quickly it looked like his eyeballs would burst. Diaz, the fiery new leader of the *Guardia de Hacienda*, pushed morale among the *Guardia's* roughly 2,000 men to new highs with his John Wayne bravado and hands-on leadership. Now six of his men were dead, tortured and shot somewhere in the mountains near Cuilco. Their informants insisted the Civilian Self-Defense Patrol murdered them when they climbed too close to an opium plantation with their machetes. Diaz rounded up about 125 men in Cuilco, then charged up the mountain in the dark, with me bringing up the rear with my M-16.

The soldiers leading the column were natives of the area and scrabbled up the mountains like goats. My legs cramped up after a few hours of marching uphill in the thin air, bringing a few snickers from the young recruits. I returned the chuckles a few hours later when they started cramping too. When I started spitting blood, I realized how out of shape I had become. But at daybreak, I was rewarded with a breathtaking view. They called this part of the mountains *Las Nubes*: The Clouds. White, misty masses drifted just below us, parting around the rocky barrier before melting together on the other side.

We met a small Civilian Patrol squad just after sunrise. The half-dozen armed peasants confronted Diaz, belligerently ordering him off their mountain. Diaz looked like he had been slapped. They argued for a few minutes, then Diaz ended the discussion by spraying the ground around their feet with his automatic. They retreated, leaving the panting invaders to push upward.

Those same lanky men were waiting when we reached the opium plantation. They lifted small flute-like instruments to their lips and blew a few shrill notes. Suddenly, we were surrounded by what looked like every villager on the mountain. Hundreds of Indians lined a nearby ridge like Apaches in a western, watching the *Guardia* chop down their poppies. The sniper fire began as we hacked down the stalks. I yelled into my walkie-talkie, trying to find a friendly voice with an aircraft. A CIA helicopter found us, spotted the Indians, then lifted to a safe altitude and watched the villagers chase us all the way down the mountain. We reached Cuilco after eight hours, carrying soldiers with broken ankles and fractured legs. I passed out on a sidewalk, exhausted. The villagers made it very clear: Unless we marched into their plantations with an army, they were kings of this mountain.

* * *

In the fall of 1987, something finally went right.

On September 25, G2 picked up a conversation on their illegal wiretap of Garcia de Paz's phone. The Colombians planned to fly to Puerto Barrios, a port on the Guatemala's eastern coast, to drop off a large cocaine shipment.

The four-month investigation leading up to this point tested my patience at every turn. We got our first break when I bluffed Derek Mata by threatening to extradite him on conspiracy charges. He spent the next three days spilling everything he knew about drug smuggling within the Guatemalan government. He named more than a dozen officials dealing with the Colombian cartels, including Garcia de Paz. Mata claimed his high-ranking half brother and President Cerezo knew about the trafficking, and allowed the narcotics to pass through Guatemala unmolested. Garcia de Paz, a number of other government officials, and several military officers loyal to Cerezo actually participated in the trafficking, Mata added.

The G2 stepped in soon after, unceremoniously ousting Col. Moran. They told me their wiretap on his phone confirmed their suspicions: Moran was feeding information about my investigation to Cerezo and Garcia de Paz. They also gave me a stern warning: The Colombians knew Derek Mata was an informant. I shook my head, suddenly depressed. Few investigations could survive one major security breach, much less two.

Throughout July and August, we watched and listened as the buyers and sellers came together. On July 22, a woman representing the Chicago buyers flew in for the first of several meetings with the Guatemalan minister of defense. I always suspected the military helped the traffickers. This seemed to confirm it. Cerezo's government, with their few loyal military officials, could not protect such a large trafficking operation. The dopers needed the more powerful right wing's cooperation as well.

Soon, the other side of the equation arrived: On July 27, three Colombians and a Mexican trafficker flew in to Guatemala to oversee a small cocaine shipment. We let it go through. It was a warm-up for the mother lode in September.

On September 25, everything was in place. Dozens of G2 soldiers crawled around the Puerto Barrios hotel where Garcia de Paz was staying with the Colombians and their Mexican partner.

The *diputado* arrived in his Mercedes. He was the middleman, personally ensuring the cocaine's smooth transfer from the Colombian sellers to the Chicago buyers. It was the most boring Friday night I could remember. I watched the hotel for hours, yawning and chatting with CIA agent Randy Kapasar as well as Derek Mata. The CIA sent Kapasar to get its new narcotics section's feet wet in Central America. G2 reluctantly agreed to allow Mata to come along only after I lobbied for him. He knew all the players and could identify them at critical points.

We settled in for a long night of surveillance. Close to 100 G2 troops lingered around the hotel and the port. G2 was convinced the cocaine would arrive by boat, so they placed most of their eyes on the piers. Someone forgot to bring radios, so runners flitted from group to group, passing messages down the line.

On Saturday morning, the Colombians disappeared. The G2 commander was livid, demanding to know how so many men could allow the *traficantes* to slip past their surveillance. His men scurried around Puerto Barrios like drunken rats, hunting for the Colombians. Kapasar and I had to laugh. It would be a miracle if this operation worked.

While they searched, the mother vessel *Daring* cruised into the quiet waters of Puerto Barrios. We suspected the Panamanian-registered ship was our smuggler, but we could not be sure. We waited, listening to the scanner, hoping the Colombians would slip and reveal themselves. That night on the scanner, a voice gave an order in English: *Turn the lights off, we're coming in.* Suddenly, the *Daring*'s lights clicked off, its darkened hull vanishing against the black water. "Probably loading the cocaine now," one of the G2 officers said. The G2 troops were ready to pounce. Most of the officers wanted to move in immediately, but their commander held up his hand. "Let's wait."

On Sunday, I peered through my binoculars and cursed to myself as Garcia de Paz hopped into his Mercedes and drove away, his job apparently done. Every time I got close to nailing the the *diputado*, he wiggled away. It was like trying to catch a snake with chopsticks.

A G2 officer called to us, his eyes glued to the piers. The Colombians were back. Everything exploded. They swarmed the pier and the hotel, grabbing the Colombians, the Mexican trafficker, and two young women. The girls identified themselves as the Mexican trafficker's daughters. Their father apparently brought them along as cover: Just a middle-class family on vacation in Guatemala. G2 threw the captives in a white van and whisked them to the airport. I turned my attention elsewhere, assuming they would be flown to Guatemala City for trial.

G2 also grabbed a Guatemalan air force reservist based in Puerto Barrios who served as the dopers' air traffic controller. We asked his commander to order him to the base. As soon as the reservist realized his interrogators were G2, he turned ashen, then revealed everything. He said he directed the Colombians to a tiny airstrip at a nearby banana plantation, where they landed with 3,000 kilos of cocaine. The G2 men asked where the Colombians went the day they disappeared. They were at the plantation, he said, loading the kilos on the small train used to shuttle bananas to the port. Then, under cover of darkness, they loaded the coke onto small inflatable powerboats and shuttled it to the *Daring*.

We had enough evidence to search the ship. Randy and I convinced a local judge to sign a search warrant, then comandeered a small boat. The G2 men were behind us, ready to crack heads.

Two dozen feet shuffled over the deck as we inspected the ship, poking our heads into every hatch. The boat was something to behold. Someone had remodeled the former Canadian coast guard cutter drug lord style. Rich wood paneling covered the walls. In the mess, we found freezers crammed with beef and a refrigerator full of beer. We heard voices. Two or three Americans stood near the bow, turning meat on a barbecue and swigging beer. "Narcotics agents," I barked in English, holding up the search warrant. They looked at me, dumbstruck, as the G2 troops took them into custody and rounded up their cohorts.

I could not believe how gently the troops treated the six Americans and one Canadian on board. They were a models of restraint, snapping on handcuffs and sitting their captives down without the aid of a gun butt. I know they were tempted to resort to their tried-and-true techniques when the *norteamericanos* said they knew nothing about any cocaine. We started searching.

Randy, an expert at finding hidden drugs, soon reached his frustration threshold. He could not find the cocaine anywhere. Back on shore, the dopers were deep into negotiations with G2. The Colombians promised to tell them where they hid the cocaine, as long as G2 agreed to turn around and sell it back to them. The G2 officers were not accustomed to negotiating, especially with dopers. One of the officers later told me the Colombians were desperate to make a deal: "I'll have $5 million for you - - just let me make a phone call." The G2 officers consulted briefly, then agreed.

While Randy and I hunted for the hidden kilos, the G2 troops emerged with the Mexican trafficker in tow. He had obviously received the full treatment. He was stripped to his underwear, hogtied, bruised, and blindfolded. When they untied him, the Mexican rubbed his wrists for a minute, flinching every time anyone moved toward him. He led us into the hold and pointed to the spot where they bolted the cocaine into the ship's thick skin. One of the G2 men unbolted a 3-foot square sheet of steel. We peered into the dark space with flashlights. Nylon bags packed with cocaine lay piled between the metal skins.

The rest of the G2 force came aboard and gleefully stripped the boat clean, taking everything that wasn't nailed down. Before they could finish, a Guatemalan admiral from the Puerto Barrios naval station commandeered the boat, ordering everything pad-locked. This was his boat now.

As the admiral surveyed his new toy, we piled the coke in a on the top deck. It looked like the world's largest collection of leftovers. Every kilo was carefully packaged in a tupperware container marked "oro." Gold. I picked up a container and struggled with the wrapping. The cocaine was compressed it into a brick, then wrapped in two layers of plastic with coffee grounds in between to throw off drug-sniffing dogs. A thick skin of duct tape encased the package before it was sealed in the watertight containers.

We counted 2,404 kilos, more than two and a half tons of cocaine. The air force reservist we interrogated assured us the Colombians delivered 3,000 kilos on the nose. Almost 600 kilos were missing. I returned to the *Daring* to look for the rest. The admiral blocked my path to the hold.

"Everything is out of there," he said with a hard stare.

"I just want to look," I said.

"No. Everyone's getting off my boat now."

G2 delivered the cocaine to the *Guardia de Hacienda* in Guatemala City. In the papers, the *Guardia de Hacienda* received the credit for the Puerto Barrios bust, although they knew nothing about it before the cocaine appeared at their doorstep. G2 hated media attention.

Oscar Diaz took custody of the cocaine and happily burned it, tupperware and all. They checked every other container to make sure nobody tampered with the contraband between Puerto Barrios and Guatemala City. Amazingly, all the cocaine we found was still there.

For DEA, the Puerto Barrios raid was the largest bust ever in Central America. It was the fifth largest seizure in the world involving U.S. federal agents. It was also the first time since I had come to Central America that all the pieces fell together as they were supposed to. The bad guys were arrested; the drugs were seized; the good guys sent it up in smoke. As it turned out, the bust saved Stia's ass. He was suddenly a DEA hero, the brains behind a breakthrough seizure in Central America. The bust helped me as well. Some of the clouds hanging over me from the Contra investigation cleared. I thought I was out of the doghouse.

But in my mind, Puerto Barrios was not a complete success. In the aftermath of the raid, I learned of a dark secret the newspapers never discovered. As I prepared to leave Puerto Barrios that Sunday, a G2 lieutenant known as El Raton debriefed me. I never learned his real name - - G2 preferred aliases. El Raton told me they allowed one of the Colombians to place a phone call to his cartel bosses.

"A few hours later, a Lear jet flew in with $5 million in cash from Medellín," he said, his eyes widening with the word "cash."

G2, he said, promptly took the cash and the plane, raped the Mexican trafficker's daughters, then killed everyone. He described the carnage almost proudly, like a boss describing a job well done by his employees. The dismembered bodies, sealed in weighted 55-gallon drums, were dumped into the ocean. A couple of days later, the Colombians' car would be discovered at the Mexican border, planted to make it appear the dopers fled into Mexico.

I did not want to believe G2 slaughtered the traffickers, but long experience told me El Raton was telling the truth. The TV confirmed it. In the following weeks, I saw heart-wrenching ads on Guatemalan television. The traffickers' families appeared on the screen, pleading for the bodies of their loved ones. Their anguished faces interrupted the deodorant commercials and the daytime dramas for a few weeks, then disappeared.

On October 17, a sullen Garcia de Paz traveled to Costa Rica. He had a lot of explaining to do. The cartel wanted to know what happened to their product and their people. The G2 wiretaps picked up the conversation and called me immediately to pass on the news: Pablo Escobar himself was flying in to meet with Garcia de Paz and other cartel-corrupted government officials. The cocaine king was holding court.

G2's moles in Costa Rica called after the meeting to report their second-hand summary of Escobar's inquest. A furious Escobar held Garcia de Paz responsible for allowing the debacle at Puerto Barrios. Escobar paid a lot of protection money for that load. Someone was going to pay for this outrage.

When he returned to Colombia, Escobar sent a hit squad to assassinate anyone involved in the operation. I presumed that included me. As usual, G2 knew about it soon after the order left Escobar's lips. When the would-be assassins arrived in Guatemala, G2 hunted them one by one, leaving a lone survivor to give the boss all the gory details. It was their custom.

* * *

In July, after clicking off the Iran-Contra hearings in the middle of Oliver North's testimony, I picked up bits and pieces from the newspapers. The Congressional committees pulled witness after witness to the table, promising them immunity in exchange for their individual versions of the tangled events. North insisted he raised money for the Contras and guided the resupply operation with Poindexter's approval. Poindexter testified the buck stopped with him: He did not tell President Reagan that profits from the Iranian arms sales were used to help the Contras.

As the hearings wrapped up that summer, I slipped into despair. Poindexter's dramatic testimony in July drove Kerry's narcotics hearings to the back pages. Kerry's subcommittee hearings were overshadowed by Iran-Contra. When *The New York Times* ducked into the Dirksen Senate Office Building in Washington to cover Morales' testimony, the paper all but wrote off the speedboat smuggler's allegations of a Contra drug smuggling tie: ''The charges have not been verified by any other people and have been vigorously denied by several Government agencies.'' The third secret slipped out of the political spotlight as quickly as it appeared.

While the nation waited though the summer and fall of 1987 for the committees' final report, I received a call which told me the issue was far from dead.

On October 22, the call came in from DEA headquarters. A woman in our Freedom Of Information department asked me to keep the file on the Contras open. I was puzzled. For months, the DEA brass urged me to close those files and bury them. The woman explained: If the file remained open, Walsh's Iran-Contra investigators could be denied access to my reports under the Freedom of Information Act.

I was torn between complying and telling her to go to hell. After a moment of twitching between the two, I agreed to keep the file open. I wanted to keep my job. And I was not ready to close the book on the Contras yet.

* * *

The slaughter at Puerto Barrios should have been an aberration. When I returned to busting everyday traffickers, I learned it was the standard in Guatemala.

In the first weeks of 1988, I hopped from informant to informant, gathering enough names and numbers to keep me busy for months. After Puerto Barrios, I wanted to distance myself from G2. I preferred to work with Oscar Diaz and his *Guardia de Hacienda*, but the the spheres of influence were clearly marked: The *Guardia* helped with eradication and small raids. For large busts, the embassy wanted me to work with G2, who had the manpower, the money, and the power.

It was a terrible mistake.

I started at the bottom, meeting with small Guatemalan and Colombian cocaine suppliers looking for a Guatemalan buyer. They formed the conduit between the Colombian cocaine factories and the American consumers, using Central America as a sort of narcotics autobahn. If I busted enough of them, I knew they could give me enough evidence to build cases against the cartels. Few lived long enough to give me any information.

Every few weeks, I arranged a meeting with a doper, then called my G2 contacts to give them the time and place. The G2 commanders took down the information, thanked me, then promptly jumped the traffickers on their way to the rendezvous. The first few times it happened, I found myself waiting at the meeting place like a confused tourist, checking my watch every few minutes as the scheduled meeting time drifted further and further behind the minute hand.

In January, 1988, I called G2 to pass along an informant's tip about a Colombian drug plane scheduled to land on a clandestine airstrip outside Guatemala City. The next day, the Colombians were found shot to death near the burned-out remains of their plane. G2 blamed the killings on the guerrillas. I knew better. I described the incident in my next report, shaking my head in disbelief. Six months later, on July 20, I gave them another tip, this time about a local judge-lawyer team who offered to sell me cocaine seized by the government. The next day, both were kidnapped and found dead. G2 told me the two got what they deserved. *This isn't drug enforcement,* I thought. *It's a massacre.*

The dopers were usually dumped on the streets, their blood-smeared faces gaping sightlessly as people hustled past the stiffening corpses. When I confronted the G2 commanders, they brazenly admitted to the murders. They made no effort to lie or conceal their grisly work. They were the predators here, roaming the streets with no natural enemies. When I insisted they stop ambushing my busts, they simply changed techniques. On the next bust, they staked out the meeting spot as planned, but when the dopers showed up, the G2 stormtroopers wrestled them into the trunk of a car and screeched away. I stood rooted to the spot for ten minutes, dumbfounded. They returned a short time later. The *traficantes*, they said coldly, had been eliminated.

With every killing, G2 took stacks of cash and bags of cocaine. In a faint nod to the law, they usually turned over a portion of the confiscated dope to beef up the country's drug war numbers. They sold the rest, or saved it to frame future victims.

Noe could sense something was wrong. She prodded me gently for the reason for my deepening gloom. She wanted to know why I was so distant, why we slept together less and less, why I spent my evenings in front of the television, if I came home at all. She wanted to reach out. I recoiled. I tossed her the same answer every time: It's better if you don't know. I did not want her to worry, and if someone snatched her from the streets, anything I told her about my work could put her in greater danger.

I tried to keep my distance from the carnage. Then, in a tiny shack under a bridge, G2 dragged me into their nightmare.

My target was a high-level leftist politician from a small village near the Salvadoran border. He and his Guatemalan associates made arrangements for a group of Colombians to deliver 10 kilos of cocaine in front of a supermarket near Aurora. I almost choked when they gave me the location. I shopped at the *Paiz* supermarket regularly. The place was also a favorite with embassy staffers. I would have preferred another spot, but I hoped the high-profile location would keep the G2 operatives honest. With enough American eyes around, I felt certain they would follow procedure for once.

The operatives lingered around the front of the supermarket in street clothes, their eyes narrowing as the *politico* strolled up the sidewalk flanked by four men. The politician pumped my hand and flashed a polished smile as he checked his watch. The Colombians were due any minute with the cocaine. He did not bother making introductions -- not that it mattered. I could see the G2 team collecting behind them, reaching for their pistols. The action caught the attention of several shoppers, who lingered near the door to watch. I recognized a few embassy personnel among the onlookers. The nervous Guatemalans followed my eyes, turning just as a blanket of men jumped them.

I winced as they brought the butts of their guns down on the mens' heads with a crack, right in front of the wide-eyed embassy people. A white panel van appeared a moment later, spilling G2 troops from its back doors.

I helped them load the dopers into the van. As I pushed the last one inside, I heard the doors shut with a metallic clang. Before I could protest, the driver shifted into gear and hit the accelerator.

Shit. The last place on earth I wanted to be was in that van. The commanding officer sensed my discomfort and assured me they were merely taking the Guatemalans in for questioning. The captives sat quietly, knowing a stray word could bring another crushing gun butt. I peered through the windshield every time the van turned. If the G2 officer planned to take these men to jail, they were going the wrong direction.

The driver jerked the wheel, jumping the front tires onto a dirt road. He stopped the van momentarily while two uniformed G2 men scrambled out to stand guard. The road dropped into a ravine, its rocky walls filling the windshield as we descended. I knew this neighborhood. The bridge stretching over the ravine led to a posh neighborhood popular among Guatemalan military officers. This was a G2 nest.

The road curved under the bridge, where the overpass created a cavelike gloom. As the van ground to a halt, I could see the faint outline of two small structures in the fading light. Two G2 men silently pushed open the van's back doors as their comrades shoved the prisoners headlong into the dirt, then picked them up roughly and pointed them toward the darkened structures.

Another white van and several jeeps and pickup trucks were parked haphazardly around two wooden shacks. Several men sat in the back of the other van, looking uneasily at the gun barrels pointed at them. The Colombians. The G2 troops ordered them out of the van and lined them up with the Guatemalans. They pulled five from the line: All three Colombians, the Guatemalan politician, and one of his lieutenants. The G2 men filed inside with their captives, followed by the commander and me. We barely fit. As I inspected the inside of the barren shack, a familiar smell filled my nostrils. My eyes adjusted to the dim interior, confirming what my nose did not want to acknowledge. Dark, rusty streaks and spatters covered the rough walls.

Blood.

The captives smelled death. A low moan escaped one man's throat, then rose to a grunt as his captors ripped his shirt open, spraying buttons like birdshot. A few minutes later, the five men crouched naked in the center of the hut, their pleading eyes searching for a sympathetic face. I stared at the floor, afraid to look at them. The interrogation began.

The G2 squad took turns shouting questions at the cowering men, demanding the names of others in the politician's left-wing brood, the address of the place where they kept their cocaine, and where they hid their drug money. They punctuated each question with a two-by-four. At first, the dopers tried to take it. They clenched their teeth, their jaw muscles straining to hold back the screams. The board cracked ribs and arms, then the men cracked, blurting out names, phone numbers, addresses. A G2 agent with a notebook jotted everything down as calmly as if he were taking notes in class. A half dozen of his comrades crouched along the walls like spectators at a grisly play. The door opened again. A young soldier carried a metal bucket filled with water in one hand, and in the other, a black length of rubber cut from a car inner tube.

The G2 torturers turned their rage on the politician and his companion, beating them mercilessly. They pulled the politician to his knees, a bare flashlight beam turning his face into an anguished mask. The lead interrogator wrapped the black strip around his head and pulled until his features emerged through the rubber. He twisted the rubber tighter, squeezing a muffled groan from the politician, then leaned toward suffocating man's ear and whispered, ''You are going to die.'' I could see the rubber cave in as the captive desperately tried to draw air. When his body went limp, the interrogator released the mask. The politician flopped to the ground, his chest heaving.

A pair of hands pushed the second man's head into the bucket until the water churned with bubbles. They yanked him up by the hair, splashing my feet. He coughed water from his lungs, then spit out every detail of the cocaine operation he could think of. It didn't matter. The interrogator pulled his head back and repeated the sentence: ''You're going to die.''

''But why? I'm telling you everything,'' the man wailed, terror pinching his voice into a childlike squeak.

The agent, a dark-skinned man with vaguely oriental features, said, ''Because you're a coward.''

The men realized their lives were about to come to a violent end. They pleaded: We have wives, families. The G2 squad continued the torture, asking more questions. Their victims ran out of answers.

From the corner of my eye, I saw a glint of steel.

The interrogator lifted the machete and brought the razor edge down across the politician's shoulder blade, opening his back. It looked like a scene from a slaughterhouse. The politician let out a long, anguished scream. ''*Mamacita linda*,'' he wailed, crying for a mother who could not hear. The blood sprayed the other men, driving home the certainty of their fate. Their eyes reflected a deep, profound horror. One of them immediately lost control of his bowels and defecated on the dirt floor. The G2 men crouched along the walls jumped to their feet, enraged. They flattened him with a board, then grabbed his legs, dragging him through his own filth while one of the soldiers fished through his uniform for a pair of pliers. Locking the sobbing man's foot under his armpit, the soldier locked the pliers on the man's toe and ripped his toenails out, exposing pearly flesh which immediately welled blood.

After a half dozen turns with the mask, the politician stopped moaning. Blood oozed from his mouth, his eyes dim from loss of blood and lack of oxygen. His tormentor again pulled the mask tight around his face. Suddenly, his legs thrashed out from under him, his hands struggling against the smothering blackness. The rubber mask heaved twice, then smoothed as his body fell limp. Two plainclothes G2 silently dragged his body outside where others waited with razor-sharp machetes and several empty steel drums. I followed them out, took one look at the semi-circle of amateur butchers, then quickly ducked back inside.

The second captive stopped fighting against the hands. His head collapsed into the bucket. The interrogator grabbed a clump of wet hair and pulled. He was dead, drowned in a couple gallons of water. Two more men rose and dragged him outside. When the door opened, the wet sound of steel on flesh drifted in with the warm air. I wondered if the remaining dopers locked up in the vehicles could see what awaited them.

I had seen enough. I pushed my way outside and told the captain I needed to get back to the supermarket for my car. A few of the men with the machetes were smoking and chatting. They were done with the politician, whose components lay scattered in the dirt like a dismantled mannequin. Others were hacking the second man apart by flashlight. The bodies would never be found.

The G2 officer whistled to one of his men and ordered him to drive me back to town. ''You know, we only found one kilo when we took the Colombians,'' he said as I pulled myself into the seat. ''The deal was for 10 kilos,'' I snapped.

The officer shrugged, then turned to watch his men leisurely toss arms and legs into the steel barrels. He turned to face me again. ''Do not tell anyone what you saw here.'' It was not a request. It was a cold threat.

''Do you think anyone would ever believe me?'' I asked. The motor roared to life.

On the way back to the grocery, the driver smiled. ''We really took 10 kilos. We need the other nine to plant on other people.'' He laughed at his commander for his little lie. G2 answered to no one.

Ten
Backlash
Guatemala City - 1988

After the Puerto Barrios bust, DEA rewarded us with more manpower in the form of agent Larry Holifield, whose slow Louisiana drawl disguised a quick mind, and agent Delphin Von Briesen Jr., a portly good old boy from Dallas. Larry immediately impressed me with his eagerness to learn the rhythms of Central America, despite his poor Spanish. Von Briesen, who everyone called Tuffy, was another story. He smothered his ignorance with a haughty attitude which set me instantly on edge. DEA, I thought, seemed intent on sending its Latin American offices a steady stream of mismatched agents.

Tuffy quickly alienated the locals, treating anyone who did not speak English as an inferior. He bulldozed his way through each day, an overweight, burr-haired giant in scuffed shoes and mismatched clothes. He barked at members of the *Guardia* de Hacienda and the National Police. Our informants complained he pretended to understand when he clearly did not follow. They did not trust him to get things right.

I tried to help them both to adjust as best I could. Larry branched out into Belize, a country we had virtually ignored, while Tuffy planted himself in Guatemala.

The arrival of two more bodies took some of the pressure off me. Unfortunately, I did not remember how to enjoy it. The stress weighed on me like layers of wet clothes: First, the Contras; then the G2 murders; then back-to-back investigations by my own agency. I knew from my encounter with Martsh OPR was watching, waiting for one misstep.

Instead of searching for some way to defuse the tension DEA surrounded me with, I buried myself deeper into my work. In addition to several major investigations, I worked countless small cases, playing my well-worn role in Guatemala City's bars and restaurants: Smile big; tell some jokes; gain their trust; seal the deal, then bust them. Move on to the next one. Often I worked until 2 a.m., dragged myself through the front door, then slipped into bed next to a sleeping Noe. She no longer waited up for me.

Noe told me I was killing myself for an ungrateful agency. I stopped listening. I did not want to hear the truth, particularly from my wife. For months, I drifted away from her, feeling the emotions that built our marriage crumble under the weight of a burden I could not voice to her. We did not talk much anymore. I began sleeping in the guest bedroom. Somewhere along the way, I stopped thinking of Noe as my wife, instead seeing her as the mother of my children.

After our El Salvador embassy declared the country forbidden ground, I was home more, but not as a father and a husband. After seven years of adrenaline overloads, I saw myself as the protector. I could never relax, not even during my son's second birthday party on September 19, 1987. We invited our friends from the embassy and barbecued while the kids whacked at a *piñata*. I bought C4 a pint-sized bike with training wheels, which he mounted and zoomed off with Ana scrambling behind. She tracked him like a bloodhound, the portable alarm button in her hand. When an alarm sounded anywhere on the street, every guard in the neighborhood scrambled toward the sound, guns drawn. I hated knowing we could never let him play alone. I wondered what Guatemala was doing to him and to Crystal. I began to wonder if I could ever slow down and enjoy their childhood with them.

"You're losing your family because of your job," Noe told me. It turned out to be a prophetic statement. I mumbled some pathetic reply. I had a job to do.

By early 1988, my job seemed more at risk than ever. A letter arrived on April 7 from Richard G. Smith, chairman of DEA's Board of Professional Conduct. The board wanted to suspend me for five days for two charges of improper conduct. The first was improper association with a cooperating individual. *Aparecio.* The letter quoted passages from my statements to

Martsh, including my admission that Aparecio and I loaned each other money for the FUCA unit's operational expenses. I was also admonished for staying overnight at Aparecio's house on numerous occassions, also a violation of the agency's "no social contact" rule.

The second charge surprised me: Possession of an unauthorized weapon; specifically, a Colt AR-15 rifle I bought in New York and brought to Guatemala. No argument there. But the AR-15 was not on the list of DEA's authorized shoulder weapons.

The charges amazed me. Somewhere between Washington and the front lines, the rules often became counterproductive. I trusted Aparecio with my life. How could I avoid becoming friends with him? The weapons charge was even more ridiculous. I was a decorated Vietnam veteran. I would gladly prove my skill with an AR-15 on the firing range.

Someone wanted to send me a message. After back-to-back investigations, I knew the backlash would follow sooner or later. I typed my response, explaining my side of the story. The loans were for operations, not personal use. I stayed at Aparecio's house during the Contra investigation because I honestly felt safer there than at some hotel.

A DEA bureaucrat wrote back with the agency's ruling. They dropped the weapons charge, but the improper association charge would stand. The suspension was reduced to three days, beginning August 1. I appealed it all the way to Administrator John Lawn's office, but Lawn sustained the suspension with a terse letter: My decision is final. I spent the first three days of August at home, brooding as Noe tried in vain to cheer me up. I was beyond consolation.

Aparecio felt the whip too. The national police, at the request of the embassy, stripped him of his advisor credentials, which cut him off from the FUCA unit he helped build. He remained a DEA informant. The embassy controlled our advisors, but they could not interfere with our informants.

Our FUCA recruits were bewildered when Aparecio said his goodbyes. They could not understand why the U.S. government gave them mentors, then yanked them away. The year before, Dr. Regalado was fired after Corr discovered he was on the U.S. government's blacklist of human rights violators. When Corr realized Regalado was giving shooting lessons to the FUCA unit, he chewed me out and demanded I get rid of Regalado. I had not seen *El Doctor* in months. By August, 1988, Corr's term ran out and he left too, probably glad to escape the madness. I wondered how long I could last.

Stia tried to help. Two weeks before my suspension, Stia typed out a recommendation for my promotion from a level 12 agent to level 13. He included the highlights of my DEA career, including the Puerto Barrios bust, then brushed off the suspension, writing: "The charge is technical and nebulous and depending on the judgement (sic) of the Board could have been decided either way. These charges were brought about by S/A Castillo's having to work all alone under very adverse and dangerous conditions in a country torn apart with war and insurrectionism (sic) ... His dedication to DEA's mission under those conditions should be lauded by DEA Headquarters ... Instead of recognition for these efforts he was disciplined."

* * *

The high-pitched buzz reached the G2 team's ears before the Cessna broke through the clouds. They followed the plane's downward trajectory, gripping their weapons tight in anticipation. On board, the Colombian pilot carried 356 kilos of high-grade cocaine. If he hurried, he could drop the load, refuel, and get back to Colombia before dark. He spotted his destination, an out-of-the way airstrip the local cropdusters grudgingly shared with cartel pilots, and swooped low over Guatemala's flat coastal plain.

The G2 team was waiting at the airstrip. I was waiting next to the radio at the military base in Pueblo Nuevo Tiquisate, three miles away. When Larry, Tuffy, and I arrived with a new agent on TDY from Miami, G2 handed us a radio and ordered us to stay at the base until they called. Close to 30 of them piled into trucks and set out to meet the drug plane.

I closed my eyes and thought about the blood-stained shacks. *Not again*, I thought. *It can't happen again.*

After the grisly scene under the bridge, I tried quietly shifting my alliance to the *Guardia de Hacienda* and the national police, but every time we set up a bust, G2 showed up. Their wiretaps obviously were not limited to the dopers' phones. No one could cough in Guatemala without G2 hearing.

The fact that dopers were showing up dead after I gave their names to G2 did not impress my superiors. "The embassy wants us to work strictly with G2," Stia said after I reported the first killings. He was not about to argue with policy.

I tried taking my concerns to Ambassador Alberto Martinez Piedra, who agreed to a meeting. Piedra, a short, smooth-talking Cuban-American who was on his way out when the killings began, seemed mildly irritated after hearing my story, although I could not tell if he was angry at G2 for executing traffickers or annoyed with me for bringing it up.

"Did you see them killed?"

"No." I lied. I knew if I admitted witnessing anything like this, I would be kicked out of the country. My presence under the bridge broke every rule in the book, the least of which being the regulations forbidding DEA agents from participating in arrests and interrogations. I felt certain witnessing a foreign military force murdering civilians was probably against DEA rules as well. Washington was watching. I was not about to give them more ammunition.

Piedras complained to the CIA, who complained to G2, with little effect. The killings continued.

Whenever we opened a big case in Guatemala, the ambassador seemed to forget our conversation. Despite my earlier protests, he ordered us to continue working with G2, who the U.S. government had begun referring to as "D2."

Now here we were, sitting in our Toyota four-wheel-drive at the military base, watching the drug plane drop below the treeline and into the G2 team's jaws.

After a few long minutes, the radio crackled to life. They were ready for us. I had to give them credit for efficiency. The G2 men were cleaning up when we arrived a few minutes later. While part of their force apprehended the pilot, the rest ambushed the Colombians en route to the airstrip.

The Colombians, squatting on the floor of a hangar under armed guard, looked like the losers of a whiskey brawl. The G2 guards told me to take my three companions to the other side of the hangar. I thought they were going to kill them right there. As we watched, they tossed their prisoners into the trunks of various cars and sped off toward the base, leaving us to unload the nylon bags of cocaine from the Cessna. When we caught up with them at the base, only three prisoners remained. *El Raton* walked up to us with a smile. The two missing prisoners, he said, had been executed.

By the end of 1988, I realized how hopelessly tangled DEA, the CIA, and every other U.S. entity in Central America had become with the criminals. The lines that should have defined our ethical boundaries were stepped over and scuffed until they melted into nothingness. The Piper Co. in Guatemala City served as a perfect case study of how friends and enemies fuse together from sheer convenience.

Endnote coming to support this statement. G2 knew Gregorio Valdez had branched into drugs, as did many of our informants. Valdez, the young, Polo-clad owner of Piper, threw the best parties in town. His company, with its stockpile of planes and pilots, lived off CIA and DEA contracts. To show his appreciation, Valdez frequently filled his office with hookers and dancers, then invited his friends at the CIA, DEA, and the embassy over for booze-drenched parties.

The connections boggled my mind. I needed a flow chart to keep track of all the paths crossing at Piper. Among Valdez's flock of pilots were *El Coyote*, Reina's smuggler-informant, and several others who popped up in our computer as documented traffickers. Naturally, at least two of them -- Eduardo Ruiz and a pilot called "*El Negro*" Alvarado -- flew for the Contras before North pulled the plug on the resupply operation. The CIA frequently hired his pilots and hangars at Aurora airport. DEA stored helicopters there and used his planes exclusively until Pérez and Stia purchased their plane, which was also stored at Piper.

When I ran Valdez's name in the computer, I found a case already open on him for financing a drug operation. I wondered why a man with such a solid lock on success would risk his business and reputation by working for the dopers. His father, who built the company and handed it down to his son, was a member of the respected elite. Valdez made good money from his legitimate contracts with the U.S. government.

But after a few days of surveillance, it was obvious Valdez wanted more. He was preparing to run a load of cocaine to Miami for the Colombians. When Larry and I confronted him with our evidence, he confessed immediately and signed a statement outlining his involvement with the cartel. Valdez said he was just in it for the thrill. Naturally, when I told Stia and the CIA we were renting documented drug pilots from a man who just admitted his ties with the cartels, nobody blinked. The CIA and DEA continued giving Valdez their business, and he continued giving us wild parties lasting until the wee hours. The lines were gone.

What the hell are we doing here? The question surfaced more and more as the locals manipulated us to settle scores, the traffickers used us to eliminate their competition, and the politicians coddled us to keep U.S. aid flowing.

* * *

In December, 1988, General Adolfo Blandón, the head of El Salvador's military chiefs of staff, dragged us into a political power struggle. As the military's inner circle prepared to choose someone for a cabinet position, Blandón decided to sic DEA on his chief rival, General Bustillo.

Blandón invited Stia and me to his home for a quiet luncheon. Elmore was there, with a colonel from the MilGroup. Blandón wasted no time getting to the point: He had evidence an officer at Ilopango was involved in cocaine smuggling. He wanted DEA to start an undercover investigation. Stia looked at me. I could tell what he was thinking: *Get ready to go back into El Salvador, Cele.*

I knew the officer's name well. Hugo mentioned it several times in his Contra reports. Hugo watched the suitcases pass between the Contra planes and the officer's Ilopango office for a while, then asked the pilots what they were carrying. They answered openly: The suitcases held cash and cocaine. Of course, that was no revelation at Ilopango. Aparecio said his buddies in the Salvadoran air force knew about the officer's connection with the Colombians and the Contras.

Stia agreed to put me on the case, much to my chagrin. We could have nailed Bustillo's people two years earlier on drug running charges, but the general's support for the Contras made him untouchable. Obviously, Bustillo's sacred-cow designation disappeared after the Hasenfus plane went down. Blandón certainly saw the opportunity to exploit his rival's lost stature. He wanted the investigation kept quiet, but everyone knew how the military's inner circle would react when they inevitably discovered one of Bustillo's men was the subject of a drug investigation. When word of our probe leaked to Bustillo, he flew into a rage, asking how the U.S. government could stab him in the back after what he did for the Contras. Our investigation ended before it could begin. But it was too late for Bustillo. Blandón got the cabinet post.

* * *

Omar Pira-Palma pushed open the door of the steakhouse in Guatemala City and found me in a booth along the wall. The young, flashy strawberry baron and businessman seemed nervous without a phalanx of guards around him. Good. When I asked him to meet me the day before, I told him to leave his goons at home. A member of his own family had turned on Pira-Palma, revealing he was using his personal armada of boats and planes to shuttle drugs into the United States for the Cali cartel. By the end of our lunch meeting, I would know whether Pira-Palma wanted to go to jail, or cooperate and help me gather evidence against the cartel.

I put on my best bad cop face and raked Pira-Palma with the evidence we had against him. When I told him his trafficking activities were listed in detail in our computer, Pira-Palma started sobbing. Losing his visa for drug trafficking seemed to alarm him more than the thought of going to jail. He immediately tried to strike a deal: "How about if I give you 1,000 kilos right now?" The cartel delivered the cocaine some time ago, he said, and he knew where it was stored. I was interested. A thousand kilos would put a good kink in the cartel's bottom line that month.

"Let's see what you got," I replied.

The next day, Pira-Palma and I drove to Antigua Guatemala, an ancient city in the shadows of Guatemala's volcanoes. Guiding me to a small house in downtown Antigua, Pira-Palma took me to the front gate and pointed to a gasoline tanker truck parked within the concrete walls. The cocaine, he said, was inside. I could not go in without a search warrant or backup, so I rushed back to Guatemala City to give Stia the details.

Two days later, the quiet neighborhood looked like a war zone. A DEA helicopter circled overhead while two dozen *Guardia de Hacienda* lurched up to the front gate in pickups. For once, Stia agreed to let us call in the *Guardia*: Pira-Palma refused to cooperate if G2 was involved. I watched the *Guardia* bash through the front gate, then emerge a few minutes later with an old woman and a cluster of frightened kids, who were released after they convinced the *Guardia* they knew nothing about any drugs.

After rounding up such a conspicuous display of firepower, I prayed the cocaine was where Pira-Palma said it would be. It looked like half the city was there, huddled across from the front gate for a peek inside. I heard excited voices from around the tanker. They had found the cocaine. The *Guardia* pulled 1,000 kilos from the tanker's empty belly, just a fraction of the coke Pira-Palma already smuggled for the cartel.

Pira-Palma agreed to cooperate, and sat down with me to explain how his system worked. It was ridiculously easy, he boasted. Sometimes, he used the cartels' planes to fly in the cocaine. He packed it into boats. He hired drivers to take over the Texas border in loads of towels. He even stuffed it in boxes and shipped it by air freight. Anyone with a taste for money and a little ingenuity could join the game. The powder flowed through America's porous border like sand through a seive.

Back in Washington, the Senate Subcommittee on Terrorism, Narcotics and International Operations was reaching the same conclusion. After two years of witnesses, subpoenas, and stonewalling by government agencies, Sen. Kerry's subcommittee wrapped up its hearings at the end of 1988. ''The Subcommittee believes that this investigation has demonstrated that the drug cartels pose a continuing threat to national security at home and abroad, and that the United States has too often in the past allowed other foreign policy objectives to interfere with the war on drugs,'' the senators wrote.

The report contained a virtual roadmap of the connections between drug traffickers and the Contra operation. Unfortunately, many of their star witnesses were convicted felons like Morales, whose credibility came under scrutiny in the media. To this day, I wonder why they failed to call someone from DEA's Central American posts to testify.

Kerry's subcommittee never became more than an Iran-Contra sideshow. The country's attention remained fixed on the fates of North, Poindexter, and Robert McFarlane, Poindexter's predecessor, who were all indicted in March, 1988, for their role in Iran-Contra and the subsequent cover-up. Also indicted were Secord and his business partner, Albert Hakim, who each sucked about $1.5 million from the Contra gravy train while serving as the Contras' chief arms brokers.

The subcommittee released the report in the middle of North's highly publicized Washington trial. The media paid little attention. *The New York Times* buried the story on page 8. *Washington Post* readers had to dig back to page 20 for a summary of the report, which highlighted the political bickering between Kerry and Sen. Mitch McConnell, the ranking Republican on the subcommittee. A belligerent McConnell boycotted Kerry's press conference, calling parts of the report ''one-dimensional or one-sided.'' While America waited for the jury to decide North's guilt or innocence, the Contra drug scandal quietly died.

* * *

Pira-Palma called constantly to update me on the fallout from our 1,000-kilo seizure. To verify their cocaine was gone, the Cali cartel wanted Pira-Palma to send newspaper reports of the raid. Pira-Palma sent them the stories for their scrapbooks, then played dumb when they demanded to know how DEA sniffed out the cocaine in the red tanker. We had a goldmine, someone who could give us the names of the Cali's operatives throughout Central America. The roller coaster was lurching up again, carrying me out of my stress-induced gloom. But before I could gather momentum, a phone call in August, 1989, sent me plunging back into the darkness. The embassy wanted information on Col. Moran.

Moran's name had slipped out of my short-term memory, pushed away by the names and dates and events of the past two years. I had not heard a peep from the colonel since the day G2 yanked him off the Puerto Barrios investigation in 1987. The mere mention of his name made my skin crawl. After his security breach at Puerto Barrios, it was obvious Moran was part of Garcia de Paz's cocaine clique.

Months after Puerto Barrios, an immigration officer at Aurora arrested one of Moran's lieutenants slipping a suitcase full of cocaine on an Aviateca flight. The officer claimed Moran frequently ordered him to stash cocaine on commercial planes, and then Moran arranged for the bags to slip past Customs. When the airport officials called in the national police, Moran tried to pin the blame on two American tourists. But the lieutenant wilted under interrogation, ensuring Moran's airport exploits would be added to his DEA file. But Moran's stature shielded him from criminal prosecution. Nobody was going to testify against him.

Now I learned the State Department had discovered the black marks on Moran's record and denied his request for a visa, snuffing his plans to travel to the States for military training. Moran complained to President Cerezo, who called the embassy, demanding an explanation. When Ambassador James Michel, newly posted to Guatemala, called looking for everything we had on Moran, I typed out a summary of DEA's encounters with the colonel, including his Aviateca smuggling game and the leaks in the early stages of the Puerto Barrios case. The ambassador sent a copy to Cerezo. A few days later, my phone rang.

"I want you to meet me at the El Dorado," Moran said. "Right now."

I answered almost reflexively: "Okay. I'll be there in fifteen minutes."

Before I set the phone back in the cradle, I decided I was not going anywhere near the El Dorado. Moran's voice sounded pinched, angry. I knew my name did not appear anywhere on the memo the ambassador sent to Cerezo, but the edge in Moran's voice told me he figured out the source.

After half an hour, the phone rang again. I reluctantly picked it up.

"Where the hell are you?" Moran demanded.

"I've been told not to have any contact with you," I said, making things up as I went.

The line was silent for a moment, then Moran lowered his voice an octave and continued.

"Why did you give that letter to the president accusing me of those things?" he asked.

"Did you see my name on it?"

"No, but everything in there, you were involved in."

"I did not give that letter to the president," I shot back.

Moran was seething. "You have ruined my military career," he hissed. "And you will answer to me later."

I hung up with the threat lingering in the air. I thought back to the lieutenant arrested at the airport with the coke-filled suitcase. Soon after, the immigration official who apprehended the lieutenant was found shot to death. One of the national police agents involved in the investigation was also shot, but survived.

They're biting back, I thought. That month, Danillo Barillas, a prominent Christian Democrat, was assassinated by unidentified gunmen when rumors circulated he was about to reveal narcotraffickers had penetrated the party. I could easily be next.

* * *

On September 13, 1989, Larry and I walked into Guatemala's presidential palace and handed $10,000 worth of quetzales to Col. Francisco Ortega, the commander of G2.

The cash came from Pira-Palma, who wanted so desperately to distance himself from the cartel that when they gave him $10,000 expense money for the next shipment, he dumped it on my desk and asked me to give it to G2. Pira-Palma wanted protection in case the cartel discovered his betrayal, and he knew a monetary tribute to G2 was the best way to keep the Colombians at bay. Stia had no objections to giving the cash to G2. He considered it a reward for their help with our drug cases.

When I turned the money over to Stia, he asked Tuffy to stash it in the office safe.

"Do you want me to write a report on it?" I asked Stia. It was procedure to report any drug money seized.

"No, I'll take care of it," Stia replied. I returned to my desk, glad to have one less piece of paper to worry about.

Pira-Palma did not trust anyone. He insisted on meeting Stia in front of the embassy to make sure the money reached its destination. "You got the money, right?" Pira-Palma asked. "Yeah, we got the $10,000. It's in the office," Stia said. Pira-Palma looked satisfied.

The money sat in the safe for several months. After repeatedly asking Stia to file a report on the cash, I gave up and wrote it myself. By then, the dollars were gone, replaced by quetzales, the local currency. Stia dipped into the safe before his vacation to Europe, insisting he needed dollars for the trip. G2 would not know the difference.

When Larry and I gave the money to Col. Ortega, he assured us the money would be put to good use. *New machetes, colonel?* I thought contemptuously. With our errand done, I was glad to wash my hands of the cash. But the incident would come back to haunt me.

* * *

In December, three months after his thinly-veiled threat on my life, Moran sat in his office, explaining how he planned to repay me for ruining his career. He did not want to have me killed in Guatemala, where suspicion could fall on him. During one of my trips to El Salvador, Moran told the man sitting across from him, I would be ambushed on the highway. When my body was found, the murder would be blamed on the Salvadoran guerrillas.

The man listening to Moran's plot was a DEA informant from Houston, a Guatemalan whose concealed microphone picked up every word. He arranged the meeting to set up Moran. The informant wanted to arrange a cocaine delivery with the colonel. Instead, Moran launched into his plot to murder me. When the informant took the tape to his contacts at the Houston DEA office, an agent called immediately to tell me about Moran's threat.

When I received copies of the tapes, I listened to Moran's menacing voice slowly spelling out my fate. I was slowly coming unhinged. After watching so many men die, the image of my own death had never seemed so real. I had to get out of Cental America. I thought DEA would reassign me immediately, given the seriousness of the threat and the solid evidence backing it up. I waited for action from Washington, who responded with a disquieting silence.

When I took Noe and the kids home to McAllen for the holidays, I made an appointment with Armando Ramirez of DEA's Brownsville office. Noe and I met him for dinner, and for half an hour I sat stiffly next to my wife and sketched the details of my predicament in Guatemala, finishing with Moran's taped assassination plot. I wanted to come back to the Valley, and I needed Ramirez's help. I could almost feel Noe's excitement when Ramirez told me he had a position open in Brownsville, then promised to send his recommendation to headquarters. In the weeks ahead, I clung to that promise like a life preserver. I did not tell Ramirez my sanity and my marriage depended on it.

My parents knew something was wrong as we sat down to Christmas dinner at their house. Noe and I were not talking much. They could feel the tension, and I caught a few nervous glances passing between them. My mother took me aside and asked what was wrong. I pressed my lips together, holding back the words trying to burst through: *Noe and I haven't slept together in more than a year. I'm so busy trying to stay alive I can't think straight, and I don't know what to do.*

I pushed the jumbled thoughts aside and mumbled, "We're okay, mom."

* * *

When we returned to Guatemala, I dipped into my savings to hire two more guards for the house. I told Ana to keep the kids inside. Our "home" became a maximum security prison. I gave Noe a .22 pistol to carry in the car and lectured her on how to protect herself while driving. Everywhere Noe went, she carried a hand-held radio with a direct frequency to the embassy.

Stia walked into the office shortly after my return with another assignment. Newly-elected Salvadoran President Alfredo Cristiani, a member of D'Aubisson's ARENA party, wanted DEA's help. Cristiani suspected military officers were seizing weapons from the guerrillas, then selling them to the cartels. Stia asked when I could start an investigation. I bolted from my chair, feeling the blood rush to my head.

"What the hell are you talking about? Don't you remember what Moran said on that tape? The next time I set foot in El Salvador, he's going to have me whacked," I said, my voice rising in the small room.

Stia said he remembered the tape. Nobody else could work El Salvador, he added firmly.

Now I know how Jimmy Hoffa felt before they grabbed him, I thought grimly as I pushed the car toward the Salvadoran border. I scoured every inch of highway 8 between Guatemala City and San Salvador, pumping the accelerator at the slightest movement. Shrubs became crouching men. Tree branches were sniper rifles. I felt as if someone had painted a bullseye on the back of my head. As I watched my back, I caught my own sunken eyes reflected back in the rearview mirror.

DEA could not spare another agent to back me up, despite the death threat. I drafted a woman from the FUCA unit to pose as my girlfriend during the undercover meetings with the middle-man, while Aparecio and another FUCA recruit watched from nearby cars. I chose open-air restaurants so we could spot anyone suspicious approaching from the street. My nerves, stretched to the snapping point, tripped off my internal alarm whenever a bypasser glanced my way. I no longer trusted my instincts. I prayed Aparecio was watching carefully. While we watched for Moran's hit men, Moran was looking for other ways to strike.

On February 12, Stia appeared at my office door, looking solemn.

"Cele, Moran just took off to Costa Rica to meet with OPR. They're going to try to do you again."

I could not take much more of this. First Moran wants to kill me. Now he was meeting with our Gestapo.

"Goddam," I muttered. "Again?"

"This time," Stia said, "they're trying to get you for murder."

OPR called looking for the Puerto Barrios file. While I was in El Salvador, Stia took the file to Miami and met with the investigators, who repeated Moran's story. The colonel, Stia told me, accused me of executing the traffickers captured during the Puerto Barrios raid. Stia repeated to me the scenario Moran concocted: While the captives knelt in a row, Moran said I walked behind them, firing the *tiro de gracia* into the backs of their heads while declaring vengeance for another agent's murder.

I sat quietly, letting the story soak in. I could picture Moran spinning his tales to an eager OPR audience. A congress of vultures. I tried to laugh at the ridiculousness of it all. Instead, I braced myself for the next onslaught.

At the end of February, 1989, Stia finally typed a cable to Washington about Moran's death threat, a full two months after we received the tapes from the Houston office. I asked him why it took so long. Stia sounded defensive. "We had to verify everything."

I exploded. "You had the fucking tapes right here!"

Stia threw me an I'm-just-following-procedure shrug. I stalked out of the office, wondering if I could trust anyone anymore. When I pulled into the driveway that evening, I called to Noe and told her to start packing. We were getting the hell out of Guatemala.

Eleven
Post-Guatemalan Stress Disorder
Guatemala City - February, 1990

What was left of my marriage disintegrated during our hasty escape from Guatemala. While headquarters worked on how to react to Moran's death threat, I used up my savings and evacuated my family. On February 24, I drove Noe, Crystal, and C4 to the airport and put them on a plane to Texas. Noe and I did not talk much. I kissed her and said I would follow as soon as I could tie up a few loose ends.

First, I had to take care of Ana. During Moran's conversation with the DEA informant, he talked of grabbing our maid to squeeze her for information. If I left Ana behind, I was afraid Moran would turn his wrath on her. Ana watched, forlorn, as I packed my bags. I told her to stay put until the movers arrived, then I drove to the embassy to apply for a passport and a tourist visa for her. As soon as the visa was approved, she could stay in McAllen with Noe until we figured out what to do.

Ten days later, I joined Noe and the kids in the apartment she rented in McAllen. I tried spending a night with Noe, hoping the change in surroundings would spark a healing process. It was futile. The next day, I snapped my suitcase closed and trudged to my parents' house, where I slept in my old bed for the next week. Noe called several times to ask if we could talk things over. I let the opportunity slip by. I told her I had too many things on my mind.

I still believed I could straighten everything out. As soon as DEA approved my transfer to Brownsville, I could slow down, defuse, relax, then rebuild my marriage and my family. The agency crushed that faint hope with one phone call. A disembodied voice from headquarters told me the only openings were in New York City or San Francisco. The Brownsville job, the voice said perfunctorily, was closed. I would be assigned to temporary duty in San Diego until they could figure out where to banish me. Noe, not surprisingly, decided to keep the apartment in McAllen and stay behind with the kids. It was over, and it was my fault.

The two suitcases I lugged aboard the plane for San Diego contained the remains of my life. I reported to the DEA office and tried to concentrate on the assignments they happily piled on me. My tension increased with the workload. My kids, the two people in the entire world who truly made me happy, were hundreds of miles away. My marriage was over, and my career, the other pillar of my sanity, was shuddering badly.

Two weeks after I arrived, Stia called to inform me of OPR's latest move.

"Cele, my hands are tied. They're coming after you with both barrels."

"Why?" After being under OPR's microscope for three years, I wondered what they could possibly come up with next.

"Omar made some new allegations."

Now what? First, Moran accused me of murder, now Pira-Palma was pouring more gas on OPR's bonfire. According to Stia, Pira-Palma told OPR he gave me $25,000, not $10,000, then claimed I skimmed the difference off the top. I took a deep breath, fuming at the lie. *You can handle this*, I told myself. I was confident I could counter Pira-Palma's accusations. He was an admitted trafficker with a grudge against me. Several friends warned me Pira-Palma wanted to humiliate me after our first meeting. When I made him break down in the restaurant, I stripped him of his machismo in public, a mortal sin to a Latin American man. He planned to return the favor by helping OPR strip me of my job.

DEA wanted more evidence against me. In early April, OPR sent two agents to rifle through our house in Guatemala. A friend called one night to warn me about the search. "They found a whole bunch of shit in your house, and they're taking it to OPR," he said.

I quickly dialed the familiar phone number. As the line buzzed, I tried to organize my thoughts. Why would they search my house?

When Maria finally answered the phone, she sounded out of breath and upset.

"He forced me to unlock the closet," she said, breaking into a string of apologies. She was referring to my gun closet, where I stored my rifles, pistols, ammunition, and a handful of grenades I borrowed from FUCA after Moran's death threat. I kept the closet under lock and key so the kids could not stumble onto the weapons.

"Who forced you?" I interrupted.

"Senor Toofie." She mangled the name, spitting it out like a curse. I mentally moved Tuffy on the enemies list. My friends list was almost empty. I told her to keep the house locked up tight until I returned to pack our belongings.

I hung up and dialed Stia's number, praying he was not involved as well. I needed answers. They had no right to enter my house. Even in Guatemala, you needed a warrant to search a residence. Someone wanted to set me up. When Stia picked up, I heard my voice rise sharply.

"Who gave the order to search my place?"

Stia said the search order came from Anthony Ricevuto, one of OPR's senior inspectors. Another name for the enemies list.

There was more. After seizing my AR-15 -- the same rifle DEA tried, unsuccessfully, to add to my list of sins in the previous investigation -- someone in DEA had it altered from semi-automatic to fully automatic. Now it was not merely an unapproved rifle. It was an unapproved *automatic* rifle. This time, they planned to make sure the charge stuck.

I slammed down the phone and collapsed on my small bed, my mind whirling. Stia's back was clearly against the wall. If he did not cooperate, they could turn the spotlight on him in an instant. He obviously planned to play both sides, helping OPR bury me while whispering their game plan in my ear to keep me happy. He knew OPR would summon me soon enough, and I could make his life hell if I told them everything I knew about his questionable airplane investment. "Don't fuck me over," he said during our conversation. I did not know how to respond. Everything was becoming too complicated.

In mid-April, DEA decided on a new home for me. As soon as the paperwork came through, I was to report to the San Francisco office. I spent a long night wandering San Diego, restlessly weighing my options. I wanted to return home, but that was impossible. "I don't know, but they don't want you to come to Texas," Ramirez told me when I reached him in Brownsville a few days earlier. Word of my impending fall was all over the grapevine. "They're going to do you, man," he said.

"No shit," I said to no one in particular as I punched the crosswalk button at another strange intersection. I marched blindly, turning corners until the streets swallowed me. I did not want to live in San Francisco. More than anything, I wanted to see my kids. Separation from Crystal and C4 cut deeper than wounds OPR could inflict.

I stepped into an all-night diner to get a cup of coffee. Two voices dueled in my head, one telling me to cut my losses and go home, the other urging me to dig in and fight. I could hear my father: *Whatever you do, do it right.* After ten years with DEA, I could not fold now. The Contra investigation got me into this morass, and it was also the trump card that could get me out. Playing it would mean the end of my career, or what was left of it. That was fine. I was prepared to surrender my small role in the great "drug war," but not before I had a chance to clear my name. The decision made, I tossed two quarters on the table and tried to figure out where the hell I was.

* * *

In early May, Stia called again with my regular dose of bad news: Ricevuto was in Guatemala City to request a visa for Moran. The Justice Department wanted Moran to contribute to the government's growing money laundering and bribery case against the Bank of Credit and Commerce International. Moran's anti-corruption squad once investigated BCCI's Guatemala City branch, and Uncle Sam wanted to hear Moran's story.

I can't believe this, I thought, shaking my head as Stia's voice faded into an indistinct murmur. *Moran threatens to assassinate me; a few months later, my own agency wants to invite him into United States. Maybe they can give him a pistol and my home address while they're at it.*

The ambassador, Stia said, promptly refused the visa request, as flabbergasted as I was.

On May 28, when I returned to Guatemala City to oversee the packing of our household, Stia met me at the house.

"Cele, they got you, man."

"What do you mean, they *got me*?"

"They found Omar's MAC-10 in the closet."

I bounded up the stairs, with Maria firing exclamations after me. I stood in front of the empty gun closet and cursed to myself. The MAC-10, my Colt AR-15, the grenades, everything was gone.

I had taken the MAC-10 from Pira-Palma shortly after he became an informant. DEA rules prohibited informants from carrying weapons without a permit. Pira-Palma had reluctantly parted with the rifle, which was a gift from the Cali cartel. He said a friend in the military would give him a permit for the rifle. I was skeptical. The rules also said I should have put the gun in the office safe, but the safe was jammed with ammunition from a recent restocking, so rather than keep it in an unsecured locker, I told Stia I would store it in my gun closet at home until Pira-Palma received a permit. Stia had agreed. Now he was telling me DEA seized the gun as evidence.

"You knew about the gun," I said without bothering to conceal my disgust. Stia shrugged.

I called Aparecio while the movers packed our furniture for shipping. Ricevuto had come calling, he said. After the ambassador refused to give Moran a visa, Ricevuto used his remaining time in Guatemala to grill my informants. Aparecio sounded slightly amused at the sight of yet another DEA investigator coming to him for incriminating evidence against me. "I told him you were clean," Aparecio said with his usual stoicism.

Stia told me OPR wanted a written statement explaining the items seized from my home. I angrily scribbled a handwritten reply and tossed it on his desk. At least now I could see a few of OPR's cards. They obviously wanted to beat me over the head with weapons violations again. I boarded the plane to California more determined to match them charge for charge. When they brought up the weapons, I would counter with this illegal search and seizure. I knew plenty about wars of attrition, and I planned to wear them down to a stalemate.

* * *

I arrived in San Francisco July 12. After more than five years in Peru and Central America, walking through San Francisco's tilting streets brought back the sensory overload I felt during my first days in Manhattan. My last assignment for DEA was beginning much like my first: Alone in a strange city, filled with an overpowering sense of foreboding.

I walked into the office with a dark cloud over my head. I could see the discomfort in the eyes of the other agents as I introduced myself. I felt as if someone had branded an ''OPR'' stigmata into my cheek. I was assigned to Enforcement Group 6, a flock of young agents led by Richard Oakley, whose work I knew well from my days in Manhattan. He became something of a DEA legend in New Jersey, where he busted heroin and cocaine rings with uncanny undercover skills. Oakley introduced himself with a warm smile. With his light build and dark moustache, Oakley could have passed for comedian Richard Pryor. But his eyes broadcast the cool confidence of a man who had proven himself in the trenches.

Oakley did not dwell on my OPR problems. He was accustomed to working with agents under suspicion. The San Francisco office was the catch basin for DEA's outcasts and troublemakers. Several agents in Group 6 were survivors of OPR inquests, who spoke of their experiences in sour tones, like people who all got food poisoning at the same restaurant. Oakley did not let me dwell on the OPR probe. He put me to work immediately, filling my days with undercover cases. He needed a Spanish speaker badly.

The inevitable call came at the end of July. Ricevuto wanted me to fly to Washington for an interview. This would be my opportunity to respond to the charges they were gathering against me. On the last day of July, I packed a bag and drove to the airport, feeling like the proverbial fly invited into the spiders' parlor.

When I arrived at DEA headquarters the next morning with three cups of coffee tingling through my brain, a bored receptionist guided me to the interview room.

Ricevuto chugged through the door and greeted me with a warm smile. ''You must be Castillo.'' Short and dark-skinned, with black kinky hair twirling from the sides of his balding head, Ricevuto projected the air of someone trying to pack Cary Grant's charm into Danny DeVito's body. He led me to the interview room and offered me a chair. The second member of the investigative team, a tall, thin man wearing glasses, pushed a thin hand from his suit sleeve and introduced himself as Donald Petty.

Ricevuto's disposition darkened slightly when the door closed. He recited my administrative rights, then told me I was now required to answer any and all questions. The room seemed to close in around me.

The inquest lasted all day. Playing good cop-bad cop, Ricevuto and Petty tried to push words into my mouth, starting sentences with, "Isn't it true that...." As expected, they pressed accusations of embezzlement on me, then asked about the weapons found at my residence. They repeated Moran's murder accusations, and jotted copious notes as I reconstructed the Puerto Barrios raid. Obviously, Moran's death threat did not rule him out in their eyes as a credible witness against me.

They came armed with a list of accusations levelled by Tuffy, Pira-Palma, and *El Coyote*. When I denied skimming $15,000 from the money Pira-Palma gave me, they scoffed, asking why I waited so long to report the transaction. I put a silent curse on Stia for procrastinating. I would curse his name several more times as the morning dragged into the afternoon.

Ricevuto said *El Coyote* told them he bought a DEA commemorative pistol from me. I remembered the gun. Montoya was a huge gun buff, I explained, and since I had no need for the .45 I bought in 1980 from a retired agent who needed cash for his daughter's wedding, I sold it to *El Coyote*. They were digging deep for their mud. I sold Montoya the pistol when we first met, before I knew he was an informant. It was a bad idea, I admitted, but it was a sin committed by U.S. agents and military personnel everywhere. Selling a firearm overseas was against DEA regulations, but the rule was routinely ignored. Guns passed from hand to hand like small change.

El Coyote had inflated the purchase price by $2,000. Reina claimed I knew Montoya was an informant when I sold the gun. Not true, I told Ricevuto. I wanted to take my lumps for my mistakes, but I refused to admit to false charges.

When they brought up the MAC-10, Ricevuto stunned me again, telling me Stia claimed he never laid eyes on the rifle. I shook my head vigorously and repeated my explanation: When I took the gun from Pira-Palma, Stia gave me the okay to take it to my house for safekeeping because our gun safe was full. I checked my watch for the hundredth time, wondering when they would run out of accusations.

Ricevuto wanted to know why I kept a fully automatic Colt AR-15 in my house.

"First of all, I did not alter that rifle," I said. "Second, why would I bother? We had six M-16s in the office, all fully automatic." Ricevuto and Petty glanced at each other.

As their questions petered out, I asked Ricevuto why the Brownsville position suddenly closed. Ricevuto said OPR quashed the transfer request because of the "poor judgment" admonishment I received during my first days with DEA. I was floored. They were talking about my investigation of Noe's stepfather in 1980.

That's justification for separating me from my family? I thought, glaring at Ricevuto. It was the ultimate irony. They were using my relationship with Noe a decade before to separate me from my family now.

Before I could leave, Ricevuto wanted me to visit Yvonne Conner in employee relations for some sort of psychological evaluation. I was tempted to tell him to go to hell, along with the whole damn agency. If I had had a baseball bat handy, I would have broken his knees. I stalked out of the inverview room to search out Conner, leaving a trail of muttered curses behind me. I found her office, banged on the door, and found myself scowling at a tall black woman whose smile refused to wilt despite my obvious anger. She motioned to a chair, where I spent the next several hours spewing my troubles like a broken hydrant.

I left Conner's office a different man than when I entered. She was the kindest, most patient person I'd met in all my dealings with headquarters. She seemed genuinely interested in my side of the OPR inquest. Before I knew it, I was telling her about Vietnam, Harlem, the Contras, the G2 murders, and all the other searing memories I had bottled up and carried around like rough stones for the past twenty years. Under her calm gaze, I revealed memories I refused to bare to my wife, my family, even myself. The rage I brought into her office flared, ebbed, then died.

"It sounds like post-traumatic stress disorder," she said, nodding to herself and jotting a few more lines in her notebook.

"Look, I can handle it," I replied, pulling my hard veneer back into place. Conner ignored me.

"I'm going to recommend you be taken off the streets. I'll send the paperwork to San Francisco. In the meantime, when you get back there, I want you to visit Verona Fonte."

A week later, in Berkeley, I sat in another chair across from Dr. Verona Fonte, a DEA-contracted psychologist who examined a lot of agents. Fonte walked me over the same ground Conner had patiently exposed, but she seemed more interested in the clock. A typical Berkeley liberal, she only perked up when I brought up the Contra investigation. She seemed fascinated by the scandalous possibilities. When I switched to the more mundane stuff of my nightmares, her eyebrows dropped again.

I returned to work, wondering when Conner's recommendation would reach my boss. Before I left Washington, she said she might be able to pull some strings and help me transfer to a desk job in El Paso. I would still be more than 700 miles from home, but that was close enough to give me hope.

* * *

I was soon too caught up in my work to think about El Paso. The cases piled up, one running into another, with every group in San Francisco calling my name to help them infiltrate Latino drug networks. I never felt so popular. Out of perhaps 75 agents, nobody spoke Spanish, so it came as no surprise when busts often turned into deadly ad-libbed escapes. It was the Drug War Follies all over again.

During one bust, a trafficker handed me 10 ounces of heroin, then I gave the bust signal: "*Excelente.*" Nothing happened. I smiled at the man, hefted the package, and repeated the word a little louder, wondering if the microphone taped to my skin was working properly. He wanted to see the money. *Shitshitshit where are they?* The duffel bag I brought along was purely for show. There was no money, only a loaded pistol I kept in the trunk as insurance. I watched the trafficker's hand drift toward his waist, where a brown pistol grip poked from his belt. I gave the signal again, praying hard as I reached into the bag and cocked the pistol. We were about to play out a quick-draw scene from some Western, and I planned to pull the trigger first. My backup arrived a moment later and arrested the stunned trafficker. I did not waste my breath screaming at them. I slammed the trunk shut and screeched away.

In late September, I prepared for another trip to Washington, where Ricevuto waited with written statements from our August session. On September 26, I arrived at the airport early enough to call my mother, yearning for a reassuring voice. She picked up the phone on the first ring.

"Thank God it's you," she said. "DEA and the Border Patrol are at Noe's apartment. They're looking for Ana and searching the apartment."

Shit. As my mother repeated fragmented bits of the story, my fist clenched around the phone. While Noe was gone, she said, a group of men barged into the apartment and began interrogating Ana. My mother immediately had immediately called my sister Diana, at the McAllen Police Department, where she worked; she was on her way to investigate. I looked at my watch. My plane was about to leave.

The flight from San Francisco to Washington pulled me through four time zones and a million emotions. I slumped in my seat, ignoring the conversational overtures of the woman next to me, and dwelled on my helplessness. When the plane landed, I rushed to the hotel to call Diana at the police department, where she was the teen court coordinator. Diana said when she reached Noe's apartment, the kids ran to her, crying. Two men stood in the bedroom, pulling open dresser drawers. Two others questioned the maid. Ana later said they were searching for weapons. When Diana confronted them, demanding their names and their search warrant, an agent from the McAllen DEA office gave her a bogus name and snarled at her: "Listen here, we are here on official business and don't have to take any shit from you." Diana maintained her poise and took down the name of the immigration official and two men who identified themselves as DEA investigators. One was Tony Ricevuto. The other was Donald Petty. They took Ana into custody as an illegal alien, and Diana scooped up the kids and called her friends at the police department to report the illegal search.

Later, I discovered Ana's visa was confiscated at the border when she tried to cross into Texas. The papers were approved after I left Guatemala, but Stia scribbled "for employment with the Castillos in Texas" at the bottom of the tourist visa, which set off alarm bells at Customs. When they turned her away, Noe made arrangements to sneak Ana across the river. OPR got wind of it and pounced. They obviously wanted to add smuggling an illegal alien to their list of charges against me.

They did not count on my sister appearing. When DEA discovered Diana worked for the police department, the man who snapped at her backpedalled furiously, calling to offer his "sincere apologies."

When Noe found out about the search, she called the McAllen DEA office immediately to find out what happened to Ana. They passed her call to Ricevuto, who asked her to come in and answer a few questions. When I spoke to Noe after her session with Ricevuto, she said the investigator asked a few cursory questions about Ana, then focused on me: Did Cele have a lot of money put away? Was he into anything illegal? Noe was bitter about our broken marriage, but she cooly told Ricevuto as far as she knew, I had broken no laws. I thanked her and hung up, releasing a long sigh. Noe was still on my side.

I flopped on the hard hotel bed, exhausted. I felt like a marathon runner at the end of a race, praying for a second wind that refused to arrive. I tried to clear my mind, then gave up and stood with a grunt. The digital clock on the nightstand glowed a dull red. Midnight. I flipped through a magazine, then walked to the window and stared at traffic crawling through the dark streets below. I trudged to the bathroom and splashed water on my face. The man staring back in the mirror looked gaunt and lost. In a little over a month, my body had withered from 175 pounds to 145. My clothes hung on me like a scarecrow. I could hardly eat or sleep. Nausea hammered my stomach without release. Only my anger gave me focus. Ricevuto had crossed every line by dragging my family into this inquisition.

The receptionist with the bored stare told me Ricevuto was out. An hour later, as I sat listlessly in the interview room, he appeared in the doorway and silently took a seat across from me.

"We heard you were involved with smuggling the maid into the country," he said jovially, "but don't worry, we checked it out and found out you had nothing to do with it."

I stared at him coldly, picturing my kids crying on the floor while he dug through their home. For the first time in my adult life, I erupted.

"Ricevuto, if you have something against me, you come after me, but don't hurt my family," I shouted. "Because if you hurt my family, the gloves are coming off."

Ricevuto retreated, caught off guard by my outburst. He tried to explain why he searched my wife's house, but I was not listening any more.

"It's fucking wrong what you guys are doing," I growled. "It's wrong." I barely read the stack of written statements before scrawling my name at the bottom. When I left the room, I knew my career was over.

* * *

The end came slowly. Autumn and winter slipped by in a hazy blur, pushing me reluctantly into 1991. George Bush, half way through his term, stubbornly clung to the ideals of the Reagan "drug war." Interdiction remained the name of the game. It still didn't work. Every bag of heroin or cocaine I took off the streets had about the same impact as removing a cup of sand from a desert. Black tar heroin, crack, pills, blotter acid, you could get it all any time of the day or night in San Francisco.

When an undercover police officer from Eureka called asking for help with a case, I'm not sure what made me say yes. Probably nothing more than loneliness. Every time I slowed down enough to think, my depression returned. I spent my nights falling asleep in front of the TV. Weekends became two-day purgatories. I still called Noe almost every day to share a few idle words before she turned the phone over to the kids. Only their excited voices could reach through my numbness. It broke my heart knowing they did not consider my extended absence unusual. When Noe and I finally decided to divorce in March, it was several months before we could bring ourselves to tell them the separation was not just part of Daddy's job. It was permanent.

I worked my tail off throughout the week, then drove five hours north to Eureka every weekend to help the police there infiltrate a cocaine and heroin ring feeding off the illegal aliens who worked in the lumber mills.

In late April, 1991, a letter arrived from Washington. Four years after my Contra investigation, the hammer was falling.

Dear Mr. Castillo: This letter is notice of an action which is proposed to be taken in accordance with Chapter 752, Office of Personnel Management Regulations, and the authority vested in me by DEA directives. Based on the charges of Improper

Association With an Informant, Receiving/Soliciting Gifts, Mis-appropriation of Government Property, Violations of Regula-tions Relating to the Export and Sale of Firearms, Failure to Follow Written Instructions, Poor Judgment and Making a False Statement, the reasons for which are set forth below, I propose to suspend you from your position of Criminal Investigator, for 35 days...

The dry bureaucratic prose ran twelve pages and ended with the signature of Calvin G. McFarland, Jr., chairman of the Board of Professional Conduct. I read it three times. Everything from Ricevuto's rambling investigation was there, and more: The money Pira-Palma gave me to give to G2 was considered im-proper association with an informant and poor judgment; the MAC-10 I took from him was now an unauthorized gift; the pistol I sold *El Coyote* brought charges for an unauthorized weapons sale and making a false statement ("that you didn't know Luis Montoya was an informant when you sold him a .45 caliber pistol"); possession of the MAC-10 and the AR-15 constituted failing to follow writen instructions, since Stia "was not aware that you were in possession of either of these weapons."

Charge number three came from nowhere: OPR accused me of misappropriating government property, namely, a shortwave radio I gave Pira-Palma for our operation. Larry had seized the radio from a trafficker, then stored it at the office for general use. I gave it to Pira-Palma to set up a communications link between himself and the cartel, a direct line I planned to tap for leads. The radio was never given the serial number and inventory card needed to make it government property. According to OPR, I told Pira-Palma to charge the Colombians $15,000 for the radio, then give me the money.

I almost laughed. Pira-Palma was already under suspicion by the cartel for losing 1,000 kilos of their precious cocaine. They would undoubtedly become even more suspicious if he returned for an advance on his allowance.

They lined up everyone to testify against me. Statements from Stia, Reina, and Larry peppered the letter, but the bulk of the accusations came from Pira-Palma. I knew I could no longer trust anyone. I was alone, but I was going to fight the suspension. I found a lawyer in San Francisco and began writing my appeal.

My life was spinning in a tightening downward spiral, threatening to hurl me into the abyss. I prepared myself for a showdown. In their zeal to take me down, DEA conducted two illegal searches, harrassed my friends and family, and cozied up to a man who wanted me killed. The gloves were off.

After five years of almost continuous investigations, the best they could come up with was a 35-day suspension? In my appeal letter, I told headquarters I felt my aggressiveness in Central America was the reason for OPR's dogged pursuit of me. If DEA wanted to fight dirty, I told my fellow agents, I could fight dirty too. I toyed out loud with the idea of calling a press conference and blowing the whole Contra drug scandal into the limelight.

* * *

My lawyer called in September, 1991, and asked me to come to his office: Walsh's people wanted to meet me.

On September 20, I walked into his office and shook hands with Mike Foster, an FBI agent on loan to Walsh's prosecution team. Foster spoke with a pronounced eastern accent. He seemed exhausted. For the next six hours, I took him through every step of my investigation of North's Contra operation, the support it received from the CIA and the MilGroup, the visas the CIA obtained for drug pilots, and the money flowing to the Contras from drug sales. Foster flipped through the copies I had made of my reports, scribbling notes on a legal pad.

Foster shook his head increduously. When Walsh's office asked DEA for documents referring to the Contras, he said, DEA told the prosecutors there were none. "Cele, if we can prove the Contras were involved in narcotics trafficking, it would be a grand slam home run," he said.

They needed to halt their losing streak. Four days earlier, on September 16, North's conviction on three felony counts -- obstructing Congress, destroying documents, and accepting illgal gratuities -- were overturned on a technicality, stemming from his high-profile testimony before Congress. North, America's newly-christened icon, was just one who slipped through the system virtually unscathed. A month later, a judicial panel overturned Poindexter's three-count felony conviction because of the same technicality.

Secord, facing 12 felony charges, including theft, conspiracy to defraud the government, obstruction of Congress, and perjury, decided to plea bargain and cooperate with Walsh's investigators. On November 8, 1989, he pleaded guilty to one charge of lying to Congress and received a slap on the wrist: Two years of probation. Hakim was charged with five felonies, including offering North illegal gratuities. Two weeks after Secord's sentencing, Hakim pleaded guilty to one count of supplementing North's salary, paid his $5,000 fine, and took two years' probation. One by one, convictions were reversed, punished with mere probation, or erased when President George Bush pardoned six of the remaining conspirators on Christmas Eve, 1992, because their motives were ''patriotism.''

I wanted to help bring the government's drug connections to light, hoping some of those responsible for selling out the drug war would go to jail where they belonged. Foster wanted leads. I gave him the names of everyone who knew about the Contras' drug running: Aparecio, Adame, Hugo, Elmore. I also gave him copies of my reports. He closed his notebook and shook my hand again, promising my information would be included in his report.

Foster and I spoke by phone several times after our meeting. He wanted me to arrange for Aparecio and his girlfriend to fly to the U.S. for an interview. He also said he planned to fly to El Salvador to talk to Hugo. The interviews never occurred.

When Walsh released his three-volume, 2,500-page report almost two years later, the narcotics issue was nowhere to be found. The third secret would remain a vague footnote to the Iran-Contra Affair, the revelation our government could never afford to acknowledge.

I returned to Fonte's office several times for analysis. In her final report, Fonte called me ''a warrior who had been grounded without an adequate transition or support'' and diagnosed post-traumatic stress disorder. She referred me to a Berkeley psychiatrist, Dr. Donald Goldmacher, who agreed: ''As a result of chronic exposure to psychologically traumatic events, Mr. Castillo developed post-traumatic stress disorder. He continues to experience significant psychological symptomology as a result of this disorder. And, in my opinion, is totally and permanently disabled from performing his usual duties with the DEA.''

DEA finally took me off the streets in late 1991. I was banished to internal exile, shuffled from job to job. They did not bother training me for my new duties. I worked as a training officer for a few weeks, then a dispatcher, then, in the ultimate irony, a DEA recruiter. The agency wanted to bring more Hispanics into the fold, so they sent me to college job fairs across the state to sign up eager young men and women to fight the drug war.

I was done fighting. On December 6, 1991, I left San Francisco for McAllen on sick leave, an absence from which I would never return. Six more months would pass before DEA and my attorney struck a deal: If I accepted a disability retirement, they would pay me 40 percent of my current salary and forget about the proposed suspension. I signed in a heartbeat.

During my time as a recruiter, I passed out DEA literature from my booth, recited the agency line, and smiled at the energetic faces streaming past. When a young man or woman asked me what working for DEA was like, I smiled again and did my best to scare the hell out of them. I described the grinding frustration of the drug war, hit them with some of my personal heartaches, then watched, satisfied, as their enthusiasm faded like a forgotten dream.

"I'm telling you what it's really like," I said as they quietly dropped the literature back on the table. "Man, the worst thing you can do is join DEA."

ENDNOTES

Chapter 1
Taking the Stand: The Testimony of Lieutenant Colonel Oliver L. North, Pocket Books, New York, 1987, pp 8, 12-13, 25, 298-299, 558. (North's Congressional testimony).

The Economist, May 21, 1994, pp 27-28. (U.S. drug war spending).

Rolling Stone, May 5, 1994, p. 43. (price of crack in Little Rock).

"Drugs and Jail Inmates, 1989," special report by the U.S. Department of Justice, Bureau of Justice Statistics, 1989. (crimes committed for drugs).

Michael J. Sniffen, *The Associated Press*, June 2, 1994. (drug offenders in prison).

Deposition of Central American Task Force Chief, Report of the Congressional Committees Investigating the Iran-Contra Affair, 100th Congress, 1st Session, Appendix B, Vol. 3, pp 1121, 1230. (CIA knowledge of Contra drug smuggling).

"Drugs, Law Enforcement and Foreign Policy," a report prepared by the Subcommittee on Terrorism, Narcotics and International Operations of the U.S. Senate Committee on Foreign Relations (Hereafter the Kerry subcommittee report), U.S. Government Printing Office, Washington, D.C., 1989, pp 145-147. (North diaries).

"Drugs and the Contras," *The New York Times*, January 13, 1987, p. A20. (senators fear drug issue could derail Iran-Contra inquiry).

Chapter 4

"Crack's Destructive Sprint Across America," *The New York Times Magazine*, October 1, 1989, pp 41, 58. (New York crack scene).

Federal Bureau of Investigation crime statistics: New York City drug arrests for suspects over 16, 1980-1985.

"Heroin Ring Smashed - - 20 lbs. of Drug Seized," *New York Post*, November 4, 1982.

"U.S. Drug Agents Arrest 13 After Major Heroin Inquiry," *The New York Times*," November 5, 1982, p. B5.

"$8M bail set in drug bust; link to mob," *Staten Island Advance*, November 5, 1982.

"Heroin Mobster's Bound Body Found in Car Trunk," *New York Post*, February 3, 1984.

Muniz v Meese, Civil Action No. 85-2300, U.S. District Court, District of Columbia, July 18, 1985. (Class action suit filed by DEA Hispanics).

Chapter 5

Robert O'Brien and Sidney Cohen, M.D., *The Encyclopedia of Drug Abuse*, Green Springs Inc., 1984, pp 63-65.

Edmundo Morales, "The Political Economy of Cocaine Production: An Analysis of the Peruvian Case," Latin American Perspectives, fall, 1990.

Peter R. Andreas and Kenneth E. Sharpe, "Cocaine Politics in the Andes," Current History, February 1992.

"Pope Rejects a Role in Central America," *The New York Times*, February 7, 1985, p. A3. (Pope's Latin American tour).

"U.S. Drug Agent Kidnapped," *The New York Times*, February 12, 1985, p. A6. (Camarena kidnapping).

"Body of U.S. Drug Agent Believed Found in Mexico," *The New York Times*, March 7, 1985, p. A1. (Camarena murder).

Los Angeles Times, July 26, 1985, p. 2. (Judge Manuel Castro shot in Colombia).

"Car Bomb Rocks Capital as Peru Prepares for Transfer of Power," *Los Angeles Times*, July 28, 1985, p. 14. (Peruvian bombing).

The Washington Post, August 9, 1985, p. A32. (Car bomb explodes in Peru).

The Washington Post, August 11, 1985, p. A1. (North identified for Contra role).

"Peru Scores a Victory In War on Drug Traffic," *The Washington Post*, August 19, 1985. (Operation Condor).

Chapter 6

George Black, *The Good Neighbor*, Pantheon Books, New York, 1988, pp. 97-99. (1954 Guatemalan coup); p. 165 (Barry Seal incident).

Ronald Reagan, excerpts from April 15, 1985 speech as they appeared in *The New York Times*, April 16, 1985, p. A8. (Sandinista speech).

The New York Times, Oct. 16, 1985, p. A1. (Ortega suspends rights).

Ramiro Guerra's reports were placed in DEA file STG-81-0013. DEA rejected a Freedom of Information Act request for the file, citing privacy laws.

The New York Times, April 13, 1985, p. A4. (death squads).

Guatemalan officials were listed in DEA files under the following NADDIS numbers: Milton Cerezo-Garcia, #2140651; Claudia Arenas, #2627597; Alfonso Cabrera-Hidalgo, #2390984; Carlos Ramiro Garcia de Paz, #1937048.

Oliver L. North with William Novak, *Under Fire: An American Story*, HarperPaperbacks, New York, p. 308-309. (quid pro quo with Honduras).

Zabaneh is documented in DEA file GH-85-0086. DEA rejected a Freedom of Information Act request for the file, citing privacy laws.

William Clark, "Public Diplomacy (Central America)," July 1, 1983; *The Iran-Contra Scandal: The Declassified History*, The National Security Archive, The New Press, New York, 1993, p. 4, 37. (taxpayer money used for Contra propaganda).

Johnathan Miller, Memorandum for Patrick Buchanan, "White Propaganda Operation," March 13, 1985; Ibid, pp 6, 37. (Contra public relations work).

The Monitor, McAllen TX, Dec. 18, 1985, p. 1. (Gen. Singlaub's McAllen visit).

The Monitor, Dec. 21, 1985, p. 4A. (AP story on Contra drug connection).

The Contra report was placed in DEA file GF-TG-85-9999. DEA rejected a Freedom of Information Act request for the file, citing privacy laws.

Gaitan-Gaitan's activities are detailed in DEA file TG-86-0001. DEA rejected a Freedom of Information Act request for the file, citing privacy laws.

"Drugs, Law Enforcement and Foreign Policy: The Cartel, Haiti and Central America," transcript of hearings before the Subcommittee on Terrorism, Narcotics and International Communications of the U.S. Senate Foreign Relations Committee (Hereafter the Kerry subcommittee hearings), U.S. Government Printing Office, Washington, D.C., 1988, Part 3, pp 280-311. (Morales testimony)

The Kerry subcommittee report, pp 41, 147. (North suggests drug money be diverted to Contras; North diary excerpt).

Elaine Shannon, *Desperados*, Viking Penguin Inc., New York, 1988, pp 147-161 (Barry Seal).

Under Fire: An American Story, p. 315-317. (North denies Contra drug link).

Chapter 7

Guirola-Beeche is named in DEA files under NADDIS numbers 1585334 and 1744448.

"Salvadoran Archbishop Assassinated By Sniper While Officiating at Mass," *The New York Times*, March 25, 1980, p. A1. (Archbishop Romero's murder).

"Salvador is Rocked By 30 Bomb Blasts," The New York Times, March 26, 1980, p. A7. (Reaction to Romero's murder).

"Salvadoran Rightists: The Deadly Patriots," reprinted from the *Albuquerque Journal*, 1983, p.29. (D'Aubisson and ARENA).

"Brasher" is documented in DEA file TG-87-0003. The DEA rejected a Freedom of Information Act request for the file, citing privacy laws.

Theodore Draper, *A Very Thin Line*, Touchstone, 1991, pp 332-337, 345. (1986 Congressional vote on Contra aid).

Oliver North, PROFS (Professional Office System) Note to John Poindexter, "Private Blank Check," July 24, 1986; *The*

Iran-Contra Scandal: The Declassified History, The National Security Archive, The New Press, New York, 1993, p. 184. (North recommends returning operation to the CIA).

Garcia de Paz is documented in DEA file TG-86-0005:IA4C1. The DEA rejected a Freedom of Information Act request for the file, citing privacy laws.

Chapter 8

Oliver North, Memorandum for John Poindexter, ''Press Guidance re: Costa Rican Airstrip,'' September 30, 1986; *The Iran-Contra Scandal: The Declassified History*, The National Security Archive, The New Press, New York, 1993, pp. 181-183. (Santa Elena airstrip fallout and response).

A Very Thin Line, Touchstone, New York, 1991, pp. 38, 96. (Steele's role in Contra resupply operation).

''C.I.A. Recalls Costa Rica Aide,'' *The New York Times*, January 18, 1987. (Fernandez recalled from Costa Rica).

''American Is Captured After Plane Is Downed in Nicaraguan Territory,'' *The New York Times*, October 8, 1986, pp A1, A8. (Hasenfus shot down, Shultz's denial).

''Nicaragua Shows Reporters Man It Says Is Flier,'' The New York Times, October 8, 1986, p A8. (Hasenfus press conference).

Under Fire, pp 353-355. (North's shredding).

''U.S. Prisoner in Nicaragua Says C.I.A. Ran Contra Supply Flights,'' *The New York Times*, October 10, 1986, p A1. (Hasenfus says CIA headed Contra operation).

''Bush Praises Man Tied to Contra Aid,'' *The New York Times*, October 12, 1986, p A1. (Bush link to Felix Rodriguez).

The Iran-Contra Scandal: The Declassified History, The National Security Archive, The New Press, New York, 1993, pp. 186-187. (Abrams' CNN interview).

''Lack of Help Angers Poor In El Salvador,'' *The New York Times*, October 13, 1986, p A1. (Salvadoran earthquake).

''Close Aide To Bush Linked To Figure Helping Contras,'' The New York Times, October 13, 1986, p A1. (Gregg's ties to Rodriguez).

''U.S. Prisoner in Nicaragua Says C.I.A. Ran Contra Supply Flights,'' The New York Times, October 10, 1986, p A1. (Owen's card found in wallet of Contra pilot).

Kerry subcommittee report, pp 44-45. (Owen's name discovered in DC-4).

"Special Prosecutor Asked," *The New York Times*, October 17, 1986, p A10. (House Democrats request prosecutor).

Chapter 9
"Contra Arms Crew Said to Smuggle Drugs," *The New York Times*, January 20, 1987, p A1.

"Is There a Contra Drug Connection?" *Newsweek*, January 26, 1987, p. 26.

"Cache of 2 1/2 tons of cocaine seized on boat in Guatemalan port," *Miami Herald* (international edition), October 2, 1987. (Puerto Barrios raid).

"Q1,360 milliones en cocaina incautaron," *Prensa Libre*, Guatemala, September 30, 1987. (Puerto Barrios raid).

The Kerry subcommittee report, pp 39-43.

Author interview with Richard Rivera, January 16, 1993.

Chapter 10
Final Report of the Independent Counsel for Iran/Contra Matters, August 4, 1993, vol. 1, p. 162. (Secord and Hakim's Contra profits).

Tom Barry, Inside Guatemala, The Inter-Hemispheric Education Resource Center, Albuquerque, New Mexico, 1992, p. 20. (Barillas assassination).

Moran's death threat was documented in DEA file #M3-90-0053 FAI-C1.

The Kerry Subcommittee report, p. IV.

"Foreign Policy Hurt Drug War, Senators Say," *The New York Times*, April 14, 1989, p. A8. (Kerry report released).

"Reagan Aides Accused of Hampering Drug War," *Washington Post*, April 14, 1989, p. A20. (Kerry report).

Chapter 11
Notarized affidavit given by Diana Ramos, September 26, 1990 in Hidalgo County, Texas. (search of Noe's apartment).

Author's interview with Noelia Castillo, June 1, 1994. (interview with Ricevuto).